OFFICE GUIDE TO SPELLING
and
WORD DIVISION

ARCO

OFFICE GUIDE TO SPELLING
and
WORD
DIVISION

Edited by
MARGARET A. HALLER, M.A.

MACMILLAN • USA

Macmillan General Reference
A Prentice Hall Macmillan Company
15 Columbus Circle
New York, NY 10023

An Arco Book

MACMILLAN is a registered trademark of Macmillan, Inc.
ARCO is a registered trademark of Prentice-Hall, Inc.

Library of Congress Cataloging in Publication Data

Office guide to spelling and word division / edited by
Margaret A. Haller.—2nd ed.
      p. cm.
  ISBN 0-671-89663-6
  1. Spellers. 2. English language—Syllabication.
3. English language—Business English. 4. English
language—Technical English.
I. Haller, Margaret A.
PE1146.O34   1994   94-21906
421'.52—dc20   CIP

Manufactured in the United States of America

10 9 8 7 6 5 4 3

CONTENTS

FOREWORD

If all you need to know is how to spell or pronounce or divide a word correctly, this listing of 25,000 commonly used business and technical terms will provide the answer more quickly and easily than any dictionary—and in a lot less space. Just flip through the alphabetical listing until you come to the word you need and your problem is solved.

If you are concerned about forming the plural of nouns or compound terms, or deciding whether a particular word ends in *ible* or *able*, *ise* or *ize*, *cede* or *ceed* or *sede*, the section on spelling rules will tell you just what you need to know. The commonsense guidelines for word division will clear up any confusion about when and how to divide words in letters, memos, or reports.

The *Office Guide to Spelling and Word Division* may well become one of the most used and useful reference works on any office worker's desk.

SPELLING RULES

The following rules and guidelines can answer many spelling questions. A good desk dictionary is also an essential aid to the correct use and spelling of words.

1. Use preferred forms. Some words have more than one accepted spelling; you may find both listed in the dictionary. In general, use the more common form (*airplane*, not *aeroplane*) and avoid British spellings (*behavior*, not *behaviour*). It is most important to spell a word consistently throughout.
2. Foreign words carry the diacritical marks as an essential part of their spelling.

à l'américaine	crédit foncier	mère
attaché	crédit	nacré
béton	mobilier	outré
blessé	curé	passé
calèche	détente	pâté
cañada	doña	père
cañon	entrepôt	piña
chargé	exposé	précis
chargé	longéron	raisonné
d'affaires	mañana	résumé
congé	maté	touché

Some words (such as *aperitif, chateau, debris, entree, facade, ingenue, materiel, smorgasbord*) have been completely anglicized and no longer require diacritical marks. Consult your dictionary and be consistent.

Plurals

3. Nouns ending in *o* preceded by a vowel add *s* to form
   the plural; nouns ending in *o* preceded by a consonant add *es* to form the plural, except as indicated in
   the following list.

albinos	gringos	pomelos
armadillos	halos	provisos
avocados	inamoratos	quartos
banjos	indigos	salvos
cantos	juntos	sextodecimos
cascos	kimonos	sextos
centos	lassos	siroccos
didos	magnetos	solos
duodecimos	mementos	tangelos
dynamos	merinos	tobaccos
escudos	mestizos	twos
Eskimos	octavos	tyros
falsettos	octodecimos	virtuosos
gauchos	pianos	zeros
ghettos	piccolos	

4. In forming the plurals of compound terms, the significant word takes the plural form.

Significant word first:	brothers-in-law
adjutants general	chargés d'affaires
aides-de-camp	commanders in chief
ambassadors at large	comptrollers general
attorneys at law	consuls general
attorneys general	courts-martial
billets-doux	crepes suzette
bills of fare	daughters-in-law

governors general
grants-in-aid
heirs at law
inspectors general
men-of-war
ministers-designate
mothers-in-law
notaries public
pilots-in-command
postmasters general
presidents-elect
prisoners of war
rights-of-way
secretaries general
sergeants at arms
sergeants major
surgeons general

Significant word in middle:
assistant attorneys general
assistant chiefs of staff
assistant comptrollers general
assistant surgeons general
deputy chiefs of staff

Significant word last:
assistant attorneys
assistant commissioners
assistant corporation counsels

assistant directors
assistant general counsels
assistant secretaries
brigadier generals
deputy judges
deputy sheriffs
general counsels
judge advocates
judge advocate generals
lieutenant colonels
major generals
provost marshals
provost marshal generals
quartermaster generals
trade unions
under secretaries
vice chairmen

Both words of equal significance:
Bulletins Nos. 27 and 28; *but* Bulletin No. 27 or 28
coats of arms
masters at arms
men buyers
men employees
secretaries-treasurers
women aviators
women students
women writers

No word significant in itself:

forget-me-nots	man-of-the-earths
hand-me-downs	pick-me-ups

5. When a noun is hyphened with an adverb or preposition, the plural is formed on the noun.

comings-in	hangers-on	makers-up
fillers-in	listeners-in	passers-by
goings-on	lookers-on	

6. When neither word is a noun, the plural is formed on the last word.

also-rans	go-betweens	run-ins
come-ons	higher-ups	tie-ins

7. Nouns ending with *ful* form the plural by adding *s* at the end; if it is necessary to express the idea that more than one container was filled, the two elements of the solid compound are printed as separate words and the plural is formed by adding *s* to the noun.

five bucketfuls of the mixture (one bucket filled
    five times)
five buckets full of earth (separate buckets)
three cupfuls of flour (one cup filled three times)
three cups full of coffee (separate cups)

8. The following list comprises other words the plurals of which may cause difficulty.

addendum, addenda	antenna, antennas
adieu, adieus	(antennae, zoology)
agendum, agenda	appendix, appendixes
alga, algae	aquarium, aquariums
alumnus, alumni	automaton,
(masc.); alumna,	automatons
alumnae (fem.)	axis, axes

bandeau, bandeaux
basis, bases
beau, beaus
cactus, cactuses
calix, calices
chassis
    (singular and plural)
cherub, cherubs
cicatrix, cicatrices
Co., Cos.
coccus, cocci
crisis, crises
criterion, criteria
curriculum,
    curriculums
datum, data
desideratum, desiderata
dilettante, dilettanti
dogma, dogmas
ellipsis, ellipses
equilibrium,
    equilibriums
    (equilibria, scientific)
erratum, errata
executrix, executrices
flambeau, flambeaus
focus, focuses
folium, folia
formula, formulas
fungus, fungi
genius, geniuses
genus, genera
gladiolus (singular and
    plural)

helix, helices
hypothesis, hypotheses
index, indexes (indices,
    scientific)
insigne, insignia
Kansas Citys
lacuna, lacunae
larva, larvae
larynx, larynxes
lens, lenses
lira, lire
locus, loci
madam, mesdames
Marys
matrix, matrices
maximum, maximums
medium, mediums *or*
    media
memorandum,
    memorandums
minimum, minimums
minutia, minutiae
monsieur, messieurs
nucleus, nuclei
oasis, oases
octopus, octopuses
opus, opera
parenthesis,
    parentheses
phenomenon,
    phenomena
phylum, phyla
plateau, plateaus
podium, podiums

procès-verbal,
   procès-verbaux
radius, radii
radix, radixes
referendum,
   referendums
sanatorium,
   sanatoriums
sanitarium, sanitariums
septum, septa
sequela, sequelae
seraph, seraphs
seta, setae
ski, skis
stadium, stadiums
stimulus, stimuli

stratum, strata
stylus, styluses
syllabus, syllabuses
symposium, symposia
synopsis, synopses
tableau, tableaus
taxi, taxis
terminus, termini
testatrix, testatrices
thesaurus, thesauri
thesis, theses
thorax, thoraxes
vertebra, vertebras
   (vertebrae, zoology)
virtuoso, virtuosos
vortex, vortexes

Endings *ible* and *able*

9. The following words end in *ible*; other words in this class end in *able*. Words with both endings indicated differ in meaning.

abhorrible
accendible
accessible
addible
adducible
admissible
appetible
apprehen-
   sible

audible
avertible
bipartible
circumscrip-
   tible
coctible
coercible
cognoscible
cohesible

collapsible
combustible
comestible
commonsen-
   sible
compactible
compatible
competible
compossible

comprehen-
 sible
compressible
conducible
conductible
confluxible
congestible
contemptible
controvertible
conversible
 (convertible)
 conversable
 (oral)
convertible
convincible
corrigible
corrodible
corrosible
corruptible
credible
crucible
cullible
decoctible
deducible
deductible
defeasible
defectible
defensible
delible
deprehensible
depressible
descendible
destructible
diffrangible

diffusible
digestible
dimensible
discernible
discerpible
discerptible
discussible
dispersible
dissectible
distensible
distractible
divertible
divestible
divisible
docible
edible
educible
effectible
effervescible
eligible
eludible
erodible
evasible
eversible
evincible
exemptible
exhaustible
exigible
expansible
explosible
expressible
extensible
fallible
feasible

fencible
flexible
fluxible
forcible
frangible
fungible
fusible
gullible
horrible
ignitible
illegible
immersible
immiscible
impartible
impatible
impedible
imperceptible
impermissible
imperscriptible
impersuasible
implausible
impossible
imprescriptible
imputrescible
inaccessible
inadmissible
inapprehensible
inaudible
incircumscrip-
 tible
incoercible
incognoscible
incombustible
incommiscible

incompatible
incomprehens-
    ible
incompressible
inconcussible
incontrovertible
inconvertible
inconvincible
incorrigible
incorrodible
incorruptible
incredible
indefeasible
indefectible
indefensible
indelible
indeprehensible
indestructible
indigestible
indiscernible
indivertible
indivisible
indocible
inducible
ineffervescible
ineligible
ineludible
inevasible
inexhaustible
inexpansible
inexpressible
infallible
infeasible
inflexible

infractible
infrangible
infusible
innascible
inscriptible
insensible
instructible
insubmergible
insuppressible
insusceptible
intactible
intangible
intelligible
interconvertible
interruptible
intervisible
invendible
invertible
invincible
invisible
irascible
irreducible
irrefrangible
irremissible
irreprehensible
irrepressible
irresistible
irresponsible
irreversible
legible
mandible
marcescible
miscible
negligible

nexible
omissible
ostensible
partible
passible (feeling)
    passable (open)
perceptible
perfectible
permissible
persuasible
pervertible
plausible
possible
prehensible
prescriptible
producible
productible
protrusible
putrescible
receptible
redemptible
reducible
reflectible
reflexible
refrangible
remissible
renascible
rendible
reprehensible
repressible
reproducible
resistible
responsible
reversible

revertible	suggestible	tripartible
risible	supersensible	unadmissible
runcible	suppressible	uncorruptible
sconcible	susceptible	unexhaustible
seducible	suspensible	unexpressible
sensible	tangible	unintelligible
sponsible	tensible	unresponsible
suasible	terrible	unsusceptible
subdivisible	thurible	vendible
submergible	traducible	vincible
submersible	transmissible	visible
subvertible	transvertible	vitrescible

Endings *ise, ize,* and *yze*

10. A large number of words have the termination *ise, ize,* or *yze.* The letter *l* is followed by *yze* if the word expresses an idea of loosening or separating, as *analyze;* all other words of this class, except those ending with the suffix *wise* and those in the following list, end in *ize.*

advertise	despise
advise	devise
affranchise	disenfranchise
apprise (to inform)	disfranchise
apprize (to appraise)	disguise
arise	emprise
chastise	enfranchise
circumcise	enterprise
comprise	excise
compromise	exercise
demise	exorcise

franchise
improvise
incise
merchandise
misadvise
mortise
premise
prise (to force)
   prize (to value)

reprise
revise
rise
supervise
surmise
surprise
televise

Endings *cede, ceed,* and *sede*

11. Only one word ends in *sede* (supersede); only three end in *ceed* (exceed, proceed, succeed); all other words of this class end in *cede* (precede, secede, etc.).

Doubled consonants

12. A single consonant following a single vowel and ending a monosyllable or a final accented syllable is doubled before a suffix beginning with a vowel.

bag, bagging
get, getting
red, reddish
rob, robbing

corral, corralled
transfer, transferred
but total, totaled
   travel, traveled

13. If the accent in a derivative falls upon an earlier syllable than it does in the primitive, the consonant is not doubled.

refer, reference
prefer, preference

infer, inference

Indefinite articles

14. The indefinite article *a* is used before a consonant and an aspirated *h*; *an* is used before silent *h* and all vowels except *u* pronounced as in *usual* and *o* pronounced as in *one*.

a historical review	an herbseller
a hotel	an hour
a human being	an honor
a humble man	an onion
a union	an oyster

15. When a group of initials begins with *b, c, d, g, j, k, p, q, t, u, v, w, y,* or *z*, each having a consonant sound, the indefinite article *a* is used.

a BLS compilation	a GAO limitation
a CIO finding	a PHS project

16. When a group of initials begins with *a, e, f, h, i, l, m, n, o, r, s,* or *x*, each having a vowel sound, the indefinite article *an* is used.

an AEC report	an NSC (en) proclamation
an FCC (ef) ruling	an RFC (ahr) loan

17. Use of the indefinite article *a* or *an* before a numerical expression is determined by the consonant or vowel sound of the beginning syllable.

an 11-year-old	a IV-F (four) category
a onetime winner	(military draft)
a III (three) group	a 4-H Club
an VIII (eight) classification	

GUIDELINES FOR WORD DIVISION

The following section is a guide to the correct pronunciation and division by syllables of about 25,000 words. An effort has been made to include both those words that are most commonly used and those that may cause difficulty. Many technical terms likely to be encountered in legal, medical, or scientific writing have been included. A representative sample shows how the various forms of a single word are divided (for example, *con•demn'*, *con'dem•na'tion, con•dem'na•to'ry*). These examples can be used as a guide to dividing other words with similar forms.

Each entry in the word list is divided into syllables indicated by a centered dot, a hyphen (which is part of the word and should not be dropped when the word is written), or a stress mark. Stress marks also help you to correctly pronounce each word. Both primary (boldface mark) and secondary (lighter mark) stress are indicated, and the appearance of two or more stress patterns for the same word indicates variations in the pronunciation, use, or meaning of that word.

In addition, the following rules for word division should be observed. The general principle behind these rules is to create a neat appearance and, more importantly, to avoid distracting or confusing the reader, even momentarily.

1. Do not divide words at the ends of more than two consecutive lines. Similarly, do not end more than two consecutive lines with the same word, symbol, group of numbers, etc.

2. The final word of a paragraph should not be divided.

3. Avoid dividing words in headings or titles.

4. Never divide a one-syllable word, no matter how long: *through, aisles, planned*.

5. Words should be divided according to pronunciation. To avoid mispronunciation, they should be divided so that the part of the word left at the end of the line will suggest the whole word: *capac-ity*, not *capa-city; extraor-dinary*, not *extra-ordinary*.

6. Although this section lists beginning and ending one-letter syllables for pronunciation purposes, under no circumstances are words to be divided on a single letter: *usu-ally*, not *u-sually*.

7. Where possible, division of short words (five or fewer letters) should be avoided: *aorta, only, radar*. Two-letter divisions should also be avoided: *dancer*, not *danc-er*.

8. Words of two syllables are split at the end of the first syllable: *dis-pelled, con-quered*. For words of three or more syllables, it is preferable to divide on the vowel: *particu-lar, sepa-rate*.

9. In words with short prefixes (such as *ac, do, de, dis, ex, pre, un*), divide on the prefix: *non-essential*, not *nones-sential*. Avoid breaking in the middle of a long prefix (such as *anti, multi over*): *inter-state*, not *in-terstate*.

10. The following suffixes are not broken: *ceous, cial, cient, cion, cious, scious, geous, gion, gious, sial, tial, tion, tious*, and *sion: egre-gious*, not *egregi-ous*.

11. Do not divide contractions: *doesn't, haven't.*
12. Divide hyphenated compounds only at the hyphen: *court-martial,* not *court-mar-tial; tax-supported,* not *tax-sup-ported.* Solid compounds are best divided between the two elements of the compound: *salesperson,* not *salesper-son.*
13. When two adjoining vowels are sounded separately, divide between them: *cre-ation, gene-ology.*
14. In the large group of words ending in *-meter,* distinction should be made between metric system terms and terms indicating a measuring instrument. When dividing metric terms, preserve the combining form *-meter: centi-meter, kilo-meter.* For measuring instruments, divide after the *m,* as long as such division reflects the pronunciation: *altim-eter, microm-eter,* but *volt-meter.*
15. In scientific formulas, the hyphen has an important function. Every effort should be made to avoid breaking the formula. If it is unavoidable, division is preferable after an original hyphen to avoid the introduction of a misleading hyphen.
16. Abbreviations and symbols should not be broken at the end of a line: *Ph.D., A.D., YMCA.*
17. Avoid dividing figures, closely connected combinations of figures and abbreviations, and single place references: *$15,000, 86 m.p.h., §31(b).*
18. Closely related abbreviations and initials in proper names should not be separated, nor should titles (such as *Rev., Ms., Esq., Jr.*) be separated from surnames.
19. Never divide the syllables in a person's name. Avoid dividing any proper name, if possible.
20. In dates, do not divide the month and day. The year may be carried over to the next line.

A

Aa′ron
Aa·ron′ic
a·back′
ab′a·cus
ab′a·lo′ne
ab·am′pere
a·ban′don
a·ban′don·ment
a·base′
a·bash′
a·bate′
a·bate′ment
ab′a·tis
ab′bess
ab′bey
ab′bot
ab·bre′vi·ate′
ab·bre′vi·a′tion
ab′di·cate′
ab′di·ca′tion
ab′do·men
ab·dom′i·nal
ab·duct′
ab·duc′tion
ab·duc′tor
ab·er′rance
ab·er′rant
a·bet′
a·bet′tor
a·bey′ance
ab·hor′

ab·hor′rence
a·bide′
a·bil′i·ty
ab·ject′, ab′ject
ab′ju·ra′tion
ab·jur′a·to′ry
ab·jure′
ab·la′tion
ab′la·tive
ab′laut
a′ble
a·bloom′
ab·lu′tion
ab′ne·gate′
ab·nor′mal
a·board′
a·bode′
a·bol′ish
ab′o·li′tion
a·bom′i·na·ble
a·bom′i·nate′
ab′o·rig′i·nal
a·bort′
a·bor′ti·cide′
a·bor′ti·fa′cient
a·bor′tion
a·bound′
a·bout′
a·bove′
ab·ra′dant
ab·rade′

A′bra·ham′
ab·ra′sion
ab′re·act′
a·breast′
a·bridge′
a·bridg′ment
ab′ro·gate′
a·brupt′
ab′scess
ab·scond′
ab′sence
ab′sen·tee′
ab′sen·tee′ism
ab′sinthe
ab′so·lute′
ab′so·lu′tion
ab·solve′
ab·sorb′
ab·sor′ben·cy
ab·sorp′tion
ab·stain′
ab·ste′mi·ous
ab·ster′sion
ab·stract′, ab′stract
ab·strac′tion
ab·stric′tion
ab·struse′
ab·surd′
a·bu′li·a
a·bun′dance
a·buse′

a·bu'sive
a·but'
a·bu'ti·lon
a·but'ter
a·buzz'
ab·volt'
a·bys'mal
a·byss'
a·ca'cia
ac·a·dem'ic
ac·a·dem'i·cal·ly
a·cad·e·mi'cian
a·cad'e·my
A·ca'di·a
ac'a·leph
ac·an·tha'ceous
a·can'thoid
a·can'thus
a cap·pel'la
ac'a·rid
a·car'pel·ous
a·cau'dal
ac·cede'
ac·ced'ence
ac·cel'er·ate'
ac·cel'er·a'tion
ac·cel'er·a'tor
ac'cent
ac·cen'tu·ate'
ac·cept'
ac·cept'a·ble
ac·cept'ance
ac·cept'ed
ac·ces'sa·ry
ac·ces'si·bil'i·ty

ac·ces'si·ble
ac·ces'sion
ac·ces'so·ry
ac'ci·dent
ac'ci·den'tal
ac·claim'
ac'cla·ma'tion
ac·cli'mate,
    ac'cli·mate'
ac·cli'ma·ti·za'tion
ac·cliv'i·ty
ac'co·lade'
ac·com'mo·date'
ac·com'pa·ni·ment
ac·com'pa·ny
ac·complice
ac·com'plish
ac·cord'
ac·cord'ance
ac·cor'di·on
ac·cost'
ac·couche'ment
ac·count'
ac·count'a·ble
ac·count'an·cy
ac·cou'ter·ments
ac·cred'it
ac·cred'it·a'tion
ac·crete'
ac·cre'tion
ac·cru'al
ac·crue'
ac·cul'tu·ra'tion
ac·cum'bent
ac·cu'mu·late'

ac'cu·ra·cy
ac'cu·rate
ac'cu·sa'tion
ac·cu'sa·to'ry
ac·cus'tom
a·ce'di·a
a·cen'tric
ac'er·ate
ac'er·bate'
a·cer'bi·ty
ac'e·tal'
ac'e·tate'
a·ce'tic
a·cet'i·fy'
ac'e·tone'
a·chieve'
a·chieve'ment
A·chil'les
ach'ro·mat'ic
ac'id
a·cid'i·ty
a·cid'u·late'
ac'i·nus
ac·knowl'edge
ac·knowl'edg·ment
ac'o·lyte'
ac'o·nite'
a'corn
a·cous'tic
ac·quaint'ance
ac·qui·esce'
ac·qui·es'cent
ac·quire'
ac·qui·si'tion
ac·quit'

ac·quit'tal
a'cre·age
ac'rid
ac·ri·mo'ni·ous
a·crit'i·cal
ac'ro·bat'ics
a·crog'e·nous
ac'ro·nym
ac'ro·pho'bi·a
a·crop'o·lis
a·cross'
a·cros'tic
a·cryl'ic
ac'tion
ac'ti·vate'
ac'ti·va'tor
ac'tive
ac·tiv'i·ty
ac'tor
ac'tu·al
ac'tu·al·i·za'tion
ac'tu·ar'i·al
ac'tu·ar'y
ac'tu·ate'
a·cu'i·ty
a·cu'men
ac'u·punc'ture
a·cute'
ad'age
a·da'gio
Ad'am
ad'a·mant'
a·dapt'a·ble
ad'ap·ta'tion
a·dap'tive

ad·den'dum
ad'der
ad'dict, ad·dict'
ad·dic'tion
Ad'di·son
ad·di'tion
ad'di·tive
ad'dle
ad·dress', ad'dress
ad'dress·ee'
ad·duce'
ad·duc'i·ble
ad·duct'
a·demp'tion
ad'e·nec'to·my
ad'e·noid'
ad'e·noi'dal
ad·ept'
ad'e·qua·cy
ad·here'
ad·her'ent
ad·he'sion
ad ho'mi·nem'
a·dieu'
ad in'fi·ni·tum
ad'i·pose'
ad'it
ad·ja'cent
ad'jec·ti'val
ad'jec·tive
ad·join'
ad·journ'
ad·ju'di·cate'
ad·ju'di·ca'tor
ad'junct

ad'ju·ra'tion
ad·jure'
ad·just'
ad'ju·tant
ad·min'is·ter
ad·min'is·trate'
ad·min'is·tra'tion
ad'mi·ra·ble
ad'mi·ral
ad'mi·ral·ty
ad·mir'er
ad·mis'si·ble
ad·mis'sion
ad·mit'tance
ad·mit'ted·ly
ad·mix'ture
ad·mon'ish
ad'mo·ni'tion
ad·mon'i·to'ry
ad nau'se·um
a·do'be
ad'o·les'cence
a·dopt'
a·dop'tion
a·dop'tive
a·dor'a·ble
ad'o·ra'tion
a·dorn'
ad·re'nal
ad·ren'al·in
a·drift'
a·droit'
ad·sorp'tion
ad'u·lar'i·a
ad'u·late'

ad'u·la'tion
a·dult', a'dult
a·dul'ter·ate'
a·dul'ter·er
a·dul'ter·y
ad'um·brate'
ad·vance'
ad·vec'tion
Ad'vent
ad·ven·ti'tious
ad·ven'ture
ad·ven'tur·ous
ad·ver'bi·al
ad'ver·sar'y
ad·verse'
ad·vert'en·cy
ad·ver'tent
ad'ver·tise'
ad'ver·tis'er
ad·vice'
ad·vis'a·bil'i·ty
ad·vised'
ad·vi'so·ry
ad'vo·ca·cy
ad'vo·cate'
aer'ate
aer·a'tion
aer'i·al
aer'ie
aer'obe
aer·o'bic
aer'o·dy·nam'ics
aer'o·nau'tics
aer'o·space'
aes'thete

aes·thet'ic
af'fa·ble
af·fair'
af·fect', af'fect
af'fec·ta'tion
af·fec'tion
af·fec·tiv'i·ty
af·fi'anced
af'fi·da'vit
af·fil'i·ate'
af·fil'i·a'tion
af·fin'i·ty
af·firm'
af'fir·ma'tion
a·firm'a·tive
af·fix'
af·flict'
af·flic'tion
af'flu·ence
af'flux
af·fran'chise'
af·fray'
af'fri·cate
af·fric'a·tive
af·fright'
af·front'
af'ghan
a·fi'cio·na'do
a·field'
a·float'
a·fore'men'tioned
a·fore'said'
a for'ti·o'ri
a·foul'
a·fraid'

a·fresh'
Af'ri·can
Af'ri·ka'ner
af'ter·ef·fect'
af'ter·im'age
af'ter·noon'
a·gain'
a·gam'ic
a'gar·ic
ag'ate
a'gen·cy
a·gen'da
a'gent' pro'vo'ca'teur'
ag·glom'er·ate'
ag·glu'ti·na'tion
ag'gran·dize'
ag'gra·vate'
ag'gre·gate
ag·gres'sion
ag·gres'sive
ag·grieve'
a·ghast'
ag'ile
a·gil'i·ty
ag'i·o·tage'
ag'i·tate'
a'gi·ta'tor
a·glit'ter
a·glow'
ag'nate
ag·no'men
ag·nos'tic
ag·nos'ti·cism
a·gon'ic
ag'o·nize'

ag'o·ra·pho'bi·a
a·grar'i·an
a·gree'a·ble
a·greed'
ag'ri·busi'ness
ag'ri·cul'ture
ag'ri·mo'ny
a·grol'o·gy
a·gron'o·my
a'gue
ai·lan'thus
ail'ment
al'a·bas'ter
a·lac'ri·ty
a·larm'ist
a'late
al'ba·tross'
al·be'it
al·bi'no
al'bum
al·bu'min
al·bur'num
al'che·my
al'ci·dine'
al'co·hol'
al'co·hol'ic
al'cove
al'der·man
a'le·a·to'ry
a·lert'
al'ex·an'drine
a·lex'in
al·fal'fa
al·fres'co
al'gae

al'ge·bra
al'i·bi'
al'ien
al'ien·a·ble
al'ien·ate'
a·lign'
a·like'
al'i·ment
al'i·men'ta·ry
al·i·mo'ny
a·live'
al'ka·li'
al'ka·line'
al'ka·lin'i·ty
al'kyd
al·lay'
al'le·ga'tion
al·lege'
al·leg'ed·ly
al·le'giance
al'le·gor'i·cal
al'le·go'ry
al·le·lu'ia
al'ler·gen
al·ler'gic
al·le'vi·ate'
al'ley
al·li'ance
al·lied', al'lied
al'li·ga'tor
al·lit'er·a'tion
al'li·um
al'lo·cate'
al'lo·morph'
al·lop'a·thy

al·lot'ment
al·low'
al·low'a·ble
al'loy
al·lude'
al·lure'
al·lu'sion
al·lu'vi·al
al'ly', al'ly
al'ma ma'ter
al'ma·nac'
al·might'y
al'mond
al·ni'co'
al'oe
a·loft'
a·lo'ha
a·lone'
a·long'
a·loof'
al'o·pe'ci·a
a·loud'
al·pac'a
al'pha
al'pha·bet'i·cal
al'pine
al·read'y
al'tar
al'ter
al'ter·ca'tion
al'ter e'go
al'ter·nate'
al·ter'na·tive
al·the'a
al·though'

al·tim′e·ter
al′ti·tude′
al′ti·tu′di·nal
al′to·cu′mu·lus
al′to·geth′er
al′to·stra′tus
al′tru·ism
al′tru·is′tic
al′u·del′
al′um
a·lu′mi·num
a·lum′nus
al′u·nite′
al·ve′o·lar
al′ways
a·lys′sum
a·mal′gam
a·mal′gam·ate′
am′a·ranth′
am′a·ran′thine
am′a·ryl′lis
a·mass′
am′a·teur′
am′a·tive
am′a·to′ry
am′au·ro′sis
a·maze′ment
am·bas′sa·dor
am′ber
am′ber·gris′
am′bi·dex′trous
am′bi·ence
am′bi·ent
am′bi·gu′i·ty
am·big′u·ous

am·bi′tion
am·biv′a·lent
am′ble
am′bo·cep′tor
am·bro′si·a
am′bu·lance
am′bu·la·to′ry
am·bus·cade′
am′bush
a·me′ba
a·mel′io·rate′
a·mel′io·ra′tion
a·me′na·ble
a·mend′ment
a·men′i·ty
a·men′or·rhe′a
a·men′ti·a
a·merce′ment
A·mer′i·ca
A·mer·in′di·an
am′e·thyst
a′mi·a·ble
am′i·ca·ble
a·mi′cus cu′ri·ae′
a·mid′
am′ide
am′i·dol′
a·mid′ships
a·mine′
a′mi·no′, a·mi′no
a·miss′
am′i·ty
am′me′ter
am·mo′ni·a
am′mo·nite′

am·mu·ni′tion
am·ne′si·a
am′nes·ty
am′ni·on
a·moe′ba
a·mok′
a·mong′
a·mor′al
am′o·rous
a·mor′phous
a′mor·ti·za′tion
a′mor·tize′
a·mount′
a·mour′
am·per′age
am′pere
am′per·sand′
am·phet′a·mine′
am·phib′i·an
am·phib′i·ous
am′phi·the′a·ter
am·pho′ra
am′ple
am′pli·fi·ca′tion
am′pli·fi′er
am′pli·fy′
am′pli·tude′
am′poule
am′pu·tate′
am′pu·tee′
a·muck′
am′u·let
a·muse′
am′yl
am′yl·ase′

am'y·tal'
An'a·bap'tist
an'a·bat'ic
an'a·bi·ot'ic
an'a·can'thous
a·nach'ro·nism
an'a·clas'tic
an'a·clit'ic
an'a·con'da
an'a·er·o'bic
an'a·gram'
a'nal
an'a·lects'
an'a·lep'tic
an'al·ge'si·a
a·nal'o·gize'
a·nal'o·gous
an'a·logue'
a·nal'o·gy
a·nal'yse'
a·nal'y·sis
an'a·lyt'i·cal
an'a·lyze'
an'a·mor·pho'sis
an·an'drous
an'a·pest'
an'arch·ist
an'arch·y
a·nath'e·ma
an'a·tom'ic
an'a·tom'i·cal
a·nat'o·my
an'ces·tor
an'ces·try
an'chor

an'cho·rite'
an'cho·vy
an'cient
an'cil·lar'y
an'con
an'da·lu'site
an'des·ite'
and'i·ron
an'dra·dite'
an'dro·gen
an·drog'y·nous
an'ec·do'tal
an'ec·dote'
a·ne'mi·a
an'e·mom'e·ter
a·nem'o·ne'
a·nent'
an'er·gy
an'er·oid'
an'es·the'si·a
an'es·the'si·ol'o·gy
an·es'the·tize'
an'eu·rysm
a·new'
an'ga·ry
an'gel
an·gel'ic
an'ger
an·gi'na
an·gi'na pec'to·ris
an'gle
An'gli·can
An'gli·cize'
An'glo·phile'
an'gry

ang'strom
an'guish
an'gu·lar
an'gu·la'tion
an·hy'dride
an·hy'drous
an'i·line'
a·nil'i·ty
an'i·mad·ver'sion
an'i·mal
an'i·mal'i·ty
an'i·mate'
an'i·ma'tion
an'i·mism
an'i·mos'i·ty
an'i·mus
an'i'on
an'ise
an'i·sette'
an'i·so·trop'ic
an'kle
an'klet
an'nals
an·neal'
an'ne·lid
an·nex', an'nex
an'nex·a'tion
an·ni'hi·late'
an·ni'hi·la'tion
an'ni·ver'sa·ry
an'no·tate'
an·nounce'
an·nounc'er
an·noy'
an'nu·al

an·nu′i·ty
an·nul′
an·nul′ment
an·nun′ci·a′tion
a·no′ci·as·so′ci·a′tion
an′ode
an′o·dyne′
a·noint′
a·nom′a·lous
a·nom′a·ly
an′o·mie
a·non′
an′o·nym′i·ty
a·non′y·mous
a′no·rak′
an·oth′er
an′ox·e′mi·a
an′ser·ine′
an′swer
an′swer·a·ble
ant·ac′id
an·tag′o·nism
an·tag′o·nist
an·tag′o·nis′tic
an·tag′o·nis′ti·cal·ly
ant·al′ka·line′
ant·arc′tic
Ant·arc′ti·ca
an′te
ant′eat·er
an′te·bel′lum
an′te·cede′
an′te·ced′ent
an′te·cham′ber
an′te·date′

an′te·di·lu′vi·an
an′te·lope′
an′te·me·rid′i·an
an′te me·ri′di·em
an·ten′na
an′te·pe′nult
an′te·pe·nul′ti·mate
an·te′ri·or
an′te·room′
ant·he′li·on
an′them
an′ther
an·thol′o·gist
an·thol′o·gy
an′thra·cite′
an′thrax
an′thro·po·cen′tric
an′thro·poid′
an′thro·po·log′i·cal
an·thro·pol′o·gy
an′thro·pom′e·try
an′thro·po·mor′phic
an′thro·po·mor′phize
an′thro·po·mor′phous
an′thro·poph′a·gous
an′ti·bac·te′ri·al
an′ti·bi·ot′ic
an′ti·bod′y
an′tic
an·tic′i·pate′
an·tic′i·pa′tion
an·tic′i·pa·to′ry
an′ti·cler′i·cal
an′ti·cli′max
an′ti·dote′

an′ti·freeze′
an′ti·gen
an′ti·his′ta·mine′
an′ti·ma·cas′sar
an′ti·mo′ny
an′ti·node′
an·ti′no·my
an′ti·pas′to
an′ti·pa·thet′ic
an·ti′pa·thy
an′ti·pe′ri·od′ic
an′ti·per·son·nel′
an·tiph′o·nal
an·tip′o·dal
an′ti·pode′
an′ti·py′rine
an′ti·quar′i·an
an′ti·quar′y
an′ti·quat′ed
an·tique′
an·tiq′ui·ty
an′ti·sep′tic
an′ti·sep′ti·cal·ly
an′ti·se′rum
an′ti·so′cial
an′ti·spas·mod′ic
an·tith′e·sis
an′ti·thet′i·cal
an′ti·tox′in
an′ti·trust′
an′ti·type′
ant′ler
an′to·nym′
an·ton′y·mous
an′trum

a·nu'cle·ar
an·u'ran
a'nus
an'vil
anx·i'e·ty
anx'ious
an'y·thing'
an'y·way'
an'y·where'
a'o·rist
a·or'ta
a·pace'
a·part'
a·part'heid
a·part'ment
ap'a·thet'ic
ap'a·thy
a'pe·ri·od'ic
a'pe·ri'tif'
ap'er·ture
a'pex
aph'a·nite'
a·pha'si·a
a·phe'li·on
a'phid
a·pho'ni·a
aph'o·rism
aph'o·ris'tic
aph'ro·dis'i·ac'
aph'tha
a'pi·an
a'pi·ar'y
ap'i·cal
a'pi·cul'ture
ap'ish

ap'la·nat'ic
ap'lite
a·plomb'
a·poc'a·lypse'
a·poc'a·lyp'tic
a·poc'ry·phal
ap'o·dal
ap'o·gee'
a·pol'o·get'ic
ap'o·lo'gi·a
a·pol'o·gize'
a·pol'o·gy
ap'o·plec'tic
ap'o·plex'y
a·pos'ta·sy
a·pos'tate
a pos·te'ri·o'ri
a·pos'tle
a'pos·tol'ic
a·pos'tro·phe
a·pos'tro·phize'
a·poth'e·car'y
ap'o·thegm'
ap'o·them'
a·poth'e·o'sis
ap·pall'
ap'pa·ra'tus
ap·par'el
ap·par'ent
ap'pa·ri'tion
ap·peal'
ap·peal'a·ble
ap·pear'
ap·pear'ance
ap·peas'a·ble

ap·pease'
ap·pease'ment
ap·pel'lant
ap·pel'late
ap'pel·la'tion
ap·pel·lee'
ap·pel'lor
ap·pend'
ap·pend'age
ap·pen·dec'to·my
ap·pen·di·ces'
ap·pen·di·ci'tis
ap·pen'dix
ap'per·cep'tion
ap'per·tain'
ap'pe·tite'
ap'pe·tiz'er
ap·plaud'
ap·plause'
ap'ple
ap·pli'ance
ap·pli·ca·bil'i·ty
ap'pli·ca·ble
ap'pli·cant
ap'pli·ca'tion
ap·plied'
ap·pli·qué'
ap·ply'
ap·point'
ap·point'ee'
ap·poin'tive
ap·por'tion·ment
ap·pos'a·ble
ap·pose'
ap'po·site

ap·prais'al
ap·praise'
ap·prais'er
ap·pre'ci·a·ble
ap·pre'ci·ate'
ap·pre'ci·a'tion
ap·pre'ci·a'tor
ap'pre·hend'
ap'pre·hen'sion
ap·pren'tice
ap·prise'
ap·proach'
ap·proach'a·ble
ap'pro·ba'tion
ap·pro'pri·ate
ap·prov'al
ap·prove'
ap·prox'i·mate'
ap·prox'i·ma'tion
ap·pur'te·nance
a'pri·cot'
a pri·o'ri
a'pron
ap'ro·pos'
ap'sis
ap'ter·yx
ap'ti·tude'
aq'ua
aq'ua·ma·rine'
aq'ua·plane'
a·quar'i·um
a·quat'ic
aq'ua·tint'
aq'ue·duct'
a'que·ous

aq'ui·line'
ar'a·besque'
Ar'a·bic
ar'a·ble
a·ra'ceous
a·rach'nid
a·rag'o·nite'
Ar'a·ma'ic
ar'bi·ter
ar'bi·tra·ble
ar'bi·trage
ar'bi·trar'i·ly
ar'bi·trar'y
ar'bi·trate'
ar'bi·tra'tion
ar'bor
ar·bo're·al
ar'bo·re'tum
ar·bu'tus
ar·cade'
ar·cane'
ar·ca'num
ar·cha'ic
ar'cha·ism
arch'an'gel
arch'bish'ᴜᴘ
arch'dea'con
arch'di'o·cese'
arch'duke'
arch'en'e·my
ar'che·ol'o·gy
arch'er
arch'er·y
ar'che·type'
Ar'chi·me'de·an

ar'chi·pel'a·go'
ar'chi·tect'
ar'chi·tec·ton'ic
ar'chi·tec'tur·al
ar'chi·tec'ture
ar'chi·trave'
ar'chives
ar'chi·vist
ar'chon
arc'tic
ar'cu·ate
ar'dent
ar'dor
ar'du·ous
ar'e·a
ar'e·ca
a·re'na
a·re'o·la
ar'gent
ar·gen'tum
ar'gon
ar'go·sy
ar'got
ar'gu·a·ble
ar'gue
ar'gu·ment
ar'gu·men·ta'tion
ar'gyle
a'ri·a
ar'id
a·rid'i·ty
a·right'
a·rise'
ar'is·toc'ra·cy
a·ris'to·crat'

a·rith′me·tic
a′rith·met′i·cal
ar·ma′da
ar′ma·dil′lo
Ar·ma·ged′don
ar′ma·ment
ar′ma·ture
ar′mi·ger
ar′mi·stice
ar·moire′
ar′mor
ar′mor·er
ar′mor·i·al
ar′mor·y
ar′my
a·ro′ma
ar′o·mat′ic
a·rose′
a·rous′al
a·rouse′
ar·peg′gio
ar·raign′
ar·raign′ment
ar·range′
ar′rant
ar′ras
ar·ray′
ar·rears′
ar·rest′
ar·rhyth′mi·a
ar·rhyth′mic
ar·ri′val
ar·rive′
ar′ro·gant
ar′ro·gate′

ar′ro·ga′tion
ar·ron′disse′ment′
ar′row
ar·roy′o
ar′se·nal
ar′se·nic
ar′se·nide′
ar·sine′
ar′son
ar′te·fact′
ar·tel′
ar·te′ri·al
ar·te′ri·o·scle·ro′sis
ar·te′ri·o·scle·rot′ic
ar′ter·y
ar·te′sian
art′ful
ar·thrit′ic
ar·thri′tis
ar′thro·pod′
Ar·thu′ri·an
ar′ti·choke′
ar′ti·cle
ar·tic′u·late′
ar·tic′u·la′tion
ar·tic′u·la′tor
ar′ti·fact′
ar′ti·fice′
ar·tif′i·cer
ar′ti·fi′cial
ar·til′ler·y
ar′ti·san
art′ist
ar·tis′tic
art′ist·ry

art′less
art′y
ar′um
as′a·fet′i·da
as·bes′tos
as·cend′
as·cend′an·cy
as·cen′sion
as·cent′
as·cer·tain′
as·cet′ic
as·cet′i·cism
as·ci′tes
a·scor′bic
as′cot
as·crib′a·ble
as·cribe′
as·crip′tion
a·sep′tic
a·sex′u·al
a·shamed′
ash′en
a·shore′
A′sian
a·side′
as′i·nine′
as′i·nin′i·ty
a·skance′
a·skew′
a·slant′
a·sleep′
a·so′cial
as·par′a·gus
as′pect
as′pen

as·per'i·ty
as·per'sion
as'phalt
as'pho·del'
as·phyx'i·a
as·phyx'i·ate'
as·phyx'i·a'tion
as'pic
as'pi·dis'tra
as'pir·ant,
   as·pir'ant
as'pi·rate'
as'pi·ra'tion
as·pire'
a·squint'
as'sa·gai'
as·sail'
as·sail'ant
as·sas'sin
as·sas'si·nate'
as·sas'si·na'tion
as·sault'
as·say'
as·sem'blage
as·sem'ble
as·sem'bly
as·sent'
as·sen'tor
as·sert'
as·ser'tion
as·ser'tive
as·sess'
as·ses'sor
as'set
as·sev'er·ate'

as·sid'u·ous
as·sign'
as'sig·na'tion
as·sign'ee'
as·sign'or'
as·sim'i·late'
as·sim'i·la'tion
as·sist'
as·sist'ant
as·size'
as·so'ci·ate'
as·so'ci·a'tion
as'so·nance
as·sort'
as·suage'
as·sum'a·ble
as·sume'
as·sump'tion
as·sur'ance
as·sure'
as·sur'ed·ly
a·stat'ic
as'ter
as'ter·isk'
a·stern'
as'ter·oid'
as·the'ni·a
as·then'ic
asth'ma
asth·mat'ic
as·tig·mat'ic
a·stig'ma·tism
a·stir'
as·ton'ish
as·tound'

a·strad'dle
as'tral
a·stray'
as·tric'tion
a·stride'
as·trin'gen·cy
as·trin'gent
as'tro·dome'
as'tro·labe'
as·trol'o·ger
as·trol'o·gy
as'tro·naut'
as·tron'o·mer
as'tro·nom'i·cal·ly
as·tron'o·my
as'tro·phys'i·cal
as'tro·phys'ics
as·tute'
a·sun'der
a·sy'lum
a'sym·met'ri·cal
a·sym'me·try
as'ymp·tote'
as'ymp·tot'ic
a·syn'chro·nism
at'a·vism
at'a·vis'tic
a·tax'i·a
at'el·ier'
a'the·ism
a'the·ist
a'the·is'ti·cal
ath'lete
ath·let'ic
a·thwart'

at'las
at'mos·phere'
at'mos·pher'ic
at'oll
at'om
a·tom'ic
at'om·ism
at'om·ize'
at'om·iz'er
a·ton'al·ism
a'to·nal'i·ty
a·tone'ment
a'tri·um
a·tro'cious
a·troc'i·ty
at'ro·phy
at'ro·pine'
at·tach'
at'ta·ché'
at·tach'ment
at·tack'
at·tain'
at·tain'a·ble
at'tar
at·tempt'
at·tend'
at·tend'ance
at·ten'tion
at·ten'tive
at·ten'u·ate'
at·test'
at'tic
at·tire'
at'ti·tude'
at'ti·tu'di·nize'

at·tor'ney
at·tract'
at·trac'tion
at·trib'ut·a·ble
at·tri'bute
at'tri·bu'tion
at·tri'tion
at·tune'
a·typ'i·cal
au'bade'
au'burn
auc'tion
auc'tion·eer'
au·da'cious
au·dac'i·ty
au'di·bil'i·ty
au'di·bly
au'di·ence
au'di·o'
au'dit
au·di'tion
au'di·tor
au'di·to'ri·um
au'di·to'ry
au'ger
aug·ment'
aug'men·ta'tion
au'gur
au'gu·ry
au·gust'
au na·tu·rel'
au'ra
au'ral
au're·ate
au're·ole'

au're·o·my'cin
au re·voir'
au'ric
au'ri·cle
au·ric'u·lar
au·ro'ra bo're·a'lis
aus·cul·ta'tion
aus'pice
aus·pi'cious
aus·tere'
aus·ter'i·ty
aus'tral
Aus·tral'ia
au'tarch·y
au·then'tic
au·then'ti·cate'
au'then·tic'i·ty
au'thor
au'thor·ess
au·thor'ri·al
au·thor'i·tar'i·an
au·thor'i·ta'tive
au·thor'i·ty
au'thor·ize'
au'tism
au·tis'tic
au'to·bi·og'ra·pher
au'to·bi'o·graph'i·cal
au'to·bi·og'ra·phy
au·toch'thon
au'to·clave'
au·toc'ra·cy
au'to·crat'
au'to·dyne'
au'to·e·rot'ic

au·tog'e·nous
au'to·graph'
au'to·harp'
au·tol'y·sis
au'to·mat'
au'to·mate'
au'to·mat'ic
au'to·mat'i·cal·ly
au'to·ma'tion
au·tom'a·ton
au'to·mo·bile'
au'to·mo'tive
au'to·nom'ic
au·ton'o·mous
au·ton'o·my
au'top·sy
au'to·sug·ges'tion
au'to·tox'in
au'tumn
au·tum'nal
au'tun·ite'
aux·il'ia·ry
a·vail'
a·vail'a·bil'i·ty
av'a·lanche'
av'a·rice

av'a·ri'cious
a·vast'
av'a·tar'
a·venge'
a've·nue'
a·ver'
av'er·age
a·ver'ment
a·verse'
a·ver'sion
a·vert'
a'vi·ar'y
a'vi·a'tion
a'vi·a'tor
a'vi·cul'ture
av'id
av'o·ca'do
av'o·ca'tion
a·void'
a·void'ance
av'oir·du·pois'
a·vouch'
a·vow'
a·vow'al
a·vun'cu·lar
a·wait'

a·wake'
a·wak'en
a·wak'en·ing
a·ward'
a·ware'
a·wash'
a·way'
a·weigh'
awe'some
aw'ful
awk'ward
awn'ing
a·woke'
a·wry'
ax'i·al
ax·il'la
ax'i·om
ax'i·o·mat'ic
ax'is
ax'le
ax'on
a·zal'ea
az'i·muth
a·zo'ic
az'ure
az'y·gous

B

bab'bitt·ry
bab'ble
Ba'bel
ba·boon'
ba'by
Bab'y·lon'
bac'ca·lau're·ate
bac'ca·rat'
bac'cha·nal
bac'cha·na'li·an
bac·chan'te
bac'ci·form'
bach'e·lor
ba·cil'lus
bac'i·tra'cin
back'ache'
back'bone'
back'fire'
back'gam'mon
back'ground'
back'hand'ed
back'lash'
back'slide'
back'stitch'
back'ward
back'wa'ter
back'woods'man
ba'con
bac·te'ri·a
bac·te'ri·al·ly
bac'te·rin

bac'te'ri·o·log'i·cal
bac'te'ri·ol'o·gy
bac·te'ri·um
ba·cu'li·form'
badg'er
bad'i·nage
bad'lands'
bad'min·ton
baf'fle
bag'a·telle'
ba'gel
bag'gage
bag'gy
bag'man
bag'pipe'
ba·guette'
Ba·ha'i
Ba·ha'ism
bail'a·ble
bail'ee'
bail'iff
bail'i·wick'
bail'ment
bail'or'
ba'ke·lite'
bak'er·y
bak'sheesh'
bal'a·lai'ka
bal'ance
bal'co·ny
bal'der·dash'

bald'pate'
bal'dric
ba·leen'
bale'ful
Bal'kans
balk'y
bal'lad
bal·lade'
bal'lad·mon'ger
bal'lad·ry
bal'last
bal'le·ri'na
bal'let
bal·lis'tic
bal·loon'
bal·loon'ist
bal'lot
ball'room'
bal'ly·hoo'
balm'i·ness
balm'y
ba·lo'ney
bal'sam
bal·sam'ic
Bal'tic
bal'us·trade'
bam·bi'no
bam·boo'
bam·boo'zle
ba'nal, ba·nal'
ba·nal'i·ty

ba·nan'a
band'age
ban·dan'na
ban·deaux'
ban'di·coot'
ban'dit
band'mas'ter
band'wag'on
ban'dy
bane'ful
ban'gle
ban'ish
ban'is·ter
ban'jo
bank'a·ble
bank'book'
bank'er
bank'rupt
bank'rupt'cy
ban'ner
ban'nock
ban'quet
ban·quette'
ban'shee
ban'tam·weight'
ban'ter
ban'yan
ba'o·bab'
bap'tism
bap·tis'mal
Bap'tist
bap'tize'
bar·bar'i·an
bar'ba·rism
bar'ba·rous

Bar'ba·ry
bar'bate
bar·be·cue'
bar'bell'
bar'ber
bar'ber'ry
bar·bette'
bar·bi'tu·rate
bard'ic
bare'faced'
bare'foot'
bare'hand'ed
bare'ly
bar'fly'
bar'gain
bar'ic
bar'ite
bar'i·tone'
bar'i·um
bar'keep'er
bark'er
bar'ley
bar'maid'
bar'na·cle
barn'storm'er
barn'yard'
ba·rom'e·ter
bar'o·met'ric
bar'on
bar'on·ess
bar'on·et
ba·ro'ni·al
ba·roque'
bar'o·scope'
ba·rouche'

bar'rack
bar·rage'
bar'ra·try
bar'rel
bar'ren
bar'ren·ness
bar·rette'
bar'ri·cade'
bar'ri·er
bar'ris·ter
bar'room'
bar'row
bar'tend'er
bar'ter
Bart'lett
bas'al
ba·salt'
base'ball'
base'board'
base'ment
bash'ful
bas'ic
bas'i·cal·ly
bas'il
bas'i·lar
ba·sil'i·ca
bas'i·lisk'
ba'sin
ba'sis
bas'ket
bas'ket·ball'
bas'ket·ry
bas'set
bas'si·net'
bas'so

bas·soon'
bas'tard
bas'tard·i·za'tion
bas'tar·dy
bas·tille'
bas'ti·na'do
bas'tion
ba·teau'
ba·the'tic
bath'i·nette'
bath'o·lith'
ba·thom'e·ter
ba'thos
bath'robe'
bath'room'
bath'y·scaph'
bath'y·sphere'
ba·tik'
ba·tiste'
ba·ton'
ba·tra'chi·an
bat·tal'ion
bat'ten
bat'ter
bat'ter·y
bat'ting
bat'tle
bat'tle·dore'
bat'tle·field'
bat'tle·ment
bat·tue'
bat'ty
bau'ble
baux'ite
Ba·var'i·an

bawd'i·ness
bawd'ry
bawd'y·house'
bay'ard
bay'ber'ry
bay'o·net
bay'ou
ba·zaar'
ba·zoo'ka
beach'comb'er
beach'head'
bea'con
bea'dle
bead'y
bea'gle
bean'stalk'
bear'a·ble
bear'er
beast'li·ness
beat'en
be'a·tif'ic
be·at'i·fi·ca'tion
be·at'i·fy'
be·at'i·tude'
beat'nik'
beau·i·de'al
beau'te·ous
beau·ti'cian
beau'ti·fi·ca'tion
beau'ti·ful
beau'ty
bea'ver
be·calm'
be·came'
be·cause'

bé'cha·mel'
beck'et
beck'on
be·cloud'
be·come'
be·com'ing
Bec'que·rel'
be·daz'zle
bed'bug'
bed'ding
be·deck'
be·dev'il
be·dev'il·ment
be·dew'
bed'fel'low
be·dim'
be·diz'en
bed'lam
bed'lam·ite'
Bed'ou·in
bed'pan'
be·drag'gle
bed'rid'den
bed'rock'
bed'side'
bed'spread'
bed'time'
beech'en
beech'wood'
beef'eat'er
beef'i·ness
beef'y
bee'hive'
bee'line'
Be·el'ze·bub'

beer′y
bees′wax′
bee′tle
bee′tling
be·fall′
be·fit′ting
be·fog′
be·fore′
be·fore′hand
be·foul′
be·friend′
be·fud′dle
be·gan′
be·get′
be·get′ter
beg′gar
be·gin′
be·gin′ner
be·gone′
be·go′ni·a
be·got′ten
be·grime′
be·grudge′
be·guile′
be·guile′ment
be·gun′
be·half′
be·have′
be·hav′ior
be·hav′ior·ism
be·hav′ior·is′tic
be·head′
be·held′
be·he′moth
be·hest′

be·hind′
be·hold′
be·hold′en
be·hoove′
be′ing
be·jew′el
be·la′bor
be·lat′ed
be·lay′
bel can′to
bel′dam
be·lea′guer
bel′fry
Bel′gian
be·lie′
be·lief′
be·liev′a·ble
be·lieve′
be·liev′er
be·lit′tle
bel′la·don′na
bell′boy′
bel·let′rist
bel′le·tris′tic
bell′hop′
bel′li·cose′
bel′lied
bel·lig′er·ence
bel·lig′er·ent
bel′low
bell′weth′er
bel′ly
be·long′
be·long′ings
be·lov′ed

be·low′
be·lu′ga
bel′ve·dere′
be·mire′
be·moan′
be·mused′
ben′a·dryl
bend′er
be·neath′
ben′e·dict′
Ben′e·dic′tine
ben′e·dic′tion
ben′e·fac′tion
ben′e·fac′tor
ben′e·fice
be·nef′i·cence
be·nef′i·cent
ben′e·fi′cial
ben′e·fi′ci·ar′y
ben′e·fit
be·nev′o·lence
be·nev′o·lent
be·night′ed
be·nign′
be·nig′nant
ben′i·son
ben′ton·ite′
ben′ze·drine′
ben′zene
ben′zi·dine′
ben′zine
ben′zo·caine′
ben·zo′ic
be·queath′
be·quest′

be·rate'
ber'ber·ine'
be·reave'
be·reave'ment
be·reft'
be·ret'
ber'ga·mot'
be·rib'boned
ber'i·ber'i
berke'li·um
ber·lin', ber'lin
ber'ried
ber'ry
ber·seem'
ber'serk, ber·serk'
ber'serk·er,
    ber·serk'er
ber'yl
be·ryl'li·um
be·seech'
be·seem'
be·set'
be·set'ting
be·side'
be·sides'
be·siege'
be·smirch'
be'som
be·sot'ted
be·sought'
be·spat'ter
be·speak'
be·spec'ta·cled
be·spoke'
Bes'se·mer

bes'tial
bes'ti·al'i·ty
bes'ti·ar'y
be·stir'
be·stow'
be·stow'al
be'ta
be'ta·ine'
be·take'
be'ta·tron'
beth'el
be·think'
be·tide'
be·times'
be·to'ken
be·tray'
be·tray'al
be·troth'al
be·trothed'
bet'ter
bet'ter·ment
bet'ting
bet'tor
be·tween'
be·twixt'
bev'el
bev'er·age
bev'y
be·wail'
be·ware'
be·wil'der
be·wil'der·ment
be·witch'
be·yond'
be·zique'

bi'as
bi'au·ric'u·late
bi·ax'i·al
bib'cock'
bib'li·og'ra·pher
bib'li·o·graph'i·cal
bib'li·og'ra·phy
bib'li·ol'a·try
bib'li·o·ma'ni·a
bib'li·o·phile'
bib'u·lous
bi·cam'er·al
bi·car'bon·ate
bi'cen·te'nar·y
bi'cen·ten'ni·al
bi'ceps
bi·chlo'ride
bi·cip'i·tal
bick'er
bi·cus'pid
bi'cy·cle
bid'der
bid'ding
bid'dy
bi·det'
bi·en'ni·al
bi'fid
bi·fo'cal, bi·fo'cal
bi·fo'li·ate
bi·fur·cate'
bi·fur·ca'tion
big'a·mist
big'a·my
big'ot
big'ot·ry

big'wig'
bi'jou
bi·la'bi·al
bil'an·der
bi·lat'er·al
bil'ber'ry
bi·lin'gual
bil'ious
bill'a·ble
bill'board'
bil'let
bill'fold'
bil'liard
bil'lings·gate'
bil'lion
bil'lion·aire'
bil'low
bil'low·y
bil'ly
bi·loc'u·lar
bi·man'u·al
bi·met'al·ism
bi·month'ly
bi'na·ry
bin·au'ral
bind'er
bind'er·y
bin'dle
bin'go
bin'na·cle
bin·oc'u·lar
bi·no'mi·al
bi·nu'cle·ate'
bi'o·as'tro·nau'tics
bi'o·chem'i·cal

bi'o·chem'is·try
bi'o·cide'
bi'o·de·grad'a·ble
bi'o·gen'e·sis
bi'o·ge·og'ra·phy
bi·og'ra·pher
bi·og'ra·phy
bi'o·log'i·cal
bi'o·log'i·cal·ly
bi·ol'o·gist
bi·ol'o·gy
bi'o·lu'mi·nes'cence
bi'o·met'rics
bi'o·nom'ics
bi'o·phys'i·cal
bi'o·phys'ics
bi'op·sy
bi·o'ta
bi·ot'ic
bi'o·type'
bi·pa'rous
bi·par'ti·san
bi·par'tite
bi'ped
bi·pe·dal
bi·pin'nate
bi·plane'
bi·po'lar
bi·quar'ter·ly
bi·ra'di·al
birch'en
bird'seed'
bi'reme
bi·ret'ta
birl'ing

birth'day'
birth'mark'
birth'place'
birth'right'
bis'cuit
bi·sect'
bi·sec'tion
bi·sec'tor
bi·sex'u·al
bish'op
bish'op·ric
bis'muth
bi'son
bis'tro
bi·sym·met'ri·cal
bi·sym'me·try
bit'ing
bit'ten
bit'ter
bit'tern
bit'ter·sweet'
bi·tu'men
bi·tu'mi·nous
bi·va'lence
bi·va'lent
bi'valve'
biv'ou·ac'
bi·week'ly
bi·zarre'
blab'ber
black'ber'ry
black'bird'
black'board'
black'en
black'guard

black'jack'
black'mail'
black'out'
black'top'
blad'der
blad'der·nose'
blade'bone'
blam'a·ble
blame'a·ble
blame'wor'thy
blanc·mange'
blan'dish·ment
blan'ket
blank'ly
blar'ney
bla·sé'
blas·pheme'
blas'phe·mous
blas'phe·my
blas·te'ma
blas'to·derm'
blas'to·gen'e·sis
blas'tu·la
bla'tan·cy
bla'tant
blath'er
blaz'er
bla'zon
bla'zon·ry
bleach'ers
blear'y
bleed'er
blem'ish
bless'ing
blight'er

blind'er
blind'fold'
blink'er
bliss'ful
blis'ter
blith'er·ing
blitz'krieg'
bliz'zard
bloat'er
block·ade'
block'age
block'bust'er
block'head'
block'ish
blood'cur'dling
blood'hound'
blood'i·ly
blood'let'ting
blood'y
bloom'er
blos'som
blotch'y
blot'ter
blot'to
blow'er
blow'out'
blow'torch'
blowz'y
blub'ber
blub'ber·y
blud'geon
blue'ber'ry
blue'fish'
blue'grass'
blue'nose'

bluff'er
blu'ing
blu'ish
blun'der
blun'der·buss'
blur'ry
blush'er
blus'ter
blus'ter·y
board'er
board'ing·house'
board'walk'
boar'ish
boast'ful
boat'house'
boat'swain
bob'bin
bob'bi·net'
bob'by
bob'cat'
bob'o·link'
bob'sled'
bob'sleigh'
bob'tail'
bob'white'
bod'ice
bod'ied
bod'i·ly
bod'ing
bod'kin
bod'y
bod'y·guard'
bo'gey
bog'gle
bog'gy

bo'gie
bo'gus
bo'gy
bo·he'mi·an
boil'er
bois'ter·ous
bo'la
bold'ness
bo·le'ro
bo'lide
bol'i·var
bol'lix
bol'she·vism
bol'son
bol'ster
bo'lus
bom·bard'
bom'bard·ier'
bom·bard'ment
bom'bast
bom·bas'ti·cal·ly
bom'ba·zine'
bomb'er
bomb'shell'
bo'na fi'de
bo·nan'za
bon'bon'
bond'age
bond'ed
bonds'man
bone'less
bon'fire'
bon'go
bon'ho·mie'

bon'hom·mie'
bon'i·face'
bon'i·ness
bon'net
bon'ny
bon·sai'
bo·nus
bon vi·vant'
bon voy·age'
bon'y
boo'by
boo'dle
boo'gie-woo'gie
boo'hoo'
book'ish
book'keep'ing
book'let
book'mak'er
book'mo·bile'
book'rack'
book'store'
boom'er·ang
boon'docks'
boon'dog'gle
boor'ish
boost'er
boot'black'
boot'ee
boot'leg'ger
boo'ty
booz'i·ly
booz'y
bo'ra
bo'ra·cite'

bor'age
bo'rat·ed
bo'rax
bor·del'lo
bor'der
bor'der·land'
bor'der·line'
bo're·al
bore'dom
bor'er
bo'ric
bo'ride
bor'ing
bor'ne·ol'
born'ite
bo'ron
bor'ough
bor'row
bor'zoi
bos'cage
bos'ket
bosk'y
bos'om
bos'quet
boss'ism
boss'y
Bos'ton
bo'sun
bo·tan'i·cal
bot'a·nist
bot'a·ny
both'er
both'er·a'tion
both'er·some

bot'ry·o·my·co'sis
bot'tle
bot'tle·neck'
bot'tom
bot'tom·less
bot'u·lin
bot'u·li'nus
bot'u·lism
bou·clé'
bou'doir
bouf·fant'
bou'gie
bouil'la·baisse'
bouil'lon
boul'der
boul'e·vard'
boul'ter
bounc'er
bound'a·ry
bound'er
bound'less
boun'te·ous
boun'ti·ful
boun'ty
bou·quet'
bour'bon
bour·geois'
bour'geoi·sie'
bour'rée'
bou'stro·phe'don
bou'ton·niere'
bo'vine
bowd'ler·ize'
bow'el

bow'er
bow'er·y
bow'fin'
bow'ie
bow'leg'ged
bowl'er
bow'line
bowl'ing
bow'sprit'
bow'string'
box'car'
box'er
box'haul'
box'ing
boy'ar'
boy'cott'
boy'ish
boy'sen·ber'ry
brab'ble
brace'let
brac'er
bra'chi·al
bra'chi·ate
bra'chi·o·pod'
brach'y·ce·phal'ic
bra·chyl'o·gy
brac'ing
brack'en
brack'et
brack'ish
brad'y·car'di·a
brag'ga·do'ci·o
brag'gart
brag'ger

Brah'min
braid'ing
brain'less
brain'storm'ing
brain'wash'
brain'y
brake'age
brake'man
bram'ble
bram'bly
bran'chi·ae'
bran'chi·o·pod'
bran'died
bran'dish
bran'dy
bra'sier
brass'age
bras·siere'
brass'i·ness
brass'ware'
brass'y
brat'tice
bra·va'do
brav'er·y
bra·vis'si·mo'
bra'vo
bra·vu'ra
brawl'ing
brawn'i·ness
brawn'y
brax'y
bra'zen
bra'zen·faced'
bra'zier

bra·zil'wood'
bread'bas'ket
bread'fruit'
bread'win'ner
break'a·ble
break'age
break'down'
break'er
break'fast
break'neck'
break'through'
break'wa'ter
breast'work'
breath'a·ble
breath'er
breath'ing
breath'less
breath'y
brec'ci·a
breech'cloth'
breech'es
breech'ing
breech'load'er
breed'er
breed'ing
breez'i·ly
breez'y
breg'ma
breth'ren
bre'vi·ar'y
brev'i·ty
brew'age
brew'er
brew'er·y

brew'is
bri'ar
brib'a·ble
brib'er·y
brick'lay'er
brick'work'
bri·cole'
brid'al
bride'groom'
brides'maid'
bridge'head'
bridg'ing
bri'dle
bri·doon'
bri'er
bri·gade'
brig'a·dier'
brig'and
brig'and·age
brig'an·tine'
bright'en
bright'ness
bril'liance
bril'lian·cy
bril'liant
bril'lian·tine'
brim'stone'
brin'dled
Bri·nell'
brink'man·ship'
brin'y
bri'oche
bri'o·lette'
bri·quette'

bri·quet'
bris'ket
bris'tle
bris'tly
brits'ka
brit'tle
broad'ax'
broad'brim'
broad'cast'
broad'cast'er
broad'cloth'
broad'en
broad'leaf'
broad'loom'
broad'side'
bro·cade'
bro'ca·tel'
bro'ca·telle'
broc'co·li
bro·chette'
bro·chure'
brock'et
bro'gan
broil'er
bro'kage
bro'ken
bro'ken·heart'ed
bro'ker
bro'ker·age
bro'ma
bro'mal
bro'mic
bro'mide
bro'mine

bro'mism
bron'chi·a
bron'chi·al
bron'chi·ole'
bron·chi'tis
bron'cho·scope'
bron'chus
bron'co
bron'co·bust'er
bron'to·sau'rus
brood'er
brood'y
brook'let
broom'stick'
broth'el
broth'er
broth'er·hood'
broth'er·ly
brou'ha'ha'
brow'beat'
Brown'i·an
brown'ie
brown'out'
brown'stone'
brows'ing
bruc'ine
bru'in
bruis'er
bru'mal
bru'mous
bru·nette'
brush'wood'
brush'work'
brusque'ness

bru'tal
bru·tal'i·ty
bru'tal·ize'
brut'ish
bry·ol'o·gy
bry'o·ny
bry'o·zo'an
bub'ble
bub'bly
bu'bo
bu·bon'ic
buc'cal
buc'ca·neer'
buc'ci·na'tor
buck'a·roo'
buck'board'
buck'et
buck'eye'
buck'le
buck'ler
buck'ram
buck'shot'
buck'skin'
buck'toothed'
Bud'dhism
Bud'dhist
bud'dle
bud'dy
budg'er·i·gar'
budg'et
budg'et·ar'y
budg'ie
buf'fa·lo'
buff'er

buf'fer
buf'fet,
  buf·fet'
buf'fo
buf·foon'
buf·foon'er·y
bug'a·boo'
bug'bane'
bug'bear'
bug'ger
bug'ger·y
bug'gy
bu'gle
bu'gler
bu'gloss
build'er
build'ing
bul·ba'ceous
bulb'ous
bul'bul
bulg'ing
bulg'y
bu·lim'i·a
bulk'head'
bulk'i·ness
bulk'y
bul'la
bull'dog'
bull'doze'
bull'doz'er
bul'let
bul'le·tin
bul'let·proof'
bull'fight'

bull'fight'er
bull'finch'
bull'head'ed
bul'lion
bull'ish
bul'ly
bul'rush'
bul'wark
bum'ble·bee'
bump'er
bump'i·ness
bump'kin
bump'tious
bump'y
bu'na
bunch'y
bun'combe
bun'dle
bun'ga·low'
bun'gle
bun'ion
bunk'er
bunk'mate'
bun'kum
bun'ny
Bun'sen
bunt'ing
bunt'line
buoy'an·cy
buoy'ant
bu·ran'
bur'ble
bur'bot
bur'den

bur'den·some
bur'dock'
bu'reau
bu·reauc'ra·cy
bu'reau·crat'
bu'reau·crat'i·cal·ly
bu·ret'
bu·rette'
burg'age
bur'geon
bur'gess
burgh'er
bur'glar
bur'glar·ize'
bur'gla·ry
bur'go·mas'ter
bur'i·al
bur'lap
bur·lesque'
bur'li·ness
bur'ly
burn'er
bur'net
burn'ing
bur'nish
bur'nish·er
bur·noose'
burn'out'
bur'ro
bur'row
bur'sa
bur'sal
bur'sar
bur'sa·ry

bur'seed'
bur·si'tis
bur'ton
bur'weed'
bur'y
bush'el
bush'ham'mer
bu'shi·do'
bush'i·ness
bush'man
bush'whack'er
bush'y
bus'i·ly
busi'ness
busi'ness·like'
busi'ness·wom'an
bus'kin
bus'man
bus'tard
bust'er
bus'tle
bus'y
bus'y·bod'y
bus'y·ness
bu'ta·di·ene
bu'tane, bu·tane'
butch'er
butch'er·y
bu'tene
but'ler
but'ter
but'ter·ball'
but'ter·cup'
but'ter·fin'gers

but'ter·fly'
but'ter·y
but'tock
but'ton
but'ton·hole'
but'tress
bu'tyl
bu'tyl·ene'

bu'tyn
bux'om
buy'er
buz'zard
buz'zer
by'gone'
by'law'

by'pass'
by'road'
by'stand'er
by'way'
by'word'
By·zan'tine,
   By'zan·tine'

C

ca·bal′
cab′a·la, cab·a′la
cab′a·list
cab′a·lis′tic
ca·bal·le′ro
ca·ba′na
cab′a·ret′
cab′bage
cab′by
ca′ber
cab′in
cab′i·net
cab′i·net·mak′er
ca′ble
ca′ble·gram′
cab′man
ca·bo·chon′
ca·boo′dle
ca·boose′
ca·bril′la
cab′ri·o·let′
ca·ca′o
cach′a·lot′
ca·chet′
ca·chex′i·a
cack′le
cack′ling
cac′o·dyl
ca·cog′ra·phy
ca·coph′o·nous
ca·coph′o·ny

cac′tus
ca·cu′mi·nal
ca·das′tre
ca·dav′er
ca·dav′er·ous
cad′die
cad′dish
cad′dy
ca·delle′
ca′dence
ca′den·cy
ca·den′za
ca·det′
ca·det′cy
cadg′y
cad′mi·um
ca′dre
ca·du′ce·an
ca·du′ce·us
ca·du′cous
cae·cil′i·an
cae′cum
Cae·sar′e·an
Cae·sar′i·an
cae·su′ra
ca·fé′
caf′e·te′ri·a
caf′feine
caf′tan
cag′er
cage′y

cag′i·er
cag′i·ly
cais′son
cai′tiff
ca·jole′
ca·jol′er·y
cake′walk′
cal′a·bash′
cal′a·boose′
cal′a·mine′
ca·lam′i·tous
ca·lam′i·ty
cal·car′e·ous
cal′cic
cal′ci·fi·ca′tion
cal′ci·fy′
cal′ci·mine′
cal′cine′
cal′cite′
cal′ci·um
cal·cog′ra·phy
cal′cu·la·bil′i·ty
cal′cu·la·ble
cal′cu·late′
cal′cu·lat′ing
cal′cu·la′tion
cal′cu·la′tor
cal′cu·lus
cal·dar′i·um
cal·de′ra
cal′dron

cal'e·fa'cient
cal'e·fac'tion
cal'e·fac'to·ry
cal'en·dar
cal'en·der
cal'ends
ca·len'du·la
cal'en·ture'
ca·les'cent
calf'skin'
cal'i·ber
cal'i·brate'
cal'i·bra'tion
cal'i·bra'tor
cal'i·ces'
cal'i·co'
ca'lif
cal'if·ate'
cal'i·for'ni·um
ca·lig'i·nous
cal'i·pash'
cal'i·per
ca'liph
cal'iph·ate'
cal'is·then'ics
ca'lix
calk'er
cal'la
call'a·ble
call'board'
call'er
cal·lig'ra·phy
call'ing
cal·li'o·pe
cal·los'i·ty

cal'lous
cal'low
cal'lus
cal'ma·tive
cal'o·mel
ca·lor'ic
cal'o·ric'i·ty
cal'o·rie
cal'o·ri·met'ric
cal'o·rim'e·try
ca·lotte'
cal'o·yer
cal'trop
cal'trap
cal'u·met'
ca·lum'ni·ate'
cal'um·ny
cal·var'i·a
Cal'vin·ism
cal'y·ces'
ca·lyp'so
ca'lyx
ca'ma·ra'de·rie
cam'a·ril'la
cam'ber
cam'bist
cam'bi·um
Cam'bri·an
cam'bric
cam'el
ca·mel'li·a
ca·mel'o·pard'
Cam'em·bert'
cam'e·o'
cam'er·a

cam'er·al
cam'er·a lu'ci·da
cam'er·a ob·scu'ra
cam'er·lin'go
cam'i·sole'
cam'let
cam'o·mile'
cam'ou·flage'
cam·pa'gna
cam·paign'
cam·paign'er
cam·pa'ni·le
cam·pe·si'no
camp'fire'
camp'ground'
cam'phene
cam'phol
cam'phor
cam'phor·at'ed
cam'pi·on
cam'po
cam'pus
Ca·na'di·an
ca·naille'
ca·nal'
ca·nal'boat'
can'a·lic'u·late
can'a·lic'u·lus
ca·nal'i·za'tion
ca·na·pé
ca·nard'
ca·nar'y
ca·nas'ta
can'can'
can'cel

can'cel·la'tion
can'cer
can'cer·ous
can'croid
can'de·la'brum
can'dent
can·des'cent
can'did
can'di·da·cy
can'di·date
can'died
can'dle
can'dle·fish'
can'dle·light'
can'dle·wood'
can'dor
can'dour
can'dy
cane'brake'
ca·nel'la
ca·nes'cent
can'field'
ca·nic'u·lar
can'is·ter
can'ker
can'ker·ous
can'ker·worm'
can'na
can'na·bin
can'na·bis
can'nel
can'ner
can'ner·y
can'ni·bal
can'ni·bal·is'tic

can'ni·bal·ize'
can'ni·ly
can'ni·ness
can'ning
can'non
can'non·ade'
can'nu·la
can'ny
ca·noe'
can'on
can'on·ess
ca·non'i·cal
can'on·i·za'tion
can'on·ized'
ca·no'pic
can'o·py
can·ta'bi·le'
can·ta·loupe'
can·tan'ker·ous
can·ta'ta
can·teen'
can'ter
can'tha·ris
can'thus
can'ti·cle
can'ti·le'ver
can·ti'na
can'tle
can'to
can'ton, can·ton'
can'tor
can'tus fir'mus
can'vas
can'vass
can'yon

can'zo·net'
ca'pa·bil'i·ty
ca'pa·ble
ca'pa·bly
ca·pa'cious
ca·pac'i·tate'
ca·pac'i·tor
ca·pac'i·ty
ca·par'i·son
cap'e·lin
ca'per
cap'ful'
ca'pi·as
cap'il·lar'y
cap'i·tal
cap'i·tal·ism
cap'i·tal·ist
cap'i·tal'i·za'tion
cap'i·tal·ize'
cap'i·tate'
cap'i·ta'tion
cap'i·tol
ca·pit'u·lar
ca·pit'u·late'
ca·pit'u·la'tion
ca·pit'u·lum
ca'pon
cap'per
ca·price'
ca·pri'cious
cap'ri·ole'
ca·pro'ic
cap·sa'i·cin
cap·size'
cap'stan

cap'su·late'
cap'sule
cap'tain
cap'tain·cy
cap'tion
cap'tious
cap'ti·vate'
cap'ti·va'tion
cap'tive
cap·tiv'i·ty
cap'tor
Cap'u·chin'
car'a·bi·neer'
ca'ra·bi·nie'ri
car'a·cole'
car'a·cul
ca·rafe'
car'a·mel
car'a·mel·ize'
car'a·pace'
car'at
car'a·van
car'a·van'sa·ry
car'a·van'se·rai'
car'a·vel'
car'a·way'
car'bide
car'bine
car'bi·nol'
car'bo·hy'drate
car·bol'ic
car'bon
car'bo·na'ceous
car'bo·na'do
car'bon·ate'

car'bon·at'ed
car'bon·a'tion
car·bon'ic
car·bon··if'er·ous
car'bon·i·za'tion
car'bon·ize'
car·bo·run'dum
car'boy
car'bun·cle
car'bu·ret'
car'bu·re'tor
car'bu·rize'
car'byl·a·mine'
car'cass
car·cin'o·gen
car'ci·no'ma
car'ci·no'ma·to'sis
car'da·mom
car'da·mon
card'board'
card'er
car'di·ac'
car'di·gan
car'di·nal
card'ing
car'di·o·gram'
car'di·o·graph'
car'di·ol'o·gy
card'sharp'
ca·reen'
ca·reer'
ca·reer'ist
care'free'
care'ful
care'less

ca·ress'
care'tak'er
care'worn'
car'fare'
car'go
car'hop'
car'i·bou'
car'i·ca·ture
car'i·ca·tur·ist
car'ies
car'il·lon'
car'il·lon·neur'
ca·ri'na
car'i·nat'ed
car'i·o'ca
car'i·ole'
car'i·ous
cark'ing
car'ling
car'load'
car'ma·gnole'
car'man
Car'mel·ite'
car'mine
car'nage
car'nal
car·nal'i·ty
car'nall·ite'
car·nas'si·al
car·na'tion
car·nel'ian
car'ni·val
car'ni·vore'
car·niv'o·rous
car'no·tite'

car'ob
ca·roche'
car'ol
car'ol·ing
car'ol·ling
Car'o·lin'gi·an
car'o·lus
car'om
car'o·tene'
ca·rot'e·noid'
ca·rot'id
ca·rous'al
ca·rouse'
ca·rous'er
car'pel
car'pel·lar'y
car'pen·ter
car'pen·try
car'pet
car'pet·bag'
car'pet·bag'ger
carp'ing
car'po·go'ni·um
car'port'
car'pus
car'rack
car'ra·geen'
car'rel
car'rell
car'riage
car'rick
car'ri·er
car'ri·on
car'rom
car'ron

car'rot
car'rou·sel'
car'ry
car'ry·all'
car'ry·ing
cart'age
car·tel'
car'ter
Car·te'sian·ism
car'ti·lage
car'ti·lag'i·nous
cart'load'
car'to·gram'
car·tog'ra·pher
car·tog'ra·phy
car'ton
car·toon'
car·toon'ist
car·touche'
car'tridge
car'un·cle
ca·run'cu·lar
car'va·crol'
carv'er
carv'ing
car'y·a'tid
ca·sa'ba
ca'sa·no'va
cas'bah
cas·cade'
ca'se·ase'
ca'se·ate'
ca'se·a'tion
ca'se·fy'
ca'se·in

ca'se·in'o·gen'
case'ment
ca'se·ous
case'worm'
cash'ew
cash·ier'
cash'mere
cas'ing
ca·si'no
cas'ket
cas·sa'ba
cas·san'dra
cas·sa'tion
cas·sa'va
cas'se·role'
cas'sia
cas'si·mere'
cas·sit'er·ite'
cas'sock
cas'so·war'y
cas'ta·nets'
cast'a·way'
cas'tel·lan
cas'tel·lat'ed
cast'er
cas'ti·gate'
cas'ti·ga'tion
cas'ti·ga'tor
cast'ing
cas'tle
cas'tor
cas·to're·um
cas·tra·me·ta'tion
cas'trate
cas·tra'tion

cas'u·al
cas'u·al·ty
cas'u·ist
cas'u·is'tic
cas'u·ist·ry
ca·sus·bel'li
cat'a·bol'ic
ca·tab'o·lism
cat'a·caus'tic
cat'a·chre'sis
cat'a·cli'nal
cat'a·clysm
cat'a·clys'mal
cat'a·clys'mic
cat'a·comb'
cat'a·falque'
cat'a·lase'
cat'a·lep'sy
cat'a·lep'tic
cat'a·log'
cat'a·logue'
cat'a·logu'er
ca·tal'pa
ca·tal'y·sis
cat'a·lyst
cat'a·lyt'ic
cat'a·ma·ran'
cat'a·mite'
cat'a·mount'
cat'a·pla'si·a
cat'a·pult'
cat'a·ract'
ca·tarrh'
ca·tas'tro·phe
cat'a·stroph'ic

ca·tas'tro·phism
cat'a·to'ni·a
cat'a·ton'ic
cat'bird'
cat'call'
catch'all'
catch'er
catch'i·er
catch'y
cat'e·chism
cat'e·chis'mal
cat'e·chist
cat'e·chi·za'tion
cat'e·chize
cat'e·chu'men
cat'e·chu'me·nal
cat'e·gor'i·cal
cat'e·gor'i·cal·ly
cat'e·gor·ize'
cat'e·go'ry
cat'e·nate
ca'ter
ca'ter·er
cat'er·pil'lar
cat'er·waul'
cat'er·waul'ing
cat'fish'
ca·thar'sis
ca·thar'tic
ca·the'dral
cath'e·ter
cath'ode
Cath'o·lic
Ca·thol'i·cism
cath'o·lic'i·ty

cat'i'on
cat'kin
cat'like'
cat'nip'
ca·top'tric
ca·top'tri·cal
cat'rigged'
cat'sup
cat'tail'
cat'ti·ness
cat'tle
cat'tle·man
cat'ty
cat'walk'
cau·ca'sian
cau'cus
cau'dal
cau'date
cau'dex
cau'dle
caul'dron
cau'li·flow'er
cau'line
caulk'er
caulk'ing
caus'al
cau·sal'i·ty
cau·sa'tion
cause cé·lèbre'
cause'less
cause'way'
caus'tic
caus'ti·cal·ly
cau'ter·i·za'tion
cau'ter·ize'

cau'ter·y
cau'tion
cau'tion·ar'y
cau'tious
cav'al·cade'
cav'a·lier'
cav'a·lier'ly
cav'al·ry
cav'al·ry·man
cav'a·ti'na
ca've·at'
ca've·at' emp'tor
cav'en·dish
cav'ern
cav'ern·ous
cav'i·ar'
cav'il
cav'il·er
cav'il·ler
cav'i·ty
ca·vort'
ca'vy
cay·enne'
cease'less
ce'dar
ce·dil'la
ce'i·ba'
ceil'ing
cel'e·brant
cel'e·brate'
cel'e·brat'ed
cel'e·bra'tion
ce·leb'ri·ty
ce·ler'i·ty
cel'er·y

ce·les'ta
ce·les'tial
cel'es·tite'
cel'i·ba·cy
cel'i·bate
cel'lar
cel'lar·age
cel'list
cel'lo
cel'lo·phane'
cel'lu·lar
cel'lu·late'
cel'lule
cel'lu·loid'
cel'lu·lose'
cel'o·tex'
Cel'si·us
cel'tic
ce·ment'
ce'men·ta'tion
cem'e·ter'y
cen'o·bite'
ce'no·bit·ism
ce'no·gen'e·sis
cen'o·taph'
Ce'no·zo'ic
cen'ser
cen'sor
cen·so'ri·al
cen·so'ri·ous
cen'sor·ship'
cen'sur·a·ble
cen'sure
cen'sus
cen'taur

cen·ta'vo
cen'te·nar'i·an
cen'te·nar'y
cen·ten'ni·al
cen'ter
cen'ter·board'
cen'ter·piece'
cen·tes'i·mal
cen'ti·are'
cen'ti·grade'
cen'ti·gram'
cen'ti·li'ter
cen'time
cen'ti·me'ter
cen'ti·pede'
cen'tral
cen'tral·ism
cen'tral·ist
cen·tral'i·ty
cen·tral·i·za'tion
cen'tral·ize'
cen'tral·ly
cent're
cen'tric
cen·tric'i·ty
cen·trif'u·gal
cen'tri·fuge'
cen·trip'e·tal
cen'trist
cen'troid
cen'tro·some'
cen'tro·sphere'
cen'trum
cen·tu'pli·cate'
cen·tu'ri·al

cen·tu'ri·on
cen'tu·ry
ce·phal'ic
ceph'a·lom'e·ter
ceph'a·lom'e·try
ceph'a·lo·pod'
ce·ra'ceous
ce·ram'ic
cer'a·mist
ce'rate
ce'rat·ed
ce're·al
cer'e·bel'lar
cer'e·bel'lum
cer'e·bral
cer'e·brate'
cer'e·bra'tion
cer'e·brum
cere'cloth'
cere'ment
cer'e·mo'ni·al
cer'e·mo'ni·ous
cer'e·mo'ny
ce're·us
ce'ri·a
ce·rif'er·ous
ce·rise'
ce'rite
ce'ri·um
ce'ro·type'
cer'tain
cer'tain·ly
cer'tain·ty
cer'ti·fi'a·ble
cer·ti·fi·cate

cer'ti·fi·ca'tion
cer'ti·fied'
cer'ti·fi'er
cer'ti·fy'
cer·ti·o·ra'ri
cer'ti·tude'
ce·ru'le·an
ce·ru'men
cer'vi·cal
cer'vi·ces'
cer'vi·ci'tis
cer'vine
cer'vix
Ce·sar'e·an
Ce·sar'i·an
ce'si·um
ces·sa'tion
ces'sion
cess'pit'
cess'pool'
ces'tode
ces'tus
ce·su'ra
ce'tane
cha·conne'
chaf'er
chaf'fer
chaff'y
chaf'ing
cha·grin'
chain'stitch'
chair'man
chair'per'son
chair'wom'an
chal·ced'o·ny

chal'cid
chal'co·cite'
chal'dron
cha·let'
chal'ice
chalk'i·ness
chalk'y
chal'lenge
chal'leng·er
cha·lyb'e·ate
cha·made'
cham'ber
cham'ber·lain
cham'ber·maid'
cham'bray
cha·me'le·on
cham'fer
cham'ois
cham·pagne'
cham·paign'
cham'per·ty
cham·pi'gnon
cham'pi·on
cham'pi·oned
cham'pi·on·ship'
chan'cel·ler·y
chan'cel·lor
chan'cel·lor·ship'
chan'cer·y
chan'cre
chan'croid
chanc'y
chan·de·lier'
chan·delle'
chan'dler·y

change′a·bil′i·ty
change′a·ble
change′less
change′ling
chan′nel
chant′er
chan′teuse′
chan′tey
chan′ti·cleer′
chan·til′ly
chan′try
chant′y
cha′os
cha·ot′ic
cha·ot′i·cal·ly
chap·ar′ral′
chap′book′
cha·peau′
chap′el
chap′er·on′
chap′er·one′
chap′fall′en
chap′i·ter
chap′lain
chap′lain·cy
chap′let
chap′ter
char′a·banc′
char′ac·ter
char′ac·ter·is′tic
char′ac·ter·is′ti·cal·ly
char′ac·ter·i·za′tion
char′ac·ter·ize′
cha·rade′
char′coal

charge′a·ble
char·gé′ d′af·faires′
charg′er
charg′ing
char′i·ot
char′i·ot·eer′
char′i·ta·ble
char′i·ty
char′la·tan
charm′er
charm′ing
char′nel
char′ter
chart′less
char·treuse′
chart′room
char′tu·lar′y
char′wom′an
char′y
chas′er
chas′ing
chas·seur′
chas′sis
chas′ten
chas′tise′
chas′tise·ment
chas′ti·ty
chas′u·ble
châ·teau′
chat′e·lain′
chat′e·laine′
cha·toy′ant
chat′tel
chat′ter
chat′ter·box′

chat′ter·er
chat′ti·ness
chat′ty
chauf·fer′
chauf·feur′
chau′vin·ism
chau′vin·ist
chau′vin·is′tic
chau′vin·is′ti·cal·ly
chaz′an
cheap′en
cheap′ly
cheat′er
check′book′
check′er
check′er·board′
check′ered
check′ers
check′mate′
check′off′
check′rein′
check′room′
check′up′
ched′dar
chedd′ite
cheek′bone′
cheek′i·ly
cheek′i·ness
cheek′y
cheer′ful
cheer′i·ly
cheer′i·o′
cheer′less
cheer′y
cheese′cake′

cheese'cloth'
chees'y
chee'tah
che'la
che'late
Chel'le·an
che·lo'ni·an
chem'i·cal
chem'i·cal·ly
che·min' de fer
che·mise'
chem'ist
chem'is·try
chem'o·syn'the·sis
chem'o·ther'a·pist
chem'o·ther'a·py
chem'ur·gy
che·nille'
cheq'uers
cher'ish
cher'ish·es
cher'no·zem'
Cher'o·kee'
che·root'
cher'ry
chert'y
cher'ub
che·ru'bic
che·ru'bi·cal·ly
cher'u·bim
cher'u·bin
cher'vil
Chesh'ire
chess'board'
chess'man'

chest'nut
chest'y
chev'a·lier'
chev'ron
chev'y
chew'ing
chew'y
chi·a'ro·scu'ro
chi·as'ma
chi·as'mal
chi·as'mus
chi·cane'
chi·can'er·y
chick'a·dee'
chick'en
chick'weed'
chi'co
chic'o·ry
chief'ly
chief'tain
chif·fon'
chif'fo·nier'
chig'ger
chi'gnon
chi·hua'hua
chil'blain'
child'bear'ing
child'bed'
child'birth'
child'hood
child'ish
child'like'
chil'dren
chil'e
chil'e con car'ne

chil'i
chil'i·ad'
chil'i·asm
chil'i·ast'
chill'i·ness
chil'ly
chi'lo·pod'
chi·mae'ra
chim'er
chi·me'ra
chi·mer'i·cal
chim'ney
chim·pan·zee'
chi'na
chi'na·ber'ry
chi'na·ware'
chin·chil'la
Chi·nese'
chi'no
chin·qua·pin
chip'munk'
Chip'pen·dale'
chip'per
chip'py
chi·rog'ra·pher
chi·rog'ra·phy
chi·ro·man'cer
chi·ro·man'cy
chi·rop'o·dist
chi·rop'o·dy
chi·ro·prac'tic
chi·ro·prac'tor
chir'rup
chis'el
chis'eled

chis'elled
chis'e·ler
chis'el·ler
chit'chat'
chi'tin
chi'tin·ous
chi'ton
chit'ter
chit'ter·lings
chiv'al·ric
chiv'al·rous
chiv'al·ry
chla'mys
chlo'ral
chlo'ra·mine'
chlo'rate
chlo'ric
chlo'ride
chlo'rin·a'tion
chlo'rine
chlo'ro·form'
chlo'ro·my·ce'tin
chlo'ro·phyll'
chlo'ro·plast'
chlo·ro'sis
chlo'rous
chlor·prom'a·zine'
chock'a·block'
choc'o·late
choir'boy'
choir'mas'ter
choke'ber'ry
choke'bore'
choke'cher'ry
chok'er

chok'ing
chol'e·cyst'
chol'er
chol'er·a
chol'er·ic
cho·les'ter·ol'
cho'line
chon'dri·o·some'
chon·dro'ma
choos'y
chop'fal'len
cho·pine'
chop'per
chop'py
chop'sticks'
cho'ral
cho·rale'
chor'date
cho·re'a
chor'e·og'ra·phy
cho'ri·amb'
cho'ric
cho'rine
cho'ri·on'
chor'is·ter
cho'roid
chor'tle
cho'rus
cho'sen
chow'der
chres·tom'a·thy
chris'om
chris'ten
chris'ten·ing
Chris'tian

Chris'ti·an'i·ty
Christ'mas
chro'ma
chro'mate
chro·mat'ic
chro·mat'i·cal·ly
chro'ma·tin
chro'ma·tism
chro'mite
chro'mi·um
chro'mo·gen
chro'mo·gen'ic
chro'mo·lith'o·graph'
chro'mo·li·thog'ra·phy
chro'mo·pho·tog'ra·phy
chro'mo·plast'
chro'mo·so'mal
chro'mo·some'
chro·nax'i·a
chron'ic
chron'i·cal·ly
chron'i·cle
chron'i·cled
chron'i·cler
chron'o·log'i·cal
chro·nol'o·gist
chro·nol'o·gy
chro·nom'e·ter
chron'o·met'ric
chrys'a·lis
chrys·an'the·mum
chrys'o·lite'
chrys'o·prase'
chtho'ni·an
chub'bi·ness

chub'by
chuck'hole'
chuck'le
chuk'ka
chum'my
chunk'i·ness
chunk'y
church'go'er
church'go'ing
church'man
church'ward'en
church'yard'
churl'ish
churn'ing
chut'ney
chy·la'ceous
ci·bo'ri·um
ci·ca'da
cic'a·trice
cic'a·trix
cic'a·tri·za'tion
cic'a·trize'
cic'e·ly
ci'ce·ro'ne
Cic'e·ro'ni·an
ci'der
ci·gar'
cig'a·rette'
cil'i·a
cil'i·ar'y
cil'i·ate
cil'ice
cil'i·um
ci'mex
Cim·me'ri·an

cinc'ture
cin'der
Cin'der·el'la
cin'der·y
cin'e·ma
cin'e·mat'ic
cin'e·mat'i·cal·ly
cin'e·ma·tog'ra·pher
cin'e·ma·tog'ra·phy
cin'e·ole'
cin'e·ra'ri·a
cin'e·ra'ri·um
cin'er·ar'y
cin'er·a'tor
cin'gu·lum
cin'na·bar
cin'na·mon
cinque'foil'
ci'pher
cip'o·lin
cir'ca
cir'ci·nate'
cir'cle
cir'clet
cir'cuit
cir·cu'i·tous
cir'cuit·ry
cir·cu'i·ty
cir'cu·lar
cir·cu·lar'i·ty
cir'cu·late'
cir'cu·lat'ing
cir'cu·la'tion
cir'cu·la'tor
cir'cu·la·to'ry

cir'cum·am'bi·ent
cir'cum·am'bu·late'
cir'cum·cise'
cir'cum·ci'sion
cir·cum'fer·ence
cir'cum·flex'
cir·cum'flu·ent
cir·cum'fu·sion
cir'cum·lo·cu'tion
cir'cum·nav'i·gate'
cir'cum·nav'i·ga'tor
cir'cum·po'lar
cir'cum·scribe'
cir'cum·spect'
cir'cum·spec'tion
cir'cum·stance'
cir'cum·stan'tial
cir'cum·stan'ti·al'i·ty
cir'cum·vent'
cir'cum·ven'tion
cir'cus
cir'rate
cir·rho'sis
cir·rhot'ic
cir'ri·ped'
cir'rose
cir'rus
cis·al'pine
Cis·ter'cian
cis'tern
cit'a·ble
cit'a·del
ci·ta'tion
cith'a·ra
cith'er

cith'ern
cit'i·fied'
cit'i·zen
cit'i·zen·ry
cit'i·zen·ship'
cit'ral
cit'rate
cit'ric
cit'rine
cit'ron
cit'ron·el·la
cit'rous
cit'rus
cit'y
civ'et
civ'ic
civ'ics
civ'il
ci·vil'ian
ci·vil'i·ty
civ'i·li·za'tion
civ'i·lize'
civ'i·lized'
civ'il·ly
civ'ism
clab'ber
clack'er
claim'ant
claim'ing
clair·voy'ance
clair·voy'ant
cla'mant
clam'bake'
clam'ber
clam'mi·ness

clam'my
clam'or
clam'or·ous
clam'our
clamp'er
clam'shell'
clan·des'tine
clan'gor
clan'gor·ous
clank'ing
clan'nish
clans'man
clap'board
clap'per
clap'trap'
clar'a·bel'la
clar'ence
clar'en·don
clar'et
clar'i·fi·ca'tion
clar'i·fy'
clar'i·net'
clar'i·on
clar'i·ty
cla'ro
clasp'ing
clas'sic
clas'si·cal
clas'si·cal'i·ty
clas'si·cal·ly
clas'si·cism
clas'si·cist
clas'si·fi'a·ble
clas'si·fi·ca'tion
clas'si·fied'

clas'si·fi'er
clas'si·fy'
clas'sis
class'mate'
class'room'
class'y
clas'tic
clat'ter
claus'al
claus'tral
claus'tro·pho'bi·a
cla'vate
clav'i·chord'
clav'i·cle
cla'vi·er
clay'ey
clay'more'
clean'er
clean'li·ness
clean'ly
clean'ness
cleans'er
clean'up'
clear'ance
clear'head'ed
clear'ing
clear'ing·house'
cleav'a·ble
cleav'age
cleav'er
cleis·tog'a·my
clem'a·tis
clem'en·cy
clem'ent
cle·o'me

clep'sy·dra
clere'sto'ry
cler'gy
cler'gy·man
cler'ic
cler'i·cal
cler'i·sy
clerk'ship'
cleve'ite
clev'er
clev'er·ly
clev'er·ness
clev'is
cli·ché'
cli'ent
cli'en·tele'
cli·mac'ter·ic
cli·mac'tic
cli'mate
cli·mat'ic
clio·mat'i·cal·ly
cli'ma·tol'o·gy
cli'max
climb'er
climb'ing
clinch'er
cling'ing
clin'ic
clin'i·cal
clin'i·cal·ly
cli·ni'cian
clink'er
clink'stone'
cli·nom'e·ter
cli'no·met'ric

clin'quant
clip'per
clip'ping
cli'to·ris
clo·a'ca
clo·a'cal
cloak'room'
clob'ber
clock'wise'
clock'work'
clod'dish
clod'hop'per
cloi'son·né'
clois'ter
clois'tered
clon'ic
clon'ing
close'ly
close'ness
clos'er
clos'et
clo'sure
clothes'horse'
clothes'line'
cloth'ier
cloth'ing
clo'ture
cloud'burst'
cloud'i·ness
cloud'less
cloud'y
clo'ven
clo'ver
clo'ver·leaf'
clown'ing

clown'ish
club'foot'
club'house'
club'room'
club'wom'an
clum'ber
clump'ish
clump'y
clum'si·ly
clum'sy
Clu'ny
clus'ter
clut'ter
Clydes'dale'
clys'ter
coach'man
co·ac'tion
co·ac'tive
co·ad'ju·tant
co·ad'ju·tor
co·ag'u·la·ble
co·ag'u·lant
co·ag'u·late'
co·ag'u·la'tion
co·ag'u·la'tor
co·ag'u·lin
coal'bin'
coal'er
co'alesce'
co'ales'cent
co'a·li'tion
co'ap·ta'tion
co·arc'tate
coars'en
coast'al

coast'er
coat'ed
coat'ing
coat'tail'
co·au'thor
coax'ing
co·ax'i·al
co'balt
cob'ble
cob'bled
cob'bler
cob'ble·stone'
co'bra
cob'web'
co·caine'
coc'cid
coc'cus
coc'cyx
coch'i·neal'
coch'le·a
cock·ade'
cock'a·lo'rum
cock'a·too'
cock'a·trice
cock'crow'
cock'er
cock'eyed'
cock'fight'ing
cock'i·ly
cock'le
cock'le·shell'
cock'ney
cock'pit'
cock'roach'
cocks'comb'

cock'sure'
cock'tail'
cock'y
co'coa
co'co·nut'
co·coon'
co'cotte'
co'da
cod'dle
co'dec·li·na'tion
co'de·fend'ant
co'deine'
co'dex
cod'fish'
co'di·ces'
cod'i·cil
cod'i·fi·ca'tion
cod'i·fy'
co'ed'
co'ed·u·ca'tion·al
co'ef·fi'cient
coe'la·canth'
co·emp'tion
coe'nes·the'sis
co·en'zyme
co·e'qual
co·erce'
co·er'cion
co·er'cive
co'es·sen'tial
co'e·ter'nal
co·e'val
co·ex·ec'u·tor
co'ex·ist'
co'ex·ist'ence

co'ex·tend'
co'ex·ten'sion
co'ex·ten'sive
cof'fee
cof'fee cake'
cof'fee·pot'
cof'fer
cof'fin
co'gen·cy
co'gent
cog'i·tate'
cog'i·ta'tion
cog'i·ta'tor
co'gnac
cog'nate
cog·na'tion
cog·ni'tion
cog'ni·tive
cog'ni·zance
cog'ni·zant
cog·no'men
co'gno·scen'ti
cog·no'vit
cog'wheel'
co·hab'it
co·hab'i·ta'tion
co·heir'
co·here'
co·her'ence
co·her'ent
co·her'er
co·he'sion
co·he'sive
co'hort
coif·fure'

coin'age
co·in·cide'
co·in'ci·dence
co·in'ci·dent
co·in'ci·den'tal
coin'er
co·i'tion
co'i·tus
col'an·der
co·lat'i·tude'
col'chi·cine'
co·lec'to·my
cole'man·ite'
co'le·op'ter·ous
cole'slaw'
col'e·us
cole'wort'
col'ic
col'ick·y
col'i·se'um
co·li'tis
col·lab'o·rate'
col·lab'o·ra'tion
col·lab'o·ra'tive
col·lab'o·ra'tor
col·lage'
col'la·gen'
col·lapse'
col·laps'i·ble
col·laps'ing
col'lar
col'lard
col·late'
col·lat'er·al
col·la'tion

col·la'tive
col'league
col·lect'
col·lect'a·ble
col·lect'ed
col·lect'i·ble
col·lec'tion
col·lec'tive
col·lec'tive·ly
col·lec'tiv·ism
col·lec'tiv·ist
col·lec'tiv·ize'
col·lec'tor
col'leen
col'lege
col·le'gi·al
col·le'gi·an
col·le'gi·ate
col'let
col·lide'
col'lie
col'lier
col'li·gate'
col'li·mate'
col'li·ma'tor
col·lin'e·ar
col·li'sion
col'lo·cate'
col'lo·ca'tion
col·lo'di·on
col'loid
col·loi'dal
col'lop
col·lo'qui·al
col·lo'qui·al·ism

col·lude'
col·lu·nar'i·um
col·lu'sive
co·logne'
co'lon
colo'nel
colo'nel·cy
co·lo'ni·al
co·lo'ni·al·ism
co·lo'ni·al·is'tic
co·lon'ic
co'lo·nist
col'o·ni·za'tion
col'o·nize'
col'on·nade'
col'o·ny
col'o·phon'
col'or
col'or·a·ble
col'or·a'tion
col'o·ra·tu'ra
col'or·ful
col'or·im'e·ter
col'or·ing
col'or·ist
col'or·less
co·las'sal
col·os·se'um
co·los'sus
co·los'to·my
co·los'trum
col'our
col·pi'tis
col'ter
colt'ish

col'u·brine'
col'um·ba'ri·um
col'um·bar'y
col'um·bine'
co·lum'bite
col'u·mel'la
col'umn
co·lum'nar
col'umned
col'um·nist
co'ma
co'mate
com'a·tose'
com'bat
com'bat·ant
com·ba'tive
comb'er
com·bi·na'tion
com·bi·na'tion·al
com'bi·na'tive
com·bin'ing
com'bo
com·bust'
com·bus'ti·bil'i·ty
com·bus'ti·ble
com·bus'tion
come'back'
co·me'di·an
co·me'di·enne'
com'e·dy
come'li·ness
come'ly
com'er
co·mes'ti·ble
com'et

come'up'pance
com'fort
com'fort·a·ble
com'fort·a·bly
com'fort·er
com'fort·ing
com'fort·less
com'frey
com'ic
com'i·cal
com'i·cal·ly
com'ing
com'i·ty
com'ma
com·mand'
com'man·dant'
com'man·deer'
com·mand'er
com·mand'er·ship'
com·mand'ing
com·mand'ment
com·man'do
com·mem'o·rate'
com·mem'o·ra'tion
com·mem'o·ra'tive
com·mence'
com·mence'ment
com·mend'
com·mend'a·ble
com·mend'a·bly
com'men·da'tion
com·mend'a·to'ry
com·men'sal
com·men'su·ra·bil'i·ty
com·men'su·ra·ble

com·men'su·rate
com'ment
com'men·tar'y
com'men·ta'tor
com'merce
com·mer'cial
com·mer'cial·ism
com·mer'cial·i·za'tion
com·mer'cial·ize'
com·mer'cial·ly
com'mi·nate'
com'mi·na'tion
com'mi·nute'
com·mis'er·ate'
com·mis'er·a'tion
com'mis·sar'
com'mis·sar'i·at
com'mis·sar'y
com·mis'sion
com·mis'sioned
com·mis'sion·er
com·mis·sure'
com·mit'
com·mit'ment
com·mit'ta·ble
com·mit'tal
com·mit'tee
com·mit'tee·per'son
com·mode'
com·mo'di·ous
com·mod'i·ty
com'mo·dore'
com'mon
com'mon·al·ty
com'mon·er

com'mon·ly
com'mon·place'
com'mons
com'mon·weal'
com'mon·wealth'
com·mo'tion
com·mu'nal
com·mu'nal·ism
com·mu'nal·is'tic
com'mune
com·mu'ni·ca·bil'i·ty
com·mu'ni·ca·ble
com·mu'ni·cant
com·mu'ni·cate'
com·mu'ni·ca'tion
com·mu'ni·ca'tive
com·mu'ni·ca'tor
com·mun'ion
com·mu'ni·qué'
com'mu·nism
com'mu·nist
com'mu·nis'tic
com·mu'ni·ty
com'mu·ni·za'tion
com·mut'a·bil'i·ty
com·mut'a·ble
com'mu·tate'
com'mu·ta'tion
com'mu·ta·tive
com'mu·ta'tor
com·mute'
com·mut'er
com'pact,
  com·pact'
com·pan'ion

com·pan'ion·a·bil'i·ty
com·pan'ion·a·bly
com·pan'ion·ate
com·pan'ion·ship'
com'pa·ny
com·pa·ra·bil'i·ty
com'pa·ra·ble
com·par'a·tive
com·par'a·tive·ly
com·pare'
com·par'i·son
com·part'ment
com·part'men'tal
com'pass
com·pas'sion
com·pas'sion·ate
com·pat'i·bil'i·ty
com·pat'i·ble
com·pa'tri·ot
com·peer'
com·pel'
com·pel·la'tion
com·pel'ling
com·pen'di·ous
com·pen'di·um
com·pen'sa·ble
com'pen·sate'
com'pen·sa'tion
com'pen·sa'tion·al
com'pen·sa'tive
com·pen'sa·to'ry
com·pete'
com'pe·tence
com'pe·ten·cy
com'pe·tent

com'pe·ti'tion
com·pet'i·tive
com·pet'i·tor
com'pi·la'tion
com·pile'
com·pla'cen·cy
com·pla'cent
com·plain'
com·plain'ant
com·plaint'
com·plai'sance
com·plai'sant
com·plect'
com'ple·ment
com'ple·men'ta·ry
com·plete'
com·plete'ly
com·ple'tion
com·plex',
  com'plex
com·plex'ion
com·plex'ioned
com·plex'i·ty
com·pli'ance
com·pli'ant
com'pli·cate'
com'pli·ca'tion
com·plic'i·ty
com'pli·ment
com'pli·men'ta·ry
com'plin
com·ply'
com·po'nent
com·port'
com·port'ment

com·pose'
com·posed'
com·pos'ed·ly
com·pos'er
com·pos'ite
com'po·si'tion
com·pos'i·tor
com'pos men'tis
com'post
com·po'sure
com'pote
com'pound,
   com·pound'
com·pound'ing
com'pre·hend'
com'pre·hen'si·bil'i·ty
com'pre·hen'si·bly
com'pre·hen'sion
com'pre·hen'sive
com·press',
   com'press
com·pressed'
com·press'i·ble
com·pres'sion
com·pres'sor
com·prise'
com'pro·mise'
com'pro·mis'ing
comp·trol'ler
com·pul'sion
com·pul'sive
com·pul'so·ry
com·punc'tion
com'pur·ga'tion
com'pur·ga'tor

com·put'a·ble
com'pu·ta'tion
com·pute'
com·put'er
com·put'er·ized'
com'rade
con'a·tive
co·na'tus
con·cat'e·nate'
con'cat·e·na'tion
con·cave'
con·cav'i·ty
con·ceal'
con·ceal'ment
con·cede'
con·ceit'
con·ceiv'a·bil'i·ty
con·ceiv'a·ble
con·ceive'
con'cen·trate'
con'cen·tra'tion
con'cen·tra'tor
con·cen'tric
con·cen'tri·cal·ly
con'cen·tric'i·ty
con'cept
con·cep'tion
con·cep'tive
con·cep'tu·al
con·cep'tu·al·ism
con·cep'tu·al·ize'
con·cern'
con·cerned'
con·cern'ment
con·cert', con'cert

con·cert'ed
con'cer·ti'na
con'cert·mas'ter
con·cer'to
con·ces'sion
con·ces'sion·aire'
con·ces'sive
con'cha
con·chol'o·gy
con·ci·erge'
con·cil'i·ate'
con·cil'i·a'tion
con·cil'i·a·to'ry
con·cin'ni·ty
con·cise'
con·ci'sion
con'clave
con·clude'
con·clu'sion
con·clu'sive
con·coct'
con·coc'tion
con·com'i·tance
con·com'i·tant
con'cord
con·cord'ance
con·cord'ant
con·cor'dat
con'course
con·crete'
con·cre'tion
con'cret·ize'
con·cu'bi·nage
con'cu·bine'
con·cu'pis·cence

con·cu'pis·cent
con·cur'
con·cur'rence
con·cur'rent
con·cus'sion
con·cus'sive
con·demn'
con'dem·na'tion
con·dem'na·to'ry
con·den'sa·ble
con'den·sa'tion
con·dense'
con·dens'er
con·den'si·bil'i·ty
con·den'si·ble
con'de·scend'
con'de·scend'ing
con'de·scen'sion
con·dign'
con'di·ment
con·di'tion
con·di'tion·al
con·di'tion·al·ly
con·di'tioned
con·di'tion·er
con·do'la·to'ry
con·dole'
con·do'lence
con'dom
con'do·na'tion
con·done'
con'dor
con·duce'
con·du'cive
con'duct, con·duct'

con·duct'i·bil'i·ty
con·duct'i·ble
con·duc'tion
con·duc'tive
con'duc·tiv'i·ty
con·duc'tor
con'duit
con'dy·lo'ma
Con'el·rad'
con·fab'u·late'
con·fab'u·la'tion
con·fec'tion
con·fec'tion·ar'y
con·fec'tion·er
con·fec'tion·er'y
con·fed'er·a·cy
con·fed'er·ate
con·fed'er·a'tion
con·fer'
con'fer·ee'
con'fer·ence
con·fer'ment
con·fer'ra·ble
con·fer'rer
con·fess'
con·fess'ed·ly
con·fes'sion
con·fes'sion·al
con·fes'sor
con·fet'ti
con'fi·dant'
con'fi·dante'
con·fide'
con'fi·dence
con'fi·den'tial

con·fid'ing
con·fig'u·ra'tion
con·fin'a·ble
con·fine'
con·fine'a·ble
con·fine'ment
con·firm'
con'fir·ma'tion
con·firm'a·tive
con·firm'a·to'ry
con·firmed'
con'fis·ca·ble
con'fis·cate'
con'fis·ca·to'ry
con·fit'e·or'
con'fla·gra'tion
con·flate'
con·fla'tion
con·flict', con'flict
con'flu·ence
con'flu·ent
con'flux
con·form'
con·form'a·ble
con'for·ma'tion
con·form'ist
con·form'i·ty
con·found'
con·found'ed
con'fra·ter'ni·ty
con'frere
con·front'
con'fron·ta'tion
Con·fu'cian·ism
con·fuse'

con·fused'
con·fus'ed·ly
con·fu'sion
con·fu'ta'tion
con·fut'a·tive
con·fute'
con'ga
con'gé
con·geal'
con·gen'ial
con·ge'ni·al'i·ty
con·gen'i·tal
con·gen'i·tal·ly
con'ger
con·ge'ri·es
con·gest'
con·ges'tion
con·ges'tive
con·glom'er·ate
con·glom'er·a'tion
con·glu'ti·na'tion
con·grat'u·late'
con·grat'u·la'tion
con·grat'u·la·to'ry
con'gre·gate'
con'gre·ga'tion
con'gre·ga'tion·al
Con'gre·ga'tion·al·ist
con'gress
con·gres'sion·al
con'gress·man
con'gress·wom'an
con'gru·ence
con'gru·en·cy
con'gru·ent

con·gru'i·ty
con'gru·ous
con'ic
con'i·cal
co'ni·fer
co·nif'er·ous
co'nine
con·jec'tur·al
con·jec'ture
con·join'
con'ju·gal
con'ju·gal'i·ty
con'ju·gate
con'ju·ga'tion
con'junct
con·junc'tion
con·junc·ti'val
con·junc'tive
con·junc'ti·vi'tis
con·junc'ture
con'ju·ra'tion
con'jure
con'jur·er
con'nate
con·nect'
con·nec'tion
con·nec'tive
con·nec'tor
conn'ing
con·nip'tion
con·niv'ance
con·nive'
con·nois·seur'
con'no·ta'tion
con'no·ta'tive

con·note'
con·nu'bi·al
con·nu'bi·al'i·ty
con'quer
con'quer·or
con'quest
con·quis'ta·dor'
con·san·guin'e·ous
con·san·guin'i·ty
con'science
con'sci·en'tious
con'scion·a·ble
con'scious
con'scious·ness
con'script,
   con·script'
con·scrip'tion
con'se·crate'
con'se·cra'tion
con'se·cra'tor
con'se·cu'tion
con·sec'u·tive
con·sen'su·al
con·sen'sus
con·sent'
con·sen'tient
con'se·quence'
con'se·quent'
con'se·quen'tial
con'se·quent'ly
con·serv'a·ble
con'ser·va'tion
con'ser·va'tion·ist
con·serv'a·tism
con·serv'a·tive

con·ser'va·to'ry
con·serve'
con·si'der
con·sid'er·a·ble
con·sid'er·ate
con·sid'er·a'tion
con·sid'ered
con·sid'er·ing
con·sign'
con'sig·na'tion
con'sign·ee'
con·sign'ment
con·sign'or
con·sist'
con·sist'en·cy
con·sis'tent
con·sis'to·ry
con·sol'a·ble
con'so·la'tion
con·sol'a·to'ry
con·sole'
con·sol'i·date'
con·sol'i·da'tion
con·sol'i·da'tor
con'sols
con'som·mé'
con'so·nance
con'so·nant
con'so·nan'tal
con'sort, con·sort'
con·sor'ti·um
con·spec'tus
con·spic'u·ous
con·spir'a·cy
con·spir'a·tor

con·spir'a·to'ri·al
con·spire'
con'sta·ble
con·stab'u·lar'y
con'stan·cy
con'stant
con'stant·an'
con'stel·late'
con'stel·la'tion
con'ster·na'tion
con'sti·pate'
con'sti·pa'tion
con·stit'u·en·cy
con·stit'u·ent
con'sti·tute'
con'sti·tu'tion
con'sti·tu'tion·al
con'sti·tu'tion·al'i·ty
con'sti·tu'tion·al·ly
con·strain'
con·strained'
con·strain'ed·ly
con·straint'
con·strict'
con·stric'tion
con·stric'tor
con·strin'gent
con·stru'a·ble
con·struct
con·struc'tion
con·struc'tion·ist
con·struc'tive
con·struc'tor
con·strue'
con'sub·stan'tial

con'sub·stan'ti·a'tion
con'sue·tude'
con'sul
con'su·lar
con'su·late
con'sul·ship'
con·sult'
con·sult'ant
con'sul·ta'tion
con·sult'ing
con·sum'a·ble
con·sume'
con·sumed'
con·sum'ed·ly
con·sum'er
con·sum'mate',
  con·sum'mate
con'sum·ma'tion
con·sump'tion
con·sump'tive
con'tact
con·ta'gion
con·ta'gious
con·tain'
con·tain'er
con·tain'ment
con·tam'i·nate'
con·tam'i·na'tion
con·tam'i·na'tor
con·temn'
con'tem·plate'
con'tem·pla'tion
con'tem·pla'tive,
  con·tem'pla·tive
con·tem'po·ra·ne'i·ty

con·tem'po·ra'ne·ous
con·tem'po·ra'ry
con·tempt'
con'tempt'i·ble
con·temp'tu·ous
con·tend'
con·tent',
   con'tent
con·tent'ed
con·ten'tion
con·ten'tious
con·tent'ment
con'test
con·test'ant
con'text
con·tex'tu·al
con·tex'tu·al·ly
con·ti·gu'i·ty
con·tig'u·ous
con'ti·nence
con'ti·nent
con'ti·nen'tal
con·tin'gen·cy
con·tin'gent
con·tin'u·al
con·tin'u·al·ly
con·tin'u·ance
con·tin'u·a'tion
con·tin'ue
con·ti·nu'i·ty
con·tin'u·ous
con·tin'u·um
con·tort'
con·tor'tion
con·tor'tion·ist

con'tour
con'tra
con'tra·band'
con'tra·bass'
con'tra·cep'tion
con'tra·cep'tive
con'tract,
   con·tract'
con·tract'ed
con·tract'i·ble
con·trac'tion
con'trac·tor
con·trac'tu·al
con'tra·dict'
con'tra·dic'tion
con'tra·dic'to·ry
con'tra·dis·tinc'tion
con'tra·in'di·cate'
con'tra·in'di·ca'tion
con·tral'to
con'tra·po·si'tion
con·trap'tion
con'tra·pun'tal
con'tra·ri·ly
con·trar'i·ous
con'tra·ri·wise'
con'tra·ry
con'trast,
   con·trast'
con'tra·vene'
con'tra·ven'tion
con'tre·temps'
con·trib'ut·a·ble
con'tri·bu'tion
con·trib'u·tor

con·trib'u·to'ry
con·trite'
con·tri'tion
con·triv'ance
con·trive'
con·trol'
con·trol'la·ble
con·trol'ler
con'tro·ver'sial
con'tro·ver'sy
con'tro·vert'
con'tro·vert'i·bly
con'tu·ma'cious
con'tu·ma·cy
con'tu·me·ly
con·tu'sion
co·nun'drum
con'ur·ba'tion
con'va·lesce'
con'va·les'cence
con'va·les'cent
con·vec'tion
con·vec'tive
con·vec'tor
con·vene'
con·ven'er
con·ven'ience
con·ven'ient
con'vent
con·ven'ti·cle
con·ven'tion
con·ven'tion·al
con·ven'tion·al'i·ty
con·verge'
con·ver'gence

con·ver′gent
con·verg′ing
con·vers′a·ble
con′ver·sant
con′ver·sa′tion
con′ver·sa′tion·al·ly
con′verse,
   con·verse′
con′verse·ly,
   con·verse′ly
con·ver′sion
con′vert, con·vert′
con·vert′i·bil′i·ty
con·vert′i·ble
con·vex′
con·vex′i·ty
con·vey′
con·vey′ance
con·vey′er
con·vey′or
con′vict, con·vict′
con·vic′tion
con·vince′
con·vinc′ing
con·viv′i·al
con·viv′i·al′i·ty
con′vo·ca′tion
con′vo·ca′tor
con·voke′
con′vo·lute′
con′vo·lut′ed
con′vo·lu′tion
con′voy
con·vulse′
con·vul′sion

con·vul′sive
co′ny
cook′book′
cook′er·y
cook′out′
cool′ant
cool′er
coo′lie
coop′er
co·op′er·ate′
co·op′er·a′tion
co·op′er·a′tive
co·op′er·a′tor
co·or′di·nate′
co·or′di·nat′ing
co·or′di·na′tion
co·or′di·na′tor
co′pal
co′palm
co·par′ce·nar′y
co·par′ce·ner
co·part′ner
Co·per′ni·can
co′pe·set′ic
cope′stone′
cop′i·er
co′pi′lot
cop′ing
co′pi·ous
co·pla′nar
co·pol′y·mer
co·pol′y·mer·i·za′tion
cop′per
cop′per·head′
cop′pice

cop′ro·lite′
cop·rol′o·gy
cop′ro·phil′i·a
cop′u·la
cop′u·late′
cop′u·la′tion
cop′u·la′tive
cop′y
cop′y·book′
cop′y·cat′
cop′y·ist
cop′y·read′er
cop′y·right′
cop′y·writ′er
co′quet·ry
co·quette′
co·quet′tish
cor′a·cle
cor′al
cor′al·loid′
cor′beil
cor′bel
cor′bie
cord′age
cord′ed
cor′dial
cor·dil′le·ra
cord′ing
cord′ite
cor′don
cor′du·roy′
cord′wood′
co′re·spond′ent
co′ri·an′der
Co·rin′thi·an

co'ri·um
cork'er
cork'ing
cork'screw'
cor'mo·phyte'
cor'mo·rant
corn'cob'
corn'crib'
cor'ne·a
cor'ne·al
cor'nel
cor'ne·ous
cor'ner
cor'nered
cor'ner·stone'
cor·net'
corn'fed'
corn'husk'ing
cor'nice
cor·nic'u·late'
cor·nu·co'pi·a
corn'y
cor·ol'la
cor'ol·lar'y
co·ro'na
cor'o·nal
cor'o·nar'y
cor'o·na'tion
cor'o·ner
cor'o·net'
cor'po·ral
cor'po·ral·cy
cor'po·ral'i·ty
cor'po·rate
cor'po·rate·ly

cor'po·ra'tion
cor·po're·al
cor·po're·al'i·ty
corps'man
cor'pu·lence
cor'pu·lent
cor'pus
cor'pus·cle
cor·pus'cu·lar
cor'pus de·lic'ti
cor'pus ju'ris
cor'pus lu'te·um
cor'pus stri·a'tum
cor·ral'
cor·rect'
cor·rec'tion
cor·rec'tion·al
cor·rec'tive
cor·rec'tor
cor're·late'
cor're·la'tion
cor·rel'a·tive
cor're·spond'
cor're·spond'ence
cor're·spond'ent
cor'ri·dor
cor'ri·gen'dum
cor'ri·gi·ble
cor·ri'val
cor·rob'o·rant
cor·rob'o·rate'
cor·rob'o·ra'tion
cor·rob'o·ra'tor
cor·rode'
cor·ro'sion

cor·ro'sive
cor'ru·gate'
cor'ru·gat'ed
cor'ru·ga'tion
cor·rupt'
cor·rupt'i·bil'i·ty
cor·rupt'i·ble
cor·rup'tion
cor·sage'
cor'sair
cor'set
cor·tege'
cor'tex
cor'ti·cal
cor'ti·cate
cor'ti·ces'
cor'tin
cor'ti·sone'
co·run'dum
cor'us·cate'
cor'us·ca'tion
cor'vine
cor'ymb
co·se'cant
co·sig'na·to'ry
co'sine'
cos·met'ic
cos·met'i·cal·ly
cos·me·tol'o·gy
cos'mic
cos'mi·cal·ly
cos'mism
cos·mog'o·ny
cos·mog'ra·pher
cos·mog'ra·phy

cos·mol'o·gy
cos'mo·naut'
cos'mo·pol'i·tan
cos·mop'o·lite'
cos'mos
cos'mo·tron'
cos'set
cos'tal
cos'tate
cos'ter·mon'ger
cos'tive
cost'ly
cos'tume
cos'tum·er
co'sy
co·tan'gent
co'tan·gen'tial
co·tem'po·ra'ne·ous
co·ten'ant
co'te·rie
co·ter'mi·nous
co·til'lion
cot'tage
cot'tag·er
cot'ter
cot'ton
cot'ton·seed'
cot'ton·tail'
cot'ton·y
couch'ant
cou'gar
cou'lee
cou·lisse'
cou·lomb'
coun'cil

coun'ci·lor
coun'cil·lor
coun'sel
coun'se·lor
coun'sel·lor
count'down'
coun'te·nance
count'er (thing
    that counts,
    table)
coun'ter (against,
    opposite)
coun'ter·act'
coun'ter·ac'tion
coun'ter·at·tack'
coun'ter·bal'ance
coun'ter·charge'
coun'ter·claim'
coun'ter·claim'ant
coun'ter·clock'wise'
coun'ter·dem'on·
    stra'tion
coun'ter·es'pi·
    on·age'
coun'ter·feit'
coun'ter·in·tel'li·
    gence
coun'ter·man
coun'ter·mand'
coun'ter·of·fen'sive
coun'ter·part'
coun'ter·point'
coun'ter·rev'o·
    lu'tion·ar'y
coun'ter·sign'

count'ess
count'ing
count'less
coun'tri·fied'
coun'try
coun'try·side'
coun'ty
cou·pé'
cou'ple
cou'pler
cou'plet
cou'pling
cou'pon
cour'age
cou·ra'geous
cou'ri·er
cours'er
cours'ing
cour'te·ous
cour'te·san
cour'te·sy
court'house'
cour'ti·er
court'li·ness
court'ly
court'room'
court'yard'
cous'in
cou·ture'
cou'tu·rier'
cou·vade'
co·va'lence
cov'e·nant
cov'er
cov'er·age

cov′er·all′
cov′ered
cov′er·let
cov′ert
cov′er·ture
cov′et
cov′et·ous
cov′ey
cov′in
cow′ard
cow′ard·ice
cow′ard·li·ness
cow′bird′
cow′catch′er
cow′er
cow′girl′
cow′herd′
cow′lick′
cowl′ing
cow′pox′
cow′slip′
cox′a
cox·al′gi·a
cox′comb′
cox′swain
coy′ote
coz′en
coz′en·age
co′zi·ly
co′zi·ness
co′zy
crab′ber
crab′by
crack′brained′
crack′er

crack′er·jack′
crack′le
crack′ling
crack′pot′
cra′dle
craft′i·ly
crafts′man
craft′y
crag′gi·ness
crag′gy
cram′pon
cran′ber′ry
cra′ni·al
cra·ni·ol′o·gy
cra·ni·ot′o·my
cra′ni·um
crank′i·ness
cran′kle
crank′shaft′
crank′y
cran′nied
cran′ny
crap′pie
crap′u·lence
crap′u·lous
cra′ter
cra·vat′
cra′ven
crav′ing
craw′fish′
crawl′ly
cray′fish′
cray′on
cra′zi·ly
cra′zi·ness

cra′zy
creak′y
cream′er
cream′er·y
cream′i·ness
cream′y
cre·ate′
cre′a·tine′
cre·a′tion
cre·a′tion·ist
cre·a′tive
cre·a′tiv·i·ty
cre·a′tor
crea′ture
cre′dence
cre·den′tial
cred′i·bil′i·ty
cred′i·ble
cred′it
cred′it·a·ble
cred′it·a·bly
cred′i·tor
cre′do
cre·du′li·ty
cred′u·lous
creep′er
creep′y
cre′mate
cre·ma′tion
cre′ma·tor
cre′ma·to′ri·um
cre′ma·to′ry
cre′nate
cren′u·late
cren′u·la′tion

cre'o·dont'
Cre'ole
cre'ol·ized'
cre'o·sote'
crep'i·tate'
crep'i·ta'tion
cre·pus'cle
cre·pus'cu·lar
cre·scen'do
cres'cent
cre'sol
cres'set
crest'ed
cre·ta'ceous
cre'tin
cre'tin·ism
cre'tin·ous
cre·vasse'
crev'ice
crev'iced
crew'el
crib'bage
crib'ber
crick'et
crick'et·er
cri'er
Cri·me'an
crim'i·nal
crim'i·nal'i·ty
crim'i·nol'o·gist
crim'i·nol'o·gy
crimp'y
crim'son
crin'gle
cri'nite

crin'kle
crin'kly
cri'noid
crin'o·line
crip'ple
cri'sis
cris·pa'tion
crisp'y
criss'cross'
cri·ter'i·a
cri·ter'i·on
crit'ic
crit'i·cal
crit'i·cism
crit'i·cize'
cri·tique'
croak'er
croak'y
Cro·a'tian
cro·chet'
cro·cid'o·lite'
crock'er·y
croc'o·dile'
cro'cus
crom'lech
cro'ny
crook'ed
crook'neck'
croon'er
crop'per
cro·quet'
cro·quette'
cro'sier
cross'bar'
cross'bow'

cross'bred'
cross'ing
cross'o'ver
cross'road'
cross'walk'
cross'word'
crotch'et
crotch'et·y
cro'ton
cro·ton'ic
crou'pi·er
croup'y
crou·ton', crou'ton
crow'bar'
crowd'ed
crow'foot'
cru'ces
cru'cial
cru'ci·ate
cru'ci·ble
cru'ci·fix'
cru'ci·fix'ion
cru'ci·form'
cru'ci·fy'
cru'di·ty
cru'el
cru'el·ty
cru'et
cruis'er
crul'ler
crum'ble
crum'bly
crum'my
crum'pet
crum'ple

crum'pled
crunch'y
crup'per
cru·sade'
cru·sad'er
crus·ta'cean
crus·ta'ceous
crus'tal
crust'ed
crust'i·ness
crust'y
cry'ba by
cry'ing
cry'o·gen'ics
cry'o·hy'drate
cry'o·lite'
cry'o·ther'a·py
cryp'tic
cryp'to·clas'tic
cryp'to·gram'
cryp'to·graph'ic
cryp·tog'ra·phy
cryp·tol'o·gy
crys'tal
crys'tal·line
crys'tal·li·za'tion
crys'tal·lize'
crys'tal·log'ra·phy
crys'tal·loid'
cte'noid
cten'o·phore'
cub'age
cu'ba·ture
cub'by·hole'
cu'bic

cu'bi·cal·ly
cu'bi·cle
cu'bi·form'
cub'ism
cub'ist
cu'bit
cu'boid
cuck'old
cuck'old·ry
cuck'oo'
cu'cul·late'
cu'cum·ber
cud'dle
cud'dle·some
cud'dly
cud'dy
cudg'el
cues'ta
cui·rass'
cui·sine'
cu'lex
cu'li·nar'y
cul'mi·nate'
cul'mi·na'tion
cu·lottes'
cul'pa·bil'i·ty
cul'pa·ble
cul'pa·bly
cul'prit
cul'ti·vate'
cul'ti·vat'ed
cul'ti·va'tion
cul'ti·va'tor
cul'tur·al
cul'ture

cul'tured
cul'tur·ist
cul'ver
cul'vert
cum'ber
cum'ber·some
cum lau'de
cum'mer·bund'
cu'mu·late'
cu'mu·la'tion
cu'mu·la'tive
cu'mu·lus
cu'ne·ate
cu·ne'i·form'
cun'ning
cup'board
cup'cake'
cu'pel
cup'ful'
cu'pid
cu·pid'i·ty
cu'po·la
cup'ping
cu'pric
cu'prous
cu'prum
cur'a·ble
cu'ra·cy
cu·ra're
cu'rate
cur'a·tive
cu'ra·tor
curb'ing
curb'stone'
cur'dle

curd'y
cu·ret'tage
cu·rette'
cur'few
cu'ri
cu'ri·al
cu'ri·os'i·ty
cu'ri·ous
cu'ri·um
curl'er
cur'lew
curl'i·cue'
curl'i·ness
curl'y
cur·mudg'eon
cur'rant
cur'ren·cy
cur'rent
cur'ri·cle
cur·ric'u·lar
cur·ric'u·lum
cur'ri·er
cur'ry
cur'sive
cur'so·ry
cur·tail'
cur·tail'ment
cur'tain
cur'te·sy
cur'ti·lage
curt'sy
cu'rule
cur'va·ture
cur'vi·lin'e·ar

cu'sec
cush'ion
cush'y
cus'pid
cus'pi·date'
cus'pi·dor'
cus'tard
cus·to'di·al
cus·to'di·an
cus'to·dy
cus'tom
cus'tom·ar'i·ly
cus'tom·ar'y
cus'tom·er
cus'tom·house'
cu·ta'ne·ous
cut'back'
cut'i·cle
cu'tin'
cu'tin·ize'
cut'lass
cut'ler
cut'ler·y
cut'let
cut'tage
cut'ter
cut'throat
cut'ting
cut'tle·bone'
cut'tle·fish'
cy'an·am'ide
cy·an'ic
cy'a·nide'

cy'a·no'sis
cy'ber·net'ics
cyc'la·men
cy'cle
cy'clic
cy'clist
cy·clom'e·ter
cy'clone
cy'clo·pe'di·a
cy'clo·pe'dic
cy'clops
cy'clo·ra'ma
cy'clo·tron'
cyg'net
cyl'in·der
cy·lin'dri·cal
cym'bal
cy·mom'e·ter
cyn'ic
cyn'i·cal
cyn'i·cism
cy'no·sure'
cy'press
cys·tec'to·my
cyst'ic
cys'tine
cys·ti'tis
cys'to·scope'
cy'to·gen'e·sis
cy·tol'o·gy
cy'to·plasm'
cza·ri'na
czar'ist

D

dab'ble
dachs'hund
da'cron
dac'tyl
dac·tyl'ic
dac·tyl'o·gram'
dac'ty·lol'o·gy
Da'da·ism
dad'dy
da'do
dae'dal
dae'mon
daf'fo·dil'
daf'fy
dag'ger
da·guerre'o·type'
dahl'ia
dai'ly
dain'ti·ness
dain'ty
dai'qui·ri
dair'y
dair'y·maid'
dair'y·man
da'is
dai'sy
da'leth
dal'li·ance
dal'li·er
dal'ly
dal·ma'tian

dam'age
dam'age·a·ble
dam'a·scene'
dam'ask
dam'na·ble
dam·na'tion
dam'na·to'ry
dam'ni·fy'
damn'ing
damp'en
damp'er
dam'sel
dam'son
danc'er
danc'ing
dan'de·li'on
dan'di·fied'
dan'dle
dan'druff
dan'dy
dan'ger
dan'ger·ous
dan'gle
dan'gling
dan'ish
dank'ness
dap'per
dap'pled
dare'dev'il
dar'ing
dark'en

dark'ling
dark'ness
dark'room'
dar'ling
darn'ing
dart'er
Dar·win'i·an
Dar'win·ism
dash'er
dash'ing
das'tard·ly
da'ta
dat'a·ble
dat'ed
date'less
da'tive
da'tum
daub'er
daugh'ter
daunt'less
dau'phin
dau'phin·ess
dav'en·port'
dav'it
daw'dle
daw'dling
day'break'
day'dream'
day'light'
day'time'
daz'ed·ly

daz'zle
daz'zling
dea'con
dea'con·ess
dea'con·ry
de·ac'ti·vate'
dead'beat'
dead'en
dead'en·ing
dead'head'
dead'ly
deaf'en
deaf'en·ing
deal'er
deal'ing
dean'er·y
dean'ship'
dear'ly
death'bed'
death'less
death'ly
death'watch'
de·ba'cle
de·bar'
de·bark'
de'bar·ka'tion
de·bar'ment
de·base'
de·base'ment
de·bat'a·ble
de·bate'
de·bauch'
de·bauch'ed·ly
deb'au·chee'
de·ben'ture

de·bil'i·tate'
de·bil'i·ta'tion
de·bil'i·ty
deb'it
deb'o·nair'
de·bouch'ment
de'brief'
de·bris'
debt'or
de·bunk'
de·but'
deb'u·tante'
dec'ade
de'ca·dence
de'ca·dent
dec'a·gon'
dec'a·gram'
dec'a·he'dron
de·cal'ci·fi·ca'tion
de·cal'ci·fy'
de·cal'co·ma'ni·a
de'ca·les'cence
dec'a·li'ter
Dec'a·logue'
de·camp'
dec'ane
de·cant'er
de·cap'i·tate'
de·cap'i·ta'tion
dec'a·pod'
de·car'bon·ate'
dec'are
dec'a·syl·la'bic
de·cath'lon
de·cay'

de·cease'
de·ce'dent
de·ceit'
de·ceit'ful
de·ceive'
de·cel'er·ate'
de·cel'er·a'tion
de·cen·cy
de·cen'a·ry
de·cen'ni·al
de'cent
de·cen'tral·i·za'tion
de·cen'tral·ize'
de·cep'tion
de·cep'tive
de·cern'
dec'i·bel'
de·cide'
de·cid'ed
de·cid'u·a
de·cid'u·ous
dec'i·gram'
dec'ile
dec'i·li'ter
dec'i·mal
dec'i·mate'
dec'i·ma'tion
dec'i·ma'tor
de·ci'pher
de·ci'sion
de·ci'sive
deck'house'
deck'le
de·claim'
dec'la·ma'tion

de·clam'a·to'ry
dec'la·ra'tion
de·clar'a·tive
de·clare'
dé·clas·sé'
de·clas'si·fy'
de·clen'sion
de·clin'a·ble
dec'li·na'tion
de·cline'
dec'li·nom'e·ter
de·cliv'i·ty
de·coct'
de·coc'tion
de·code'
de·co·her'er
de·co·he'sion
dé·col'le·tage'
de·com'pen·sa'tion
de·com·pose'
de·com·po·si'tion
de·com·pound'
de·com·press'
de·com·pres'sion
de·con·tam'i·nate'
de·con·trol'
dé·cor'
dec'or·ate'
dec'o·ra'tion
dec'o·ra·tive
dec'o·rous
de·co'rum
de'coy, de·coy'
de'crease,
    de·crease'

de·cree'
dec're·ment
de·crep'it
de·crep'i·ta'tion
de·crep'i·tude'
de'cre·scen'do
de·cres'cent
de·cry'
de·cum'bent
de·cus'sate
de'cus·sa'tion
ded'i·cate'
ded'i·ca'tion
ded'i·ca·to'ry
de·duce'
de·duct'
de·duct'i·ble
de·duc'tion
de·duc'tive·ly
deep'en
deer'skin'
de·face'
de·face'ment
de fac'to
de·fal'cate
de·fal·ca'tion
def'a·ma'tion
de·fam'a·to'ry
de·fame'
de·fault'
de·fault'er
de·fea'sance
de·feat'
de·feat'ist
def'e·cate'

def'e·ca'tion
de·fect,
    de·fect'
de·fec'tive
de·fend'
de·fend'ant
de·fend'er
de·fen'es·tra'tion
de·fense'
de·fen'si·ble
de·fen'sive
de·fer'
def'er·ence
def'er·en'tial
de·ferred'
de·fi'ant
de·fi'cien·cy
de'fi'cient
def'i·cit
de·fi'er
de·file'
de·file'ment
de·fin'a·ble
de·fine'
def'i·nite
def'i·ni'tion
de·fin'i·tive
de·flate'
de·fla'tion
de·fla'tion·ar'y
de·flect'
de·flec'tion
de·flec'tor
de·fo'li·ate'
de·fo'li·a'tion

de·force′
de·for′ciant
de·for′est
de·for′est·a′tion
de·form′
de·for′ma′tion
de·form′i·ty
de·fraud′
de·fray′
de·fray′al
de·fray′ment
de·frock′
de·frost′
de·funct′
de·fy′
de·gen′er·a·cy
de·gen′er·ate
de·gen′er·a′tion
deg′ra·da′tion
de·grade′
de·grad′ing
de·gree′
de·hy′drate
de·hy·dra′tion
de·ic′er
de·i·fi·ca′tion
de′i·fied′
de′i·fy′
de′i·ty
de·ject′ed
de·jec′tion
de ju′re
de·lam′i·nate′
de·late′
de·lay′

de′le
de·lec′ta·ble
de·lec·ta′tion
del′e·ga·cy
del′e·gate′
del′e·ga′tion
de·lete′
del′e·te′ri·ous
de·le′tion
de·lib′er·ate′
de·lib′er·a′tion
de·lib′er·a′tive
del′i·ca·cy
del′i·ca·tes′sen
de·li′cious
de·lict′
de·light′
de·light′ful
de·lim′it
de·lim′i·ta′tion
de·lin′e·ate′
de·lin′e·a′tion
de·lin′e·a′tor
de·lin′quen·cy
de·lin′quent
del′i·quesce′
del′i·ques′cent
de·lir′i·ous
de·lir′i·um
de·liv′er
de·liv′er·ance
de·liv′er·y
de·louse′
Del′phic
del·phin′i·um

del′ta
del′toid
de·lude′
del′uge
de·lu′sion
de·lu′sive
de·mag′net·ize′
dem′a·gog′ic
dem′a·gog′ism
dem′a·gogue′
dem′a·gog′y
de·mand′
de·man′dant
de·mar′cate
de′mar·ca′tion
de′ma·te′ri·al·ize′
de·mean′
de·mean′or
de·ment′ed
de·men′ti·a
de·mer′it
dem′e·rol′
de·mesne′
dem′i·god′
dem′i·john′
de·mil′i·ta·rized′
dem′i·mon·daine′
dem′i·monde′
de·mise′
dem′i·tasse′
dem′i·urge′
de·mo·bi·li·za′tion
de·mo′bi·lize′
de·moc′ra·cy
dem′o·crat′

dem'o·crat'ic
dem'o·crat'i·cal·ly
de'mo·graph'ic
de·mog'ra·phy
de·mol'ish
dem'o·li'tion
de'mon
de·mon'e·tize'
de·mo'ni·ac'
de·mon'ic
de'mon·ism
de'mon·ol'o·gy
de·mon'stra·bil'i·ty
de·mon'stra·ble
dem'on·strate'
dem'on·stra'tion
de·mon'stra·tive
dem'on·stra'tor
de·mor'al·ize'
de·mote'
de·mot'ics
de·mul'cent
de·mur'
de·mure'
de·mur'rage
de·mur'rer
de·nat'u·ral·ize'
de·na'ture
de·na'tur·ize'
den'dri·form'
den'drite
den'droid
den'e·ga'tion
de·ni'a·ble
de·ni'al

den'i·grate'
den'i·gra'tion
den'i·gra'tor
den'im
den'i·zen
de·nom'i·na'tion
de·nom'i·na·tive
de·nom'i·na'tor
de·no·ta'tion
de·no'ta·tive
de·note'
de·noue'ment
de·nounce'
den'si·ty
den'tal
den'tate
den·ta'tion
dent'ed
den'ti·frice'
den'tine
den'tist
den'tist·ry
den·ti'tion
den'ture
den'u·da'tion
de·nude'
de·nun'ci·ate'
de·nun'ci·a'tion
de·nun'ci·a'tor
de·ny'
de·o'dor·ant
de·o'dor·ize'
de·on·tol'o·gy
de·part'
de·part'ment

de'part·men'tal·ism
de·par'ture
de·pend'
de·pend'a·bil'i·ty
de·pend'ence
de·pend'en·cy
de·pen'dent
de·pict'
de·pic'tion
dep'i·late'
de·pil'a·to'ry
de·plete'
de·ple'tion
de·plor'a·ble
de·plore'
de·ploy'
de·ploy'ment
de·po'lar·i·za'tion
de·po'lar·ize'
de·pone'
de·pon'ent
de·pop'u·late'
de·pop'u·la'tion
de·port'
de·por·ta'tion
de·por·tee'
de·port'ment
de·pose'
de·pos'it
de·pos'i·tar'y
dep'o·si'tion
de·pos'i·tor
de·pos'i·to'ry
de'pot
dep'ra·va'tion

de·praved'
de·prav'i·ty
dep're·cate'
dep're·ca'tion
dep're·ca·to'ry
de·pre'ci·a·ble
de·pre'ci·ate'
de·pre'ci·a'tion
dep're·date'
dep're·da'tion
de·press'
de·pres'sant
de·pres'sion
de·pres'sive
de·pres'sor
dep'ri·va'tion
de·prive'
de pro·fun'dis
dep'u·ta'tion
de·pute'
dep'u·tize'
dep'u·ty
de·rac'i·nate'
de·rail'
de·rail'ment
de·range'
de·range'ment
der'by
der'e·lict'
der'e·lic'tion
de·ride'
de·ris'i·ble
de·ri'sion
de·ri'sive
der'i·va'tion

de·riv'a·tive
de·rive'
der'ma·ti'tis
der'ma·tol'o·gist
der'ma·tol'o·gy
der'mis
der'o·gate'
der'o·ga'tion
de·rog'a·tive
de·rog'a·to'ry
der'rick
der'ri·ère'
der'rin·ger
der'vish
des'cant
de·scend'
de·scend'ant
de·scend'er
de·scent'
de·scrib'a·ble
de·scribe'
de·scrip'tion
de·scrip'tive
de·scry'
des'e·crate'
des'e·crat'er
des'e·cra'tion
des'e·cra'tor
de·seg're·gate'
de·seg're·ga'tion
de·sen'si·tize'
de·sert',
  de'sert
de·sert'er
de·ser'tion

de·serve'
de·serv'ed·ly
des'ic·cate'
des'ic·ca'tion
de·sid'er·a'ta
de·sid'er·ate'
de·sid'er·a'tum
de·sign'
des'ig·nate'
des'ig·na'tion
des'ig·na'tor
de·sign'er
de·sign'ing
de·sir'a·bil'i·ty
de·sir'a·bly
de·sire'
de·sir'ous
de·sist'
des'moid
des'o·late'
des'o·la'tion
de·spair'
des'per·a'do
des'per·ate
des'per·a'tion
des'pi·ca·ble
des'pi·ca·bly
de·spise'
de·spite'
de·spoil'
de·spoil'ment
de·spo'li·a'tion
de·spond'ence
de·spond'en·cy
de·spond'ent

des'pot
des·pot'ic
des'pot·ism
des·sert'
des'ti·na'tion
des'tine
des'tin·y
des'ti·tute'
des'ti·tu'tion
de·stroy'
de·stroy'er
de·struct'i·ble
de·struc'tion
de·struc'tive
des'ue·tude'
des'ul·to'ri·ness
des'ul·to'ry
de·tach'
de·tach'a·ble
de·tach'ment
de'tail, de·tail'
de·tain'
de·tain'ment
de·tect'
de·tect'a·ble
de·tec'tion
de·tec'tive
de·tec'tor
dé'tente'
de·ten'tion
de·ter'
de·ter'gent
de·te'ri·o·rate'
de·ter'ment
de·ter'mi·na·ble

de·ter'mi·nate
de·ter'mi·na'tion
de·ter'mine
de·ter'min·ism
de·ter'rent
de·test'
de·test'a·ble
de·tes·ta'tion
de·throne'
det'i·nue'
det'o·nate'
det'o·na'tion
de'tour, de·tour'
de·tract'
de·trac'tion
de·trac'tor
det'ri·ment
det'ri·men'tal
de·tri'tion
de·tri'tus
de'us ex ma'chi·na
deu·te'ri·um
Deu'ter·on'o·my
de·val'u·ate'
de·val'u·a'tion
de·val'ue
dev'as·tate'
dev'as·ta'tion
de·vel'op
de·vel'op·er
de·vel'op·men'tal
de·vest'
de·vi'ance
de·vi'ant
de·vi·ate

de'vi·a'tion
de·vice'
dev'iled
dev'il·ish
dev'il·ry
dev'il·try
de'vi·ous
de·vise'
de·vi'tal·ize'
de·void'
de·volve'
de·volve'ment
de·vote'
de·vot'ed
dev'o·tee'
de·vo'tion
de·vour'
de·vout'
dew'y
dex·ter'i·ty
dex'ter·ous
di'a·be·tes
di'a·bet'ic
di'a·bol'ic
di'a·crit'i·cal
di'a·dem'
di'ag·nose'
di'ag·no'sis
di'ag·nos'tic
di'ag·nos·ti'cian
di·ag'o·nal
di'a·gram'
di'a·gram·mat'ic
di'a·lect'
di'a·lec'tic

di·a·logue'
di·al'y·sis
di·a·lyt'ic
di·a·mag'net·ism
di·am'e·ter
di·a·met'ri·cal·ly
di·a·mond
di·a·no·e'tic
di·a·pa'son
di·a·per
di·aph'a·nous
di·a·phragm'
di·a·rist
di·ar·rhe'a
di·ar·thro'sis
di·a·ry
di·as'po·ra
di·a·stase'
di·as'to·le'
di·as·tol'ic
di·a·ther'my
di·a·tom'ic
di·a·ton'ic
di·a·tribe'
di·a·zine'
di·a·zole'
di·bas·ic
dib'ble
di·chot'o·mize'
di·chot'o·my
di·chro·ism
di·chro'ma·tism
di·chro'mic
dick'ens
dick'er

dick'ey
di·crot'ic
di'cro·tism
dic'ta·phone'
dic'tate
dic·ta'tion
dic'ta·tor
dic·ta·to'ri·al
dic·ta·tor·ship'
dic'tion
dic'tion·ar'y
dic'tum
di·dac'tic
di·dac'ti·cism
did'dle
did'y·mous
di'e·lec'tric
di·er'e·sis
di'e·sis
di'et
di'e·tar'y
di'e·tet'ic
di'e·ti'cian
dif'fer
dif·fer·ence
dif·fer·ent
dif·fer·en'tial
dif·fer·en'ti·ate'
dif·fer·en'ti·a'tion
dif'fi·cult
dif'fi·cul·ty
dif'fi·dence
dif'fi·dent
dif·fract'
dif·frac'tion

dif·fuse'
dif·fus'i·ble
dif·fu'sion
dig'a·mous
dig'a·my
di·gas'tric
di·gen'e·sis
di·gest,
  di·gest'
di·gest'i·ble
di·ges'tion
di·ges'tive
dig'ger
dig'gings
dig'it
dig'it·al
dig'i·ta'lis
dig'it·al·ly
dig'ni·fy'
dig'ni·tar'y
dig'ni·ty
di'graph
di·gress'
di·gres'sion
di·gres'sive
di·he'dral
di·lan'tin
di·lap'i·date'
di·lap'i·da'tion
di·lat'a·ble
di·lat'ant
dil'a·ta'tion
di·late'
di·la'tion
di·la'tor

dil'a·to'ri·ness
dil'a·to'ry
di·lem'ma
dil'et·tante'
dil'et·tant'ism
dil'i·gence
dil'i·gent
dil'ly·dal'ly
di·lute'
di·lu'tion
di·lu'vi·al
di·men'sion
di·men'sion·al
di·mid'i·ate'
di·min'ish
di·min'u·en'do
dim'i·nu'tion
di·min'u·tive
dim'i·ty
dim'mer
di·mor'phism
dim'pled
dim'wit'ted
din'er
di·ner'ic
din·ette'
din'ghy
din'gi·ness
din'gle
din'go
din'gy
din'ing
din'ky
din'ner
din'ner·ware

di'no·saur'
di·oc'e·san
di'o·cese'
di'ode
Di'o·nys'i·ac
Di'o·ny'sian
di·op'ter
di'op·tom'e·ter
di·op'tric
di'o·ra'ma
di'o·rite'
di·ox'ide
diph·the'ri·a
diph'the·rit'ic
diph'thong
dip'loid
di·plo'ma
di·plo'ma·cy
dip'lo·mat'
dip'lo·mat'ic
di·po'lar
di'pole'
dip'per
dip'so·ma'ni·a
dip'so·ma'ni·ac'
dip'so·ma·ni'a·cal
dip'stick'
dip'tych
di·rect'
di·rec'tion
di·rec'tion·al
di·rec'tive
di·rect'ly
di·rec'tor
di·rec'to·ry

dire'ful
dir'i·gi·ble
dirn'dl
dirt'i·ness
dirt'y
dis·a·bil'i·ty
dis·a'ble
dis·a·buse'
dis'ad·van'tage
dis·ad'van·ta'geous
dis·af·fect'ed
dis·af·fec'tion
dis·a·gree'
dis·a·gree'a·ble
dis·a·gree'ment
dis·al·low'
dis·ap·pear'
dis·ap·pear'ance
dis·ap·point'
dis·ap·point'ed
dis·ap·pro·ba'tion
dis·ap·prov'al
dis·ap·prove'
dis·arm'
dis·ar'ma·ment
dis·arm'ing
dis·ar·range'ment
dis·ar·ray'
dis·as·sem'bly
dis·as·so'ci·ate'
dis·as'ter
dis·as'trous
dis·a·vow'
dis·a·vow'al
dis·band'

dis·bar'
dis·bur'den
dis·burse'
dis·burse'ment
dis·card'
dis·cern'
dis·cern'i·ble
dis·cern'i·bly
dis·cern'ing
dis'charge',
   dis·charge'
dis·ci'ple
dis·ci·pli·nar'i·an
dis'ci·pline'
dis·claim'
dis·claim'er
dis·cla·ma'tion
dis·close'
dis·clos'ure
dis·cog'ra·phy
dis'coid
dis·col'or
dis·col'or·a'tion
dis·com'fit
dis·com'fi·ture
dis·com'fort
dis·com'mon
dis'com·pose'
dis'con·cert'ing
dis'con·nect'
dis'con·nec'tion
dis·con'so·late
dis·con'tent'
dis'con·tin'u·a'tion
dis'con·tin'ue

dis'con·ti·nu'i·ty
dis'con·tin'u·ous
dis'cord
dis·cord'an·cy
dis'co·theque
dis'count
dis·cour'age
dis·cour'age·ment
dis'course
dis·cour'te·ous
dis·cour'te·sy
dis·cov'er
dis·cov'ert
dis·cov'er·y
dis·cred'it
dis·creet'
dis·crep'an·cy
dis·crete'
dis·cre'tion
dis·cre'tion·ar'y
dis·crim'i·nate'
dis·crim'i·na'tion
dis·crim'i·na·to'ry
dis·cur'sive
dis'cus
dis·cuss'
dis·cus'sion
dis·dain'
dis·ease'
dis'em·bark'
dis'em·bar·ka'tion
dis'em·bod'ied
dis'em·bod'y
dis'em·bow'el
dis'en·chant'ment

dis'en·cum'ber
dis'en·fran'chise
dis'en·gaged'
dis'en·tan'gle
dis'es·tab'lish
dis·fa'vor
dis·fig'ure
dis·fran'chise
dis·gorge'
dis·grace'
dis·grace'ful
dis·grun'tled
dis·guise'
dis·gust'
dis·gust'ed·ly
dis'ha·bille'
dish'cloth'
dis·heart'en·ing
di·shev'el
di·shev'eled
di·shev'elled
di·shev'el·ment
dis·hon'est
dis·hon'es·ty
dis·hon'or
dis·hon'or·a·ble
dish'wash'er
dis·il·lu'sion
dis·il·lu'sion·ment
dis'in·clined'
dis'in·fect'
dis'in·fect'ant
dis'in·gen'u·ous
dis'in·her'it
dis'in·her'i·tance

dis·in'te·grate'
dis·in'te·gra'tion
dis·in·ter'
dis·in'ter·est·ed
dis·in·ter'ment
dis·joint'ed
dis·junct'
dis·junc'tion
dis·junc'tive
dis·like'
dis·lo'cate
dis·lo·ca'tion
dis·lodge'
dis·loy'al
dis·mal
dis·man'tle
dis·may'
dis·mem'ber
dis·miss'
dis·miss'al
dis·miss'i·ble
dis·mount'
dis·o·be'di·ence
dis·o·bey'
dis·o·blige'
dis·or'der
dis·or'der·ly
dis·or'gan·ized'
dis·o'ri·ent
dis·o'ri·en·tate'
dis·own'
dis·par'age
dis·par'ag·ing
dis·pa·rate
dis·par'i·ty

dis·pas'sion·ate
dis·patch'
dis·pel'
dis·pen'sa·ble
dis·pen'sa·ry
dis·pen·sa'tion
dis·pense'
dis·per'sal
dis·perse'
dis·per'sion
dis·place'
dis·place'ment
dis·played'
dis·please'
dis·pleas'ure
dis·port'
dis·pos'a·ble
dis·pos'al
dis·pose'
dis·po·si'tion
dis·pos·sess'
dis·pos·ses'sion
dis·praise'
dis·pro·por'tion·al
dis·pro·por'tion·ate·ly
dis·prove'
dis·pu·ta·ble
dis·pu·tant
dis·pu·ta'tion
dis·pu·ta'tious
dis·pute'
dis·qual'i·fy'
dis·qui'et
dis·qui'e·tude'
dis·qui·si'tion

dis·re·gard'
dis·re·pair'
dis·rep'u·ta·ble
dis·re·pute'
dis·re·spect'
dis·re·spect'ful
dis·robe'
dis·rupt'
dis·rup'tion
dis·rup'tive
dis·sat·is·fac'tion
dis·sat·is·fac'to·ry
dis·sat'is·fy'
dis·sect'
dis·sec'tion
dis·sec'tor
dis·seize'
dis·sem'blance
dis·sem'ble
dis·sem'i·nate'
dis·sen'sion
dis·sent'
dis·sent'er
dis·ser·tate'
dis·ser·ta'tion
dis·serv'ice
dis·sev'er
dis·si·dent
dis·sim'i·lar
dis·sim'i·lar'i·ty
dis·sim'u·late'
dis·sim'u·la'tion
dis·si·pate'
dis·si·pat'ed
dis·si·pa'tion

dis·so'ci·ate'
dis·so'ci·a'tion
dis·sol'u·ble
dis'so·lute'
dis'so·lu'tion
dis·solve'
dis·sol'vent
dis'so·nance
dis·suade'
dis·sua'sion
dis·syl·lab'ic
dis'taff
dis·tain'
dis'tance
dis'tant
dis·taste'
dis·taste'ful
dis·tem'per
dis·tend'
dis·ten'sion
dis·ten'tion
dis·till'
dis'til·late
dis'til·la'tion
dis·tilled'
dis·till'er·y
dis·tinct'
dis·tinc'tion
dis·tinc'tive
dis·tinct'ly
dis·tin'guish
dis·tin'guish·a·bly
dis·tort'
dis·tor'tion
dis·tract'

dis·trac'tion
dis·train'
dis'train·ee'
dis·train'or
dis·traint'
dis·traught'
dis·tress'
dis·trib'ute
dis'tri·bu'tion
dis·trib'u·tive
dis·trib'u·tor
dis'trict
dis·trust'ful
dis·turb'
dis·turb'ance
di·sul'fide
dis·un'ion
dis'u·nite'
dis·use'
dis·val'ue
di·syl'la·ble
dith'er
dith'y·ramb'
dit'to
dit'ty
di'u·re'sis
di'u·ret'ic
di·ur'nal
di'va
di·va'lent
di·van'
div'er
di·verge'
di·ver'gence
di·ver'gent

di'vers
di·verse'
di·ver'si·fied'
di·ver'si·fy'
di·ver'sion
di·ver'sion·ar'y
di·ver'si·ty
di·ver'ti·men'to
di·vert'ing
di·vest'
di·vest'i·ture
di·vest'ment
di·vide'
di·vid'ed
div'i·dend'
di·vid'er
div'i·na'tion
di·vine'
di·vin'er
di·vin'i·ty
di·vis'i·bil'i·ty
di·vis'i·ble
di·vi'sion
di·vi'sion·al
di·vi'sive
di·vorce'
di·vor'cée'
di·vorce'ment
div'ot
di·vulge'
div'vy
diz'zi·ness
diz'zy
dob'bin
do'ber·man

dob'son
do'cent
doc'ile
do·cil'i·ty
dock'age
dock'et
dock'yard'
doc'tor
doc'tor·ate
doc'tri·naire'
doc'tri·nal
doc'trine
doc'u·ment
doc'u·men'ta·ry
doc'u·men·ta'tion
dod'der
dod'der·ing
do·de'ca·gon'
do'dec·a·he'dron
dodg'er
do'do
do'er
doe'skin'
dog'fight'
dog'ged
dog'ger·el
dog'house'
do'gie
dog'ma
dog·mat'ic
dog'ma·tism
dog'wood'
do'gy
doi'ly

do'ings
dol'ce
dol'drums
dole'ful
dol'er·ite'
dol'lar
doll'y
dol'man
dol'men
dol'o·mite'
dol'or·ous
dol'phin
dolt'ish
do·main'
do·mes'tic
do·mes'ti·cate'
do·mes'ti·ca'tion
do·mes·tic'i·ty
dom'i·cile
dom'i·nance
dom'i·nant
dom'i·nate'
dom'i·na'tion
dom'i·neer'
do·min'i·cal
do·min'ion
dom'i·no'
do'nate
do·na'tion
do·nee'
don'key
don'nish
don'ny·brook'
do'nor

do'nut
doo'dad'
doo'dle
doo'hick'ey
dooms'day'
door'bell'
door'man'
door'sill'
dope'y
Dor'ic
dor'man·cy
dor'mant
dor'mer
dor'mi·to'ry
dor'sal
dor'so·ven'tral
dor'sum
do'ry
dos'age
dos'ser
dos'si·er'
dos'sil
dot'age
do'tard
dot'ing
dot'ty
dou'ble
dou'blet
dou'bly
doubt'ful
doubt'less
dough'boy'
dough'nut'
dough'ty

dough'y
doug'las
dou·rine'
dove'cote'
dove'tail'
dow'a·ger
dow'di·ly
dow'dy
dow'el
dow'er
down'cast'
down'fall'
down'grade'
down'heart'ed
down'pour'
down'right'
down'town'
down'trod'den
down'ward
down'y
dow'ry
dows'ing
dox·ol'o·gy
dox'y
doz'en
drab'ble
drach'ma
Dra·co'ni·an
draf·tee'
draft'i·ness
drafts'man
drafts'man·ship'
draft'y
drag'gle

drag'gle·tail'
drag'net'
drag'on
drag'on·fly'
dra·goon'
drain'age
drain'er
drain'pipe'
dra'ma
Dram'a·mine'
dra·mat'ic
dra·mat'i·cal·ly
dram'a·tis
  per·so'nae
dram'a·tist
dram'a·ti·za'tion
dram'a·tize'
dram'a·tur'gy
drap'er
dra'per·y
dras'tic
dras'ti·cal·ly
draughts'man
draught'y
draw'back'
draw'bridge'
draw'ee'
draw'er
draw'ing
dray'age
dray'man
dread'ful
dread'naught'
dread'nought'

dream'er
dream'i·ly
dream'i·ness
dream'y
drear'i·ness
drear'y
dredg'er
dress'er
dress'ing
dress'mak'er
dress'y
drib'ble
drib'bling
dri'er
drift'age
drift'er
drift'wood'
drill'mas'ter
dri'ly
drink'a·ble
drink'er
drip'ping
driv'el
driv'en
driv'er
drive'way'
driv'ing
driz'zle
driz'zly
droll'er·y
drom'e·dar'y
droop'y
drop'let
drop'per

drop'si·cal
drop'sy
drosh'ky
dro·soph'i·la
dro'ver
drow'si·ness
drow'sy
drub'bing
drudg'er·y
drug'gist
drug'store'
dru'id
dru·id'i·cal
dru'id·ism
drum'beat'
drum'lin
drum'stick'
drunk'ard
drunk'en
drunk'en·ness
dry'ad
dry'er
dry'ness
du'al
du·al·is'tic
du·al·is'tic·al·ly
du·al'i·ty
du·bi'e·ty
du'bi·ous
du'bi·ta·ble
du'bon·net'
du'cal
duc'at
duch'ess

duch'y
duck'bill'
duck'ing
duck'ling
duck'pins'
duck'y
duc'tile
duct'less
dudg'eon
du'el
du'el·ist
du·en'na
du·et'
duf'fel
duf'fer
duf'fle
dug'out'
duke'dom
dul'cet
dul'ci·mer
dull'ard
dull'ness
dul'ly
dul'ness
du'ly
dumb'bell'
dum'dum
dum'found'
dum'my
dump'ling
dump'y
dun'der·head'
dun'ga·ree'
dun'geon

dun'nage
du'o·dec'i·mal
du'o·dec'i·mo'
du'o·de'nal
du'o·de'num
du'o·type'
du'ple
du'plex
du'pli·cate'
du'pli·ca'tion
du'pli·ca'tor
du·plic'i·ty
du'ra·bil'i·ty
du'ra·ble
du·ral'u·min'
du'ra ma'ter
du·ra'men
dur'ance
du·ra'tion
du·ress'
dur'ing
du'rum
dusk'y
dust'bin'
dust'er
dust'y
du'ti·a·ble
du'ti·ful
du'ty
du've·tyn'
dwarf'ish
dwell'er
dwin'dle
dwin'dling

dy'ad
dye'ing
dy'er
dy'ing
dy·nam'e·ter
dy·nam'ic
dy·nam'ics
dy'na·mism

dy'na·mite'
dy'na·mo'
dy'na·mom'e·ter
dy'nast
dy·nas'tic
dy'nas·ty
dy'na·tron'
dys'en·ter'ic

dys'en·ter'y
dys·func'tion
dys'men·or·rhe'a
dys·pep'si·a
dys·pep'tic
dys·pha'si·a
dys'tro·phy

E

ea′ger
ea′gle
ea′glet
ear′ache′
ear′drum′
ear′ful′
earl′dom
ear′ly
ear′mark′
ear′nest
earn′ings
ear′phone′
ear′ring
ear′split′ting
earth′bound′
earth′en
earth′en·ware′
earth′i·ness
earth′ling
earth′ly
earth′quake′
earth′worm′
earth′y
ear′wax′
ear′wig′
ease′ful
ea′sel
ease′ment
eas′i·ly
eas′i·ness
east′bound′

East′er
east′er·ly
east′ern
east′ern·most′
east′ward·ly
eas′y
eas′y·go′ing
eat′en
eat′ing
eaves′drop′ping
eb′on·ite′
eb′on·y
e·bul′li·ence
e·bul′li·en·cy
e·bul′li·ent
ec·bol′ic
ec·cen′tric
ec·cen′tri·cal·ly
ec′cen·tric′i·ty
ec′chy·mo′sis
Ec·cle′si·as′tes
ec·cle′si·as′ti·cal
ec′cri·nol′o·gy
ec′dy·sis
ech′e·lon′
ech′o
e·cho′ic
é·clair′
ec·lamp′si·a
ec·lec′tic
ec·lec′ti·cism

e·clipse′
e·clip′tic
ec′lo·gite′
ec′logue
ec′o·log′i·cal
e·col′o·gy
e′co·nom′ic
e′co·nom′i·cal
e′co·nom′i·cal·ly
e′co·nom′ics
e·con′o·mist
e·con′o·mize′
e·con′o·my
ec′ru
ec′sta·sy
ec·stat′ic
ec·stat′i·cal·ly
ec′to·blast′
ec′to·blas′tic
ec′to·derm′
ec′to·der′mal
ec′to·mor′phic
ec′to·plasm
ec′u·men′i·cal
ec′u·men·ism
ec′ze·ma
ec·zem′a·tous
e·da′cious
e′dam
ed′dy
e′del·weiss′

88

e·de'ma
e·dem'a·tous
e·den'ic
e·den'tate
edge'ways'
edge'wise'
edg'ing
edg'y
ed'i·ble
e'dict
ed'i·fi·ca'tion
ed'i·fice
ed'i·fi'er
ed'i·fy'
ed'i·fy'ing
ed'it
e·di'tion
ed'i·tor
ed'i·to'ri·al
ed'i·to'ri·alize'
ed'u·ca·ble
ed'u·cate'
ed'u·ca'tion
ed'u·ca'tion·al
ed'u·ca'tive
ed'u·ca'tor
e·duce'
e·duc'i·ble
e'duct
e·duc'tion
Ed·ward'i·an
eel'grass'
eel'y
ee'rie
ee'ri·ly

ee'ri·ness
ee'ry
ef·face'
ef·face'ment
ef·fect'
ef·fec'tive
ef·fec'tu·al
ef·fec'tu·al·ly
ef·fem'i·na·cy
ef·fem'i·nate
ef'fer·ent
ef'fer·vesce'
ef'fer·ves'cence
ef'fer·ves'cent
ef·fete'
ef·fi·ca'cious
ef·fi·ca·cy
ef·fi'cien·cy
ef·fi'cient
ef'fi·gy
ef'flo·resce'
ef'flo·res'cence
ef'flo·res'cent
ef'flu·ence
ef'flu·ent
ef·flu'vi·a
ef·flu'vi·um
ef'flux
ef'fort
ef'fort·less
ef·fron'ter·y
ef·ful'gent
ef·fuse'
ef·fu'sion
ef·fu'sive

e·gad'
e·gal'i·tar'i·an
e·gal'i·tar'i·an·ism
e·gest'
e·ges'tion
egg'head'
egg'nog'
egg'plant'
egg'shell'
eg'lan·tine'
e'go
e'go·cen'tric
e'go·cen·tric'i·ty
e'go·ism
e'go·ist
e'go·ma'ni·a
e'go·ma'ni·ac'
e'go·tism
e'go·tist
e'go·tis'ti·cal
e·gre'gious
e'gret
E'gyp·tol'o·gy
ei'der
ei·do'lon
Eif'fel
eight'een'
eight'eenth'
eight'fold'
eight'i·eth
eight'y
Ein·stein'i·an
ein·stein'i·um
eis·tedd'fod
ei'ther

e·jac'u·late'
e·jac'u·la'tion
e·jac'u·la'tor
e·ject'
e·jec'tion
e·jec'tor
e·lab'o·rate'
e·lab'o·ra'tion
e·lab'o·ra·tive
e'lan'
e·lapse'
e·las'tic
e·las'tic'i·ty
e·las'ti·cize'
e·late'
e·lat'ed
el'a·te'ri·um
e·la'tion
el'bow
el'bow·room'
eld'er
el'der·ber'ry
eld'er·ly
eld'est
e·lect'
e·lec'tion
e·lec'tion·eer'
e·lec'tive
e·lec'tor
e·lec'tor·al
e·lec'tor·ate
e·lec'tric
e·lec'tri·cal·ly
e·lec'tri'cian
e·lec'tric'i·ty

e·lec'tri·fi·ca'tion
e·lec'tri·fy'
e·lec'tro·car'di·o·
    gram'
e·lec'tro·chem'i·cal
e'lec'tro·cute'
e'lec'tro·cu'tion
e·lec'trode
e·lec'tro·en·ceph'a·
    lo·gram'
e·lec'tro·graph'
e·lec'trol'y·sis
e·lec'tro·lyte'
e·lec'tro·mag·net'ic
e·lec'tron
e·lec'tron'ics
e·lec'tro·plate'
e·lec'tro·scope'
e·lec'tro·stat'ics
e·lec'tro·type'
e·lec'trum
el'ee·mos'y·nar'y
el'e·gance
el'e·gant
el'e·gi'ac
el'e·gist
el'e·gize'
el'e·gy
el'e·ment
el'e·men'tal
el'e·men'ta·ry
e'len'chus
el'e·phant
el'e·phan·ti'a·sis
el'e·phan'tine

el'e·vate'
el'e·vat'ed
el'e·va'tion
el'e·va'tor
e·lev'en
e·lev'en·fold'
e·lev'enth
elf'in
elf'ish
e·lic'it
e·lide'
el'i·gi·bil'i·ty
el'i·gi·ble
el'i·gi·bly
e·lim'i·nate'
e·lim'i·na'tion
e·lim'i·na'tor
e·li'sion
e·lite'
e·lit'ist
e·lix'ir
E·liz'a·be'than
el·lipse'
el·lip'sis
el·lip'soid
el·lip'ti·cal
el·lip'tic'i·ty
el'o·cu'tion
el'o·cu'tion·ar'y
el'o·cu'tion·ist
e·lon'gate
e·lon'ga'tion
e·lope'
e·lope'ment
el'o·quence

el'o·quent
else'where'
e·lu'ci·date'
e·lu'ci·da'tion
e·lude'
e·lu'sion
e·lu'sive
e·lu'tri·ate'
elv'ish
E·ly'si·um
e·ma'ci·ate'
e·ma'ci·at'ed
e·ma'ci·a'tion
em'a·nate'
em'a·na'tion
e·man'ci·pate'
e·man'ci·pa'tion
e·man'ci·pa'tor
e·mas'cu·late'
e·mas'cu·la'tion
em·balm'
em·balm'ing
em·bank'ment
em·bar'go
em·bark'
em·bar·ka'tion
em·bar'rass
em·bar'rass·ment
em·bas·sy
em·bat'tled
em·bay'
em·bed'
em·bel'lish
em·bel'lish·ment
em'ber

em·bez'zle
em·bez'zle·ment
em·bit'ter
em·blaze'
em·bla'zon
em'blem
em·blem·at'ic
em·blem·at'i·cal·ly
em'ble·ments
em·bod'i·ment
em·bod'y
em·bold'en
em·bol'ic
em'bo·lism
em'bo·lus
em·boss'
em·boss'ing
em·bou·chure'
em·brace'
em·brace'or
em·brac'er·y
em·bran'gle
em·bra'sure
em·broi'der
em·broi'der·y
em·broil'
em·broil'ment
em'bry·o'
em'bry·og'e·ny
em'bry·ol'o·gist
em'bry·ol'o·gy
em'bry·on'ic
em'cee'
e·mend'
e'men·date'

e'men·da'tion
e'men·da'tor
e·menda'to'ry
em'er·ald
e·merge'
e·mer'gence
e·mer'gen·cy
e·mer'gent
e·merg'ing
e·mer'i·tus
e·mer'sion
em'er·y
em'e·sis
e·met'ic
em'i·grant
em'i·grate'
é'mi·gré'
em'i·nence
em'i·nen·cy
em'i·nent
e·mir'
e·mir'ate
em'is·sar'y
e·mis'sion
e·mit'
em'me·tro'pi·a
e·mol'li·ent
e·mol'u·ment
e·mote'
e·mo'tion
e·mo'tion·al
e·mo'tion·al'i·ty
e·mo'tion·al·ly
e·mo'tive
em·pan'el

em·path'ic
em'pa·thy
em'per·or
em'per·y
em'pha·sis
em'pha·size'
em·phat'ic
em'phy·se'ma
em'pire
em·pir'ic
em·pir'i·cal
em·pir'i·cism
em·pir'i·cist
em·ploy'
em·ploy'a·ble
em·ploy'ee
em·ploy'er
em·ploy'ment
em·po'ri·um
em·pow'er
em'press
emp'ti·ness
emp'ty
em'py·e'ma
em·pyr'e·al
em·py're·an
e'mu
em'u·late'
em'u·la'tion
em'u·la'tor
em'u·lous
e·mul'si·fi·er
e·mul'si·fy'
e·mul'sion
e·mul'sive

e·munc'to·ry
en·a'ble
en·act'
en·act'ment
en·am'el
en·am'or
en·am'ored
en'ar·thro'sis
en·cage'
en·camp'
en·camp'ment
en·case'
en'ce·phal'ic
en·ceph·a·li'tis
en·ceph'a·lo·gram'
en·chant'
en·chant'ment
en·chant'ress
en·chi·la'da
en·cir'cle
en'clave
en·clit'ic
en·close'
en·clo'sure
en·co'mi·ast'
en·co'mi·um
en·com'pass
en'core, en·core'
en·coun'ter
en·cour'age
en·cour'age·ment
en·cour'ag·ing
en·croach'
en·crust'
en·cum'ber

en·cum'brance
en·cy'cli·cal
en·cy'clo·pe'di·a
en·cy'clo·pe'dic
en·cy'clo·pe'dist
en·dan'ger
en·dear'
en·deav'or
en·dem'ic
en·der'mic
end'ing
en'dive
end'less
end'most'
en'do·blast'
en'do·car'di·um
en'do·cri'nal
en'do·crine'
en'do·cri·nol'o·gy
en'do·derm'
en·dog'a·mous
en·dog'a·my
en·dog'e·nous
en·dog'e·ny
en'do·morph'
en'do·mor'phism
en'do·phyte'
en'do·plasm'
en·dorse'
en·dor·see'
en·dorse'ment
en'do·sperm'
en'do·spore'
en'do·spo'ri·um
en'do·the'li·um

en'do·ther'mic
en'do·tox'in
en·dow'
en·dow'ment
en·dur'a·ble
en·dure'
en·dur'ing
end'ways'
end'wise'
en'e·ma
en'e·my
en'er·ge'sis
en'er·get'ic
en'er·get'i·cal·ly
en'er·gize'
en'er·giz'ing
en'er·gy
en'er·vate'
en'er·vat'ing
en'er·va'tion
en·face'
en·face'ment
en'fant' ter'ri·ble
en·fee'ble
en·feoff'
en'fi·lade'
en·fold'
en·fold'ing
en·force'
en·forced'
en·fran'chise
en·fran'chise·ment
en·gage'
en·gaged'
en·gag'ing

en·gage'ment
en·gen'der
en'gine
en'gi·neer'
en'gi·neer'ing
Eng'lish
en·glut'
en·gorge'
en·gorge'ment
en·graft'
en·grain'
en'gram
en·grave'
en·grav'er
en·grav'ing
en·gross'
en·gross'ing
en·gulf'
en·hance'
en·hanced'
en·hance'ment
en'har·mon'ic
e·nig'ma
e'nig·mat'ic
en·jamb'ment
en·join'
en·joy'
en·joy'a·ble
en·joy'ment
en·kin'dle
en·lace'
en·large'
en·large'ment
en·light'en
en·list'

en·list'ed
en·list'ment
en·liv'en
en·mesh'
en'mi·ty
en'ne·a·gon'
en'ne·a·he'dron
en·no'ble
en·nui'
e·nor'mi·ty
e·nor'mous
e·nough'
e·nounce'
e·now'
en·plane'
en·quire'
en·quir'y
en·rage'
en·rap'ture
en·rich'
en·rol'
en·roll'
en·roll'ment
en·rol'ment
en·sconce'
en·sem'ble
en·shrine'
en·shroud'
en'sign
en'si·lage
en·sile'
en·slave'
en·snare'
en·sue'
en·su'ing

en·sure'
en·tab'la·ture
en·ta'ble·ment
en·tail'
en·tail'ing
en·tail'ment
en·tan'gle
en·tan'gle·ment
en·tel'e·chy
en·tente'
en'ter
en·ter'ic
en'ter·ing
en'ter·on'
en'ter·prise'
en'ter·pris'ing
en'ter·tain'
en'ter·tain'er
en'ter·tain'ing
en'ter·tain'ment
en·thet'ic
en·thral'
en·thrall'
en·thrall'ment
en·thral'ment
en·throne'
en·thuse'
en·thu'si·asm
en·thu'si·as'tic
en'thy·meme'
en·tice'
en·tire'
en·tire'ly
en·tire'ty
en·ti'tle

en'ti·ty
en·tomb'
en'to·mo·log'i·cal
en'to·mol'o·gist
en'to·mol'o·gy
en·tou·rage'
en'to·zo'ic
en'trails
en·train'
en·trance',
   en'trance
en'trant
en·trap'
en·trap'ment
en·treat'
en·treat'y
en'tre·chat'
en'tree
en·trench'
en·trench'ment
en'tre·pre·neur'
en'tro·py
en·trust'
en'try
en·twine'
e·nu'cle·ate'
e·nu'mer·ate'
e·nu'mer·a'tion
e·nu'mer·a·tive
e·nu'mer·a·tor
e·nun'ci·ate'
e·nun'ci·a'tion
e·nun'ci·a'tor
en·vel'op
en've·lope'

en·vel'op·ment
en·ven'om
en'vi·a·ble
en'vi·ous
en·vi'ron
en·vi'ron·ment
en·vi'ron·men'tal
en·vi'rons
en·vis'age
en·vi'sion
en'voy
en'vy
en·wrap'
en·wrapped'
en'zo·ot'ic
en'zyme
E'o·cene'
e'o·lith'
e'o·lith'ic
e'on
e'o·sin
e'pact
ep'au·let'
ep'au·lette'
e·pee'
ep'ei·rog'e·ny
ep'en·ceph'a·lon'
ep·en'dy·ma
ep·ex'e·ge'sis
ep·ex'e·get'i·cal
e·phed'rine
e·phem'er·a
e·phem'er·al
e·phem'er·id
ep'i·blast'

ep'ic
ep'i·can'thus
ep'i·car'di·um
ep'i·cene'
ep'i·cen'ter
ep'i·cure'
Ep'i·cu·re'an
Ep'i·cu·re'an·ism
ep'i·cur·ism
ep'i·cy'cle
ep'i·cy'cloid
ep'i·dem'ic
ep'i·dem'i·cal·ly
ep'i·de'mi·ol'o·gy
ep'i·der'mal
ep'i·der'mis
ep'i·dote'
ep'i·gas'tri·um
ep'i·gene'
ep'i·gen'e·sis
ep'i·glot'tis
ep'i·gram'
ep'i·gram·mat'ic
ep'i·graph'
e·pig'ra·phy
ep'i·lep'sy
ep'i·lep'tic
ep'i·log'
ep'i·logue'
ep'i·neph'rine
e·piph'a·ny
ep'i·phe·nom'e·non'
ep'i·phyte'
ep'i·phyt'ic
e·pis'co·pa·cy

e·pis'co·pal
E·pis'co·pa'li·an
e·pis'co·pal·ism
ep'i·sode'
ep'i·sod'ic
ep'i·sod'i·cal·ly
e·pis'te·mo·log'i·cal
e·pis'te·mol'o·gy
ep'i·ster'num
e·pis'tle
e·pis'to·lar'y
ep'i·taph'
ep'i·tha·la'mi·um
ep'i·the'li·al
ep'i·the'li·um
ep'i·thet'
e·pit'o·me
e·pit'o·mize'
ep'i·zo'on
ep'i·zo·ot'ic
ep'och
ep'och·al
ep'ode
ep·on'y·mous
ep'os
ep·ox'y
ep'si·lon'
ep'som
eq'ua·ble
eq'ua·bly
e'qual
e·qual'i·tar'i·an
e·qual'i·ty
e'qual·i·za'tion
e'qual·ize'

e'qual·iz'er
e'qual·ly
e'qua·nim'i·ty
e·quate'
e·qua'tion
e·qua'tor
e'qua·to'ri·al
e·ques'tri·an
e'qui·dis'tant
e'qui·lat'er·al
e'qui·li'brate
e'qui·li'bra·tor
e'qui·lib'ri·um
e'quine
e'qui·noc'tial
e'qui·nox'
e'quip'
e'qui·page
e·quip'ment
e'qui·poise'
eq'ui·ta·ble
eq'ui·tab·ly
eq'ui·ta'tion
eq'ui·ty
e·quiv'a·lence
e·quiv'a·lent
e·quiv'o·cal
e·quiv'o·cate'
e·quiv'o·ca'tion
e'ra
e·rad'i·ca·ble
e·rad'i·cate'
e·rad'i·ca'tor
e·ras'a·ble
e·rase'

e·ras'er
E·ras'tian
e·ra'sure
er'bi·um
e·rect'
e·rec'tile
e·rec'tion
e·rec'tor
er'go
er·gom'e·ter
er'got
er·is'tic
er'mine
e·rode'
e·rog'e·nous
E'ros
e·ro'sion
e·rot'ic
e·rot'i·ca
e·rot'i·cal·ly
e·rot'i·cism
er'ran·cy
er'rand
er'rant
er·ra'ta
er·rat'ic
er·rat'i·cal·ly
er·ra'tum
er·ro'ne·ous
er'ror
er·satz'
e·ruc'tate
e·ruc·ta'tion
er'u·dite'
er'u·di'tion

e·rupt'
e·rup'tion
e·rup'tive
es'ca·drille'
es'ca·lade'
es'ca·late'
es'ca·la'tor
es'ca·pade'
es·cape'
es·cape'ment
es·cap'ism
es·cap'ist
es·carp'ment
es'char
es'cha·tol'o·gy
es·cheat'
es·cheat'age
es·chew'
es·chew'al
es'cort
es'cri·toire'
es'crow
es'cu·lent
es·cutch'eon
es'kar
es'ker
Es'ki·mo'
e·soph'a·gus
es'o·ter'ic
es·pal'ier
es·par'to
es·pe'cial
es·pe'cial·ly
Es'pe·ran'to
es·pi'al

es'pi·o·nage
es'pla·nade'
es·pous'al
es·pouse'
es·prit'
es·py'
es·quire'
es·say'
es'sence
es·sen'tial
es·sen'ti·al'i·ty
es·sen'tial·ly
es'so·nite'
es·tab'lish
es·tab'lished
es·tab'lish·ment
es·tate'
es·teem'
es'ter
es'ter·ase'
es·the'si·a
es'thete
es·thet'ic
es·thet'i·cal·ly
es·the·ti'cian
es·thet'i·cism
es·thet'ics
es'ti·ma·ble
es'ti·mate'
es'ti·ma'tion
es'ti·val
es'ti·va'tion
es·top'
es·top'pel
es·to'vers

es·trange'
es·trange'ment
es·treat'
es'tro·gen
es'trous
es'trus
es'tu·ar'y
et cet'er·a
etch'ing
e·ter'nal
e·ter'nal·ize'
e·ter'nal·ly
e·ter'ni·ty
e·te'sian
eth'ane
eth'a·nol'
e'ther
e·the're·al
e'ther·ize'
eth'ic
eth'i·cal
eth'i·cal·ly
eth'ics
E'thi·o'pi·an
eth'moid
eth'nic
eth'ni·cal·ly
eth'no·cen'trism
eth·nog'ra·pher
eth'no·graph'ic
eth·nog'ra·phy
eth'no·log'i·cal·ly
eth·nol'o·gy
e'thos
eth'yl

eth'y·lene'
e·ti·ol'o·gy
et'i·quette'
E·trus'can
et se'quens
et se·quen'ti·a
é'tude
et'y·mo·log'i·cal
et'y·mol'o·gist
et'y·mol'o·gy
eu'ca·lyp'tus
Eu'cha·rist
eu'chre
Eu·clid'e·an
eu·dae'mon·ism
eu·di·om'e·ter
eu·gen'ic
eu·gen'i·cist
eu·gen'ics
eu·he'mer·ism
eu'lo·gist
eu'lo·gis'tic
eu'lo·gize'
eu'lo·gy
eu'nuch
eu'phe·mism
eu'phe·mis'ti·cal·ly
eu·phon'ic
eu·pho'ni·ous
eu·pho'ni·um
eu'pho·ny
eu·pho'ri·a
eu·phor'ic
eu'phu·ism
eu·re'ka

Eu'rope
Eu'ro·pe'an
eu·ro'pi·um
eu·ryth'mics
eu·tec'tic
eu·tha·na'si·a
eu·then'ics
e·vac'u·ate'
e·vac'u·a'tion
e·vac'u·ee'
e·vade'
e·vag'i·nate'
e·val'u·ate'
e·val'u·a'tion
ev'a·nesce'
ev'a·nes'cence
ev'a·nes'cent
e·van'gel
e·van'gel'i·cal
e·van'gel·ism
e·van'gel·ist
e·vap'o·rate'
e·vap'o·rat'ed
e·vap'o·ra'tion
e·va'sion
e·va'sive
e·vec'tion
e'ven
e'ven·hand'ed
eve'ning
e'ven·ness
e·vent'
e·vent'ful
e'ven·tide'
e·ven'tu·al

e·ven'tu·al'i·ty
e·ven'tu·al·ly
ev'er
ev'er·glade'
ev'er·green'
ev'er·last'ing
e·ver'sion
e·vert'
ev'er·y
ev'er·y·bod'y
ev'er·y·day'
ev'er·y·one'
ev'er·y·thing'
ev'er·y·where'
e·vict'
e·vic'tion
ev'i·dence
ev'i·dent
ev'i·den'tial
ev'i·dent·ly
e'vil
e'vil·do'er
e'vil·ly
e·vince'
e·vinc'ing
e·vis'cer·ate'
e·vis'cer·a'tion
ev'i·ta·ble
ev'o·ca·ble
ev'o·ca'tion
e·voc'a·tive
e·voke'
ev'o·lu'tion
ev'o·lu'tion·ar'y
ev'o·lu'tion·ist

e·volve'
e·vul'sion
ew'er
ex·ac'er·bate'
ex·ac'er·ba'tion
ex·act'
ex·act'ing
ex·ac'tion
ex·act'i·tude'
ex·act'ly
ex·ag'ger·ate'
ex·ag'ger·a'tion
ex·alt'
ex'al·ta'tion
ex·am'i·nant
ex·am'i·na'tion
ex·am'ine
ex·am'ple
ex·as'per·ate'
ex·as'per·a'tion
ex ca·the'dra
ex'ca·vate'
ex'ca·va'tion
ex'ca·va'tor
ex·ceed'
ex·ceed'ing·ly
ex·cel'
ex'cel·lence
ex'cel·lent
ex·cel'ling
ex·cel'si·or'
ex·cept'
ex·cept'ing
ex·cep'tion
ex·cep'tion·al

ex·cerpt', ex'cerpt
ex·cess', ex'cess'
ex·ces'sive
ex·change'
ex·change'a·bil'i·ty
ex·cheq'uer
ex·cis'a·ble
ex·cise', ex'cise
ex·ci'sion
ex·cit'a·bil'i·ty
ex·cit'a·ble
ex'ci·ta'tion
ex·cite'
ex·cit'ed
ex·cit'ing
ex·claim'
ex'cla·ma'tion
ex·clam'a·to'ry
ex·clud'a·ble
ex·clude'
ex·clu'sion
ex·clu'sion·ist
ex·clu'sive
ex·com·mu'ni·cate'
ex·com·mu'ni·ca'tion
ex·co'ri·ate'
ex·co'ri·a'tion
ex'cre·ment
ex'cre·men'tal
ex·cres'cence
ex·cres'cent
ex·crete'
ex·cre'tion
ex'cre·to'ry
ex·cru'ci·ate'

ex·cru'ci·at'ing
ex'cul·pate'
ex·cul'pa·to'ry
ex·cur'sion
ex·cur'sive
ex·cur'sus
ex·cus'a·ble
ex·cuse'
ex'e·cra·ble
ex'e·crate'
ex'e·cra'tion
ex·ec'u·tant
ex'e·cute'
ex'e·cu'tion
ex'e·cu'tion·er
ex·ec'u·tive
ex·ec'u·tor
ex·ec'u·trix
ex'e·ge'sis
ex'e·get'i·cal
ex·em'plar
ex·em'pla·ry
ex·em'pli·fy'
ex·em'plum
ex·empt'
ex·emp'tion
ex'e·quy
ex'er·cise'
ex·ert'
ex·er'tion
ex'e·unt
ex·fo'li·ate'
ex·fo'li·a'tion
ex·hal'ant
ex'ha·la'tion

ex·hale'
ex·haust'
ex·haust'i·ble
ex·haust'ion
ex·haust'ive
ex·hib'it
ex'hi·bi'tion
ex'hi·bi'tion·ism
ex·hib'i·tor
ex·hil'a·rate'
ex·hil'a·ra'tion
ex·hort'
ex'hor·ta'tion
ex·hor'ta·to'ry
ex'hu·ma'tion
ex·hume'
ex'i·gen·cy
ex'i·gent
ex'ile
ex·ist'
ex·ist'ence
ex·ist'ent
ex'is·ten'tial
ex'is·ten'tial·ism
ex'it
ex'o·dus
ex·og'a·mous
ex·og'a·my
ex·og'e·nous
ex·on'er·ate'
ex·on'er·a'tion
ex'o·path'ic
ex'o·ra·ble
ex·or'bi·tance
ex·or'bi·tant

ex'or·cise'
ex'or·cism
ex'or·cist
ex·or'di·um
ex'o·skel'e·ton
ex'o·ter'ic
ex·ot'ic
ex·ot'i·cal·ly
ex·pand'
ex·pand'ed
ex·panse'
ex·pan'sion
ex·pan'sive
ex·pan'sive·ness
ex·pa'ti·ate'
ex·pa'tri·ate'
ex·pect'
ex·pect'an·cy
ex·pect'ant
ex'pec·ta'tion
ex·pec'to·rant
ex·pec'to·rate'
ex·pe'di·en·cy
ex·pe'di·ent
ex'pe·dite'
ex'pe·dit'er
ex'pe·di'tion
ex'pe·di'tous
ex·pel'
ex·pel'lant
ex·pend'
ex·pend'a·ble
ex·pend'i·ture
ex·pense'
ex·pen'sive

ex·pe′ri·ence
ex·pe′ri·en′tial
ex·per′i·ment
ex·per′i·men′tal
ex·per′i·men′tal·ly
ex·per′i·men·ta′tion
ex′pert
ex′pi·a·ble
ex′pi·ate′
ex′pi·a′tion
ex′pi·ra′tion
ex·pire′
ex·plain′
ex·pla·na′tion
ex·plan′a·to′ry
ex′ple·tive
ex·pli′ca·ble
ex′pli·cate′
ex′pli·ca′tion
ex·pli′cit
ex·plode′
ex·ploit′, ex′ploit
ex′ploi·ta′tion
ex·ploit′a·tive
ex·ploi′ter
ex′plo·ra′tion
ex·plor′a·to′ry
ex·plore′
ex·plor′er
ex·plo′sion
ex·plo′sive
ex·po′nent
ex′po·nen′tial
ex·port′, ex′port
ex′por·ta′tion

ex·port′er
ex·pose′
ex′po·sé′
ex′po·si′tion
ex·pos′i·tor
ex·pos′i·to′ry
ex·pos′tu·late′
ex·pos′tu·la′tion
ex·po′sure
ex·pound′
ex·press′
ex·press′i·ble
ex·pres′sion
ex·pres′sion·ism
ex·pres′sion·is′tic
ex·pres′sive
ex·press′ly
ex·pro′pri·ate′
ex·pro′pri·a′tion
ex·pul′sion
ex·pul′sive
ex·punge′
ex·pung′ing
ex′pur·gate′
ex′pur·ga′tor
ex′qui·site,
   ex·qui′site
ex′tant, ex·tant′
ex·tem′po·ra′ne·ous
ex·tem′po·re
ex·tend′
ex·tend′ed
ex·ten′sion
ex·ten′sive
ex·ten′sor

ex·tent′
ex·ten′u·ate′
ex·ten′u·at′ing
ex·ten′u·a′tion
ex·te′ri·or
ex·ter′mi·nate′
ex·ter′mi·na′tion
ex·ter′mi·na·tor
ex·ter′nal
ex·ter′nal·i·ty
ex·ter′nal·ize′
ex·tinct′
ex·tinc′tion
ex·tin′guish
ex·tin′guish·er
ex′tir·pate′
ex′tir·pa′tion
ex·tol′
ex·toll′
ex·tol′ler
ex·tort′
ex·tor′tion
ex·tor′tion·ar′y
ex·tor′tion·er
ex·tor′tion·ist
ex′tra
ex′tract, ex·tract′
ex·tract′a·ble
ex·trac′tion
ex·trac′tor
ex′tra·cur·ric′u·lar
ex′tra·dite′
ex′tra·di′tion
ex′tra·le′gal
ex′tra·mu′ral

ex·tra′ne·ous
ex·tra·or′di·nar′y
ex·trap′o·late′
ex·trap′o·la′tion
ex′tra·sen′so·ry
ex′tra·u′ter·ine
ex·trav′a·gance
ex·trav′a·gant
ex·trav′a·gan′za
ex·treme′
ex·trem′ism
ex·trem′ist
ex·trem′i·ty
ex′tri·cate′

ex′tri·ca′tion
ex·trin′sic
ex·trin′si·cal·ly
ex′tro·ver′sion
ex′tro·vert′
ex·trude′
ex·tru′sion
ex·u′ber·ance
ex·u′ber·ant
ex′u·da′tion
ex·ude′
ex·ult′
ex·ult′ant

ex·ul·ta′tion
ex·ur′ban
ex·ur′ban·ite′
ex·u′vi·ae′
ex·u′vi·ate′
eye′brow′
eye′ful′
eye′glass′
eye′lash′
eye′let
eye′sight′
eye′wit′ness
ey′rie

F

Fa′bi·an·ism
fa′ble
fa′bled
fab′li·au′
fab′ric
fab′ri·cate′
fab′ri·cat′ed
fab′ri·ca′tion
fab′u·list
fab′u·lous
fa·çade′
fac′et
fa·ce′tious
fa′cial
fa′ci·end′
fac′ile
fa·cil′i·tate′
fa·cil′i·ta′tion
fa·cil′i·ty
fac′ing
fac·sim′i·le
fac′tion
fac′tion·al·ism
fac′tious
fac·ti′tous
fac′tor
fac·to′ri·al
fac·to′ry
fac·to′tum
fac′tu·al
fac′ul·ta′tive

fac′ul·ty
fad′dish
fa·er′ie
fa·er′y
fag′ot
fag′ot·ing
Fahr′en·heit′
fa·ience′
fail′ing
fail′ure
fair′ing
fair′ly
fair′way′
fair′y
faith′ful
faith′less
fak′er
fa·kir′
fal′cate
fal′con
fal′con·er
fal′con·ry
fal′de·rol′
fald′stool′
fal·la′cious
fal′la·cy
fall′en
fal′li·bil′i·ty
fal′li·ble
fall′out′
fal′low

false′hood
fal·set′to
fal′si·fi·ca′tion
fal′si·fi′er
fal′si·fy′
fal′si·ty
fal′ter
fa·mil′ial
fa·mil′iar
fa·mil′i·ar′i·ty
fa·mil′iar·ize′
fam′i·ly
fam′ine
fam′ish
fa′mous
fa·na′tic
fa·nat′i·cal
fa·nat′i·cism
fan′cied
fan′ci·er
fan′ci·ful
fan′cy
fan·dan′go
fan′fare′
fan′light′
fan′ner
fan′ny
fan′on
fan·ta′si·a
fan·tas′tic
fan′ta·sy

102

far'ad
far'a·day'
far'an·dole'
far'ci·cal
far'ci·cal'i·ty
far'del
fare'well'
far'fetched'
fa·ri'na
far'i·na'ceous
farm'er
farm'house'
farm'ing
farm'yard'
far'o
far·ra'go
far'ri·er
far'row
far'see'ing
far'sight'ed
far'ther
far'thest
far'thing
far'thin·gale'
fas'ces
fas'ci·a
fas'ci·ate'
fas·cic'u·lus
fas'ci·nate'
fas'ci·na'tion
fas'cism
fas'cist
fa·scis'tic
fash'ion
fash'ion·a·ble

fash'ion·a·bly
fast'back'
fas'ten
fas'ten·er
fas·tid'i·ous
fast'ness
fa'tal
fa'tal·ism
fa'tal·ist
fa'tal·is'ti·cal·ly
fa·tal'i·ty
fa'tal·ly
fat'ed
fate'ful
fat'head'
fa'ther
fa'ther·land'
fa'ther·less
fa'ther·ly
fath'om
fath'om·less
fat'i·ga·ble
fa·tigue'
fat'ling
fat'ten
fat'tened
fat'ty
fa·tu'i·ty
fat'u·ous
fau'cet
fault'find'er
fault'i·ly
fault'i·ness
fault'less
fault'y

fau'na
fa·ve'o·late'
fa·vo'ni·an
fa'vor
fa'vor·a·ble
fa'vored
fa'vor·ite
fa'vor·it·ism
fa'vour
fe'al·ty
fear'ful
fear'less
fear'some
fea'sance
fea'si·bil'i·ty
fea'si·ble
feath'er
feath'er·bed'ding
feath'er·brained'
feath'ered
feath'er·ing
feath'er·weight'
feath'er·y
fea'ture
fea'tured
fea'ture·less
feb'ri·fuge'
fe'brile
Feb'ru·ar'y
fe'cal
fe'ces
feck'less
fec'u·lent
fe'cund
fe'cun·date'

fe·cun'di·ty
fed'er·a·cy
fed'er·al
fed'er·al·ism
fed'er·al·i·za'tion
fed'er·al·ize'
fed'er·ate
fed'er·a'tion
fe·do'ra
fee'ble
fee'bly
feed'back'
feed'er
feel'er
feel'ing
feld'spar'
fe·lic'i·tate'
fe·lic'i·ta'tion
fe·lic'i·tous
fe·lic'i·ty
fe'line
fel'lah
fell'er
fel'low
fel'low·ship'
fel'ly
fel'on
fe·lo'ni·ous
fel'o·ny
fel'site
felt'ing
fe·luc'ca
fe'male
fem'i·na·cy
fem'i·nine

fem'i·nin'i·ty
fem'i·nism
fem'i·nist
fem'i·nize'
fem'o·ral
fe'mur
fe·na'gle
fenc'er
fenc'ing
fend'ing
fe·nes'tra
fe·nes'trate
fen'es·tra'tion
Fe'ni·an
fen'nel
fen'u·greek'
fe'ral
fer'de·lance'
fer'e·to'ry
fe'ri·a
fe'ri·al
fer·ma'ta
fer'ment, fer·ment'
fer'men·ta'tion
fer'mi·um
fern'er·y
fe·ro'cious
fe·roc'i·ty
fer're·ous
fer'ret
fer'ri·age
fer'ric
fer·rif'er·ous
Fer'ris
fer'rite

fer'ro·al·loy'
fer'ro·cy'a·nide'
fer'ro·mag·net'ic
fer'ro·man'ga·nese'
fer'ro·type'
fer'rous
fer'rule
fer'ry
fer'ry·man
fer'tile
fer·til'i·ty
fer'ti·li·za'tion
fer'ti·lize'
fer'ti·liz'er
fer'u·la
fer'ule
fer'vent
fer'vid
fer'vor
fes'tal
fes'ter
fes'ti·val
fes'tive
fes·tiv'i·ty
fes·toon'
fe'tal
fetch'ing
fe'ti·cide'
fe'tish
fe'tish·ism
fe'ti·shis'tic
fet'lock'
fet'ter
fet'tle
fe'tus

feu'dal
feu'dal·ism
feu'da·to'ry
fe'ver
fe'ver·ish
fi·an·cé'
fi·an·cée'
fi·as'co
fi'at
fib'ber
fi'ber
fi'ber·glas'
fi'bril
fi'bril·lose'
fi'brin
fi·brin'o·gen
fi'brin·ous
fi'broid
fi·bro'sis
fi'brous
fib'u·la
fib'u·lar
fick'le
fic'tile
fic'tion
fic'tion·al
fic·ti'tious
fic'tive
fid'dle
fid'dler
fid'dling
fi·del'i·ty
fidg'et
fidg'et·y
fi·du'cial

fi·du'ci·ar'y
field'er
field'work'
fiend'ish
fi'er·i·ness
fi'er·y
fi·es'ta
fif'teen'
fif'teenth'
fif'ti·eth
fif'ty
fight'er
fight'ing
fig'ment
fig'u·rant'
fig'u·ra'tion
fig'ur·a·tive
fig'ure
fig'ured
fig'ure·head'
fig'u·rine'
fil'a·ment
fil'a·men'tous
fil'a·ture
fil'bert
fi·let'
fi·let' mi·gnon'
fil'i·al
fil'i·a'tion
fil'i·bus'ter
fil'i·gree'
fil'ing
Fil'i·pine'
Fil'i·pi'no
fill'er

fil'let
fill'ing
fil'lip
fil'ly
film'strip'
film'y
fi'lose
fil'ter
fil'ter·a·ble
filth'i·ness
filth'y
fil'trate
fil·tra'tion
fi'lum
fi·na'gle
fi·na'gler
fi'nal
fi·na'le
fi·nal'i·ty
fi'nal·ize'
fi'nal·ly
fi'nance
fi·nan'cial
fi·nan'cial·ly
fin'an·cier'
fin'back'
find'er
find'ing
fine'ly
fin'er·y
fi·nesse'
fin'ger
fin'gered
fin'ger·ing
fin'ger·nail'

fin′ger·print′
fin′i·al
fin′i·cal
fin′ick·y
fin′ing
fi′nis
fin′ish
fin′ished
fin′ish·ing
fi′nite
fin′i·tude′
fin′nan had′die
Finn′ish
fin′ny
fip′ple
fire′ball′
fire′brand′
fire′crack′er
fire′fly′
fire′man
fire′place′
fire′wood′
fire′works′
fir′ing
fir′kin
fir′ma·ment
firm′er
first′hand′
fis′cal
fish′bowl′
fish′er
fish′er·man
fish′er·y
fish′i·ness
fish′pond′

fish′y
fis′sile
fis′sion
fis′sion·a·ble
fis′sure
fist′ful
fis′ti·cuffs′
fis′tu·la
fis′tu·lous
fitch′ew
fit′ful
fit′ly
fit′ter
fit′ting
five′fold′
fiv′er
fix′ate
fix·a′tion
fix′a·tive
fix′ed·ly
fix′er
fix′i·ty
fix′ture
fiz′zle
fiz′zy
flab′ber·gast′
flab′bi·ly
flab′bi·ness
flab′by
flac′cid
flac·cid′i·ty
flag′el·lant
flag′el·late′
flag′el·la′tion
fla·gel′lum

flag′eo·let′
flag′ging
flag′on
flag′pole′
fla′gran·cy
fla′grant
fla·gran′te de·lic′to
flag′ship′
flag′stone′
flak′i·ness
flak′y
flam′beau
flam·boy′ance
flam·boy′ant
fla·men′co
flam′ing
fla·min′go
flam′ma·ble
flan′nel
flan′nel·ette′
flap′doo′dle
flap′jack′
flap′per
flare′back′
flar′ing
flash′er
flash′i·ness
flash′ing
flash′light′
flash′y
flat′boat′
flat′car′
flat′foot′
flat′i′ron
flat′ten

flat'ter
flat'ter·y
flat'u·lence
flat'u·lent
fla'tus
flat'ware'
flat'worm'
flau'tist
fla·ves'cent
fla'vin
fla'vor
fla'vor·ing
fla'vour
flaw'less
flax'en
flax'seed'
flea'bane'
flea'bite'
flec'tion
fledg'ling
fleec'y
fleet'ing
Flem'ish
flesh'i·ness
flesh'ly
flesh'pot'
flesh'y
flex'i·bil'i·ty
flex'i·ble
flex'i·bly
flex'ion
flex'or
flex'u·ous
flex'ure
flick'er

fli'er
flight'i·ness
flight'y
flim'flam'
flim'si·ly
flim'si·ness
flim'sy
flint'i·ness
flint'lock'
flint'y
flip'pan·cy
flip'pant
flip'per
flir·ta'tion
flir·ta'tious
flirt'y
flit'ter
fliv'ver
float'er
float'ing
floc'cu·lence
floc'cu·lent
floc'cu·lus
floc'cus
flog'ger
flood'gate'
flood'light'
floor'age
floor'ing
floor'walk'er
floo'zie
floo'zy
flop'house'
flop'py
flo'ral

Flor'ence
Flor'en·tine'
flo·res'cence
flo·res'cent
flo'ret
flo'ri·cul'ture
flo'ri·cul'tur·ist
flo'rid
Flo·rid'i·an
flo·rid'i·ty
flor'in
flo'rist
floss'y
flo'tage
flo·ta'tion
flo·til'la
flot'sam
flounc'ing
floun'der
flour'ish
flow'age
flow'er
flow'ered
flow'er·ing
flow'er·y
flow'sheet'
fluc'tu·ate'
fluc'tu·a'tion
flu'en·cy
flu'ent
fluf'fi·ness
fluf'fy
flu'id
flu·id'i·ty
fluk'ey

fluk'y
flum'mer·y
flunk'ey
flunk'ing
flunk'y
flu'o·resce'
flu'o·res'cence
flu'o·res'cent
flu'o·ri·date'
flu'o·rine'
flu'o·rite'
flur'ry
flus'ter
flut'ed
flut'ing
flut'ist
flut'ter
flut'y
flu'vi·al
flux'ior
fly'a·way'
fly'blown'
fly'ing
fly'leaf'
fly'trap'
fly'weight'
fly'wheel'
foam'i·ness
foam'y
fo'cal
fo'cal·i·za'tion
fo'cal·ize'
fo'cus
fod'der
foe'tal

foe'tus
fog'bound'
fog'gi·ness
fog'gy
fog'horn'
fo'gy
fo'gy·ish
foi'ble
foist'ed
fold'er
fol'de·rol'
fol'li·a'ceous
fo'li·age
fo'li·ate'
fo'li·a'tion
fo'lic
fo'li·um
folk'lore'
folk'lor'ist
folk'sy
folk'ways'
fol'li·cle
fol'lies
fol'low
fol'low·er
fol'low·ing
fol'ly
fo·ment'
fo'men·ta'tion
fon'dant
fon'dle
fond'ly
fon'ta·nel'
fon'ta·nelle'
food'stuffs'

fool'er·y
fool'har'di·ness
fool'har'dy
fool'ing
fool'ish
fool'ish·ness
fool'proof'
fools'cap'
foot'age
foot'ball'
foot'bridge'
foot'ed
foot'hill'
foot'hold'
foot'ing
foot'lights'
foot'note'
foot'print'
foot'step'
foot'work'
foo'zle
fop'per·y
fop'pish
for'age
for·a'men
for'ay
for·bear'
for·bear'ance
for·bid'
for·bid'dance
for·bid'den
for·bid'ding
for·bore'
forc'ed·ly
force'ful

force'meat'
for'ceps
for'ci·ble
for'ci·bly
fore'arm'
fore·bode'
fore·bod'ing
fore'brain'
fore·cast',
　　fore'cast'
fore'cast'er
fore'cas·tle
fore·close'
fore·clo'sure
fore'court'
fore'fa'ther
fore'fin'ger
fore'front'
fore'go'ing
fore·gone'
fore'hand'
fore'hand'ed
for'eign
for'eign·er
fore·know'
fore'knowl'edge
fore'leg'
fore'man
fore'most'
fore'named'
fore'noon'
fo·ren'sic
fo·ren'si·cal·ly
fore'or·dain'
fore'run'ner

fore'sail'
fore·see'
fore·shad'ow
fore·shad'owed
fore·short'en
fore'sight'
fore'skin'
for'est
fore·stall'
for'est·a'tion
for'est·ry
fore'taste'
fore·tell'
fore'thought'
fore·told'
for·ev'er
fore·warn'ing
fore·wom'an
fore'ward'
for'feit
for'fei·ture
for·fend'
for·gath'er
for·gave'
forg'er
for'ger·y
for·get'
for·get'ful
for·get'ting
forg'ing
for·giv'a·ble
for·give'
for·give'ness
for·giv'ing
for·go'

for·got'
for·got'ten
for·lorn'
for'mal
form·al'de·hyde'
for'ma·lin
for'mal·ism
for'mal·is'tic
for·mal'i·ty
for'mal·ize'
for'mal·ly
for'mat
for·ma'tion
form'a·tive
for'mer
for'mer·ly
for'mic
for'mi·da·ble
for'mi·da·bly
form'less
for'mu·la
for'mu·lar'y
for'mu·late'
for'mu·la'tion
for'mu·lis'tic
for'mu·lize'
for'ni·cate'
for'ni·ca'tion
for'ni·ca'tor
for·sake'
for·sak'en
for·swear'
for·syth'i·a
for'te
for'te-pia'no

forth'com'ing
forth'right'
forth'with'
for'ti·eth
for·ti·fi'a·ble
for·ti·fi·ca'tion
for·ti·fi'er
for·ti·fy'
for·tis'si·mo
for'ti·tude'
for'ti·tu'di·nous
fort'night
for'tress
for·tu'i·tous
for·tu'i'ty
for'tu·nate
for'tune
for'tune·tell'er
for'ty
fo'rum
for'ward
for'ward·ness
for'wards
for·zan'do
fos'sil
fos·sil·i·za'tion
fos'sil·ized'
fos'ter
fos'ter·age
fou·droy'ant
fou·lard'
foul'mouthed'
foul'ness
foun·da'tion

foun'der
found'ling
found'ry
foun'tain
four·chette'
four'flush'er
four'fold'
Fou'ri·er·ism
four'score'
four'square'
four'teen'
four'teenth'
fo've·a
fo've·a cen·tra'lis
fowl'er
fowl'ing
fox'glove'
fox'hole'
fox'hound'
fox'i·ness
fox'ing
fox'y
foy'er
fra'cas
frac'tion
frac'tion·al
frac'tious
frac'tur·al
frac'ture
frag'ile
fra·gil'i·ty
frag'ment
frag·men'tal
frag'men·tar'i·ly

frag'men·tar'y
frag'men·ta'tion
frag'ment·ed
fra'grance
fra'grant
frail'ty
frame'work'
fram'ing
fran'chise
fran'chised
Fran·cis'can
Fran'co·phile'
fran'gi·ble
fran'gi·pan'i
Frank'en·stein'
frank'furt'er
frank'in·cense'
Frank'ish
frank'lin
frank'pledge'
fran'tic
fran'ti·cal·ly
frap·pé'
fra·ter'nal
fra·ter'nal·ism
fra·ter'ni·ty
frat'er·ni·za'tion
frat'er·nize'
frat'ri·cid'al
frat'ri·cide'
fraud'u·lence
fraud'u·lent
fraz'zle
freak'ish

freak'y
freck'le
freck'ly
free'boot'er
freed'man
free'dom
free'hold'
free'load'er
Free'ma'son·ry
free'stone'
free'think'ing
free'way'
freez'er
freez'ing
freight'age
freight'er
fre·net'ic
fre'num
fren'zied
fren'zy
fre'on
fre'quen·cy
fre'quent
fre'quent·ly
fres'co
fresh'en
fresh'et
fresh'ly
fresh'man
fret'ful
fret'ted
fret'work'
Freud'i·an
fri'a·bil'i·ty

fri'a·ble
fri'ar
fri'ar·y
frib'ble
fric'an·deau'
fric'as·see'
fric'a·tive
fric'tion
Fri'day
friend'less
friend'li·ness
friend'ly
friend'ship
frig'ate
fright'en
fright'ened
fright'ful
fright'ful·ly
frig'id
fri·gid'i·ty
frill'y
frip'per·y
frisk'y
frit'ter
fri·vol'i·ty
friv'o·lous
friz'zle
friz'zly
friz'zy
frog'gy
frol'ic
frol'ick·er
frol'ic·some
fro'men·ty

frond'ed
fron·des'cence
fron·des'cent
front'age
fron'tal
fron·tier'
fron·tiers'man
fron'tis·piece'
front'let
frost'bite'
frost'bit'ten
frost'ed
frost'i·ly
frost'i·ness
frost'ing
frost'y
froth'i·ly
froth'y
frou'frou'
fro'ward
frown'ing
frow'si·ness
frow'sy
frow'zi·ness
frow'zy
fro'zen
fruc'ti·fi·ca'tion
fruc'ti·fy'
fruc'tose
fru'gal
fru·gal'i·ty
fruit'age
fruit'cake'
fruit'er

fruit'ful
fruit'i·ness
fru·i'tion
fruit'less
fruit'y
fru'men·ta'ceous
fru'men·ty
frump'ish
frump'y
frus'trate
frus·tra'tion
frus'tum
fry'er
fry'ing
fuch'si·a
fu'cus
fud'dle
fu'el
fu'el·er
fu'el·ler
fu·ga'cious
fu'gal
fu'gi·tive
fu'gle·man
ful'crum
ful·fill'
ful·fill'ment
ful'gu·rate'
ful'gu·rite'
ful·ig'i·nous
full'er
full'ness
ful'mi·nant
ful'mi·nate'

ful'mi·na'tion
ful·min'ic
ful'some
fu·mar'ic
fu'ma·to'ry
fum'ble
fum'bler
fum'bling
fu'mi·gate'
fu'mi·ga'tion
fu'mi·ga'tor
fu·nam'bu·list
func'tion
func'tion·al
func'tion·al·ism
func'tion·ar'y
fun'da·ment
fun'da·men'tal
fun'da·men'tal·ism
fun'da·men'tal·ly
fund'ed
fund'ing
fun'dus
fu'ner·al
fu·ne're·al
fun'gi·ble
fun'gi·cide'
fun'go
fun'goid
fun'gus
fu·nic'u·lar
fu·nic'u·lus
funk'y
fun'nel

fun'neled
fun'nelled
fun'ni·ly
fun'ni·ness
fun'ny
fu'ran
fur'be·low'
fur'bish
fur'cate
fur·ca'tion
fur'ri·ous
fur'long
fur'lough
fur'nace
fur'nish
fur'nish·ings
fur'ni·ture
fu'ror
fur'ri·er
fur'ri·ness
fur'ring
fur'row
fur'ry
fur'ther
fur'ther·ance
fur'ther·more'
fur'ther·most'
fur'thest
fur'tive
fu'ry
fu·sain'
fus'cous
fu'se·lage
fu'si·bil'i·ty

fu'si·ble
fu'sil
fu'sil·ier'
fu'sil·lade'
fu'sion
fuss'i·ly
fuss'i·ness

fuss'y
fus'tian
fus'tic
fust'y
fu'thark
fu'tile
fu·til'i·ty

fut'tock
fu'ture
fu'tur·ism
fu'tur·ist
fu·tu'ri·ty
fuzz'i·ness
fuzz'y

G

gab′ar·dine′
gab′ber
gab′ble
gab′bler
gab′bro
gab′by
ga′bi·on
ga′ble
ga′bled
gad′a·bout′
gad′fly′
gadg′et
gad′o·lin·ite′
gad′o·lin′i·um
Gael′ic
gaf′fer
gag′ger
gag′gle
gahn′ite
gai′e·ty
gai′ly
gain′er
gain′ful·ly
gain′ly
gain′say′
gait′ed
gai′ter
ga′la
ga·lac′ta·gogue′
ga·lac′tic
gal′an·tine′

gal′a·te′a
Ga·la′tians
gal′ax·y
gal′ba·num
ga·le′na
ga·len′ic
Gal′i·le′an
Gal′i·lee′
gal′lant
gal′lant·ry
gal′le·ass′
gal′le·on
gal′ler·y
gal′ley
gal′liard
Gal′lic
gal′lic
Gal′li·cism
gal′li·mau′fry
gall′ing
gal′li·pot′
gal′li·um
gal′li·vant′
gal′li·vant′ing
gal′lo·glass′
gal′lon
gal′lop
gal′lop·er
gal′lows
gall′stone′
ga·loot′

ga·lore′
ga·losh′es
ga·lumph′
gal·van′ic
gal′va·nism
gal′va·nize′
gal·va·no·met′ric
gal·va·nom′e·try
gam′bit
gam′ble
gam′bler
gam′bol
gam′boled
gam′bolled
gam′brel
game′cock′
game′keep′er
game′ly
game′ness
game′ster
gam′ete
ga·met′ic
gam′ic
gam′in
gam′i·ness
gam′ing
gam′ma
gam′mon
gam′ut
gam′y
gan′der

114

Gan'dhi·ism
gan'gli·a
gan'gli·at'ed
gan'gling
gan'gli·on
gan'gly
gang'plank'
gan'grene
gan'gre·nous
gang'ster
gang'way'
gan'is·ter
gan'net
gant'let
gan'try
gap'ing
ga·rage'
gar'bage
gar'ble
gar'bled
gar'çon'
gar'den
gar'den·er
gar·de'ni·a
Gar·gan'tu·an
gar'get
gar'gle
gar'gling
gar'goyle
gar'ish
gar'land
gar'land·ed
gar'lic
gar'lick·y
gar'ment

gar'ner
gar'net
gar'nish
gar'nish·ee'
gar'nish·ment
gar'ni·ture
gar'ret
gar'ri·son
gar'ri·soned
gar·rote'
gar·rot'ed
gar·rot'ted
gar·ru'li·ty
gar'ru·lous
gar'ter
gas'e·ous
gas'house'
gas'i·fi·ca'tion
gas'i·fy'
gas'ket
gas'kin
gas'light'
gas'o·line'
gas'sy
gas·tral'gi·a
gas·trec'to·my
gas'tric
gas'trin
gas·tri'tis
gas'tro·en'ter·i'tis
gas'tro·in·tes'ti·nal
gas'tro·nome'
gas'tro·nom'ic
gas·tron'o·my
gas'tru·la

gate'house'
gate'post'
gate'way'
gath'er
gath'er·ing
gau'che·rie'
gaud'i·ly
gaud'i·ness
gaud'y
gaug'er
gaug'ing
gaunt'let
gauz'i·ness
gauz'y
gav'el
ga·votte'
gawk'i·ly
gawk'i·ness
gawk'y
gay'ness
ga·ze'bo
ga·zelle'
ga·zette'
gaz'et·teer'
ge·an'ti·cli'nal
ge·an'ti·cline'
gear'box'
gear'ing
gear'shift'
gee'zer
ge·fil'te
Ge·hen'na
gei'ger
gei'sha
Geiss'ler

gel'a·tin
ge·la'ti·nate'
ge·lat'i·nous
ge·la'tion
geld'ing
gel'id
ge·lid'i·ty
gem'el
gem'i·nate'
gem'i·na'tion
gem'ma
gem·ma'tion
gen'darme
gen'dar·me·rie
gen'der
gen'e·a·log'i·cal
gen'e·a·log'i·cal·ly
gen'e·al'o·gist
gen'e·al'o·gy
gen'er·a
gen'er·al
gen'er·al·cy
gen'er·al·is'si·mo'
gen'er·al'i·ty
gen'er·al·i·za'tion
gen'er·al·ize'
gen'er·al·ly
gen'er·ate'
gen'er·a'tion
gen'er·a'tive
gen'er·a'tor
ge·ner'ic
gen'er·os'i·ty
gen'er·ous
gen'e·sis

ge·net'ic
ge·net'i·cal·ly
ge·net'i·cist
ge·net'ics
Ge·ne'van
gen'ial (pleasant)
ge·ni'al (of the
    chin)
ge'ni·al'i·ty
ge·nic'u·late
ge'nie
gen'i·tal
gen'i·ta'li·a
gen'i·tive
gen'i·to·u'ri·nar'y
gen'ius
Gen'o·a
gen'o·cide'
Gen'o·ese'
gen're
gen·teel'
gen'tian
gen'tile
gen·til'i·ty
gen'tle
gen'tle·folk'
gen'tle·man
gen'tle·man·ly
gen'tle·wom'an
gen'tly
gen'try
gen'u·flect'
gen'u·flec'tion
gen'u·ine
ge'nus

ge'o·cen'tric
ge'o·chem'is·try
ge'ode
ge'o·des'ic
ge·od'e·sy
ge'o·det'i·cal·ly
ge·od'ic
ge·og'no·sy
ge·og'ra·pher
ge'o·graph'ic
ge'o·graph'i·cal
ge·og'ra·phy
ge'o·log'ic
ge'o·log'i·cal·ly
ge·ol'o·gist
ge·ol'o·gy
ge'o·mag·net'ic
ge'o·man'cer
ge'o·man'cy
ge'o·met'ric
ge'o·met'ri·cal·ly
ge'om·e·tri'cian
ge·om'e·try
ge'o·phys'i·cal
ge'o·phys'ics
ge'o·pol'i·tics
geor·gette'
Geor'gia
Geor'gi·an
geor'gic
ge'o·stat'ics
ge'o·tax'is
ge'o·tec·ton'ic
ge'o·ther'mic
ge'o·trop'ic

ge·ot′ro·pism
ge·ra′ni·um
ger′bil
ger′i·at′rics
Ger′man
ger·mane′
Ger·man′ic
Ger·ma′ni·um
Ger·man′o·phile′
Ger·man′o·phobe′
ger′mi·cid′al
ger′mi·cide′
ger′mi·nal
ger′mi·nate′
ger′mi·na′tion
ger′on·toc′ra·cy
ger′on·tol′o·gy
ger′ry·man′der
ger′und
ge·run′di·al
ge·run′dive
Ge·stalt′
ges′tate
ges′tat·ing
ges·ta′tion
ges·tic′u·late′
ges·tic′u·la′tion
ges·tic′u·la′tive
ges′ture
Ge·sund′heit′
get′a·way′
Geth·sem′a·ne
get′ting
gew′gaw
gey′ser

gey′ser·ite′
ghast′li·ness
ghast′ly
gher′kin
ghet′to
ghost′li·ness
ghost′ly
ghoul′ish
gi′ant
gi′ant·ess
gib′ber
gib′ber·ish
gib′bet
gib′bon
gib·bos′i·ty
gib′bous
gib′er
gib′ing
gib′let
gid′di·ly
gid′di·ness
gid′dy
Gid′e·on
gift′ed
gi′gan·te′an
gi·gan′tic
gi·gan′ti·cal·ly
gi′gan·tism
gig′gle
gig′gler
gig′gly
gig′o·lo′
gig′ot
gi′la
gil′bert

gild′ed
gil′der
gild′ing
Gil′ga·mesh′
gil′lie
gil′li·flow′er
gil′ly·flow′er
gim′bals
gim′crack′
gim′el
gim′let
gim′mal
gim′mick
gim′mick·y
gimp′y
gin′ger
gin′ger·bread′
gin′ger·ly
ging′ham
gin·gi·vi′tis
gink′go
gin′ner
gin′seng
gip′sy
gi·raffe′
gir′an·dole′
gird′er
gird′ing
gir′dle
girl′hood
girl′ish
Gi·ron′dist
give′a·way′
giv′en
giv′er

giz'zard
gla·bel'la
gla'brous
gla·cé'
gla'cial
gla'ci·ate'
gla'ci·a'tion
gla'cier
gla'cis
glad'den
glad'der
glad'dest
glad'i·a'tor
glad'i·a·tor'i·al
glad'i·o'la
glad'i·o'lus
glad'ly
glam'or
glam'or·ize'
glam'or·ous
glam'our
glam'our·ous
glanc'ing
glan'der·ous
glan'ders
glan'du·lar
glan'dule
glar'ing
glar'ing·ly
glass'ful'
glass'i·ly
glass·ine'
glass'i·ness
glass'mak'er
glass'ware'

glass'work'
glass'y
glau·co'ma
glau·co'ma·tous
glau'co·nite'
gla'zier
gla'zier·y
glaz'ing
gleam'ing
glean'ings
glee'ful
glee'man
Glen·gar'ry
gle'noid
glib'ly
glib'ness
glid'er
glid'ing
glim'mer
glim'mer·ing
glimps'ing
glint'ing
gli·o'ma
gli·o'ma·tous
glis·sade'
glis·san'do
glis'ten
glis'ter
glit'ter
glit'ter·ing
glit'ter·y
gloam'ing
gloat'ing
glob'al
glo'bate

glo'bin
glob'u·lar
glob'ule
glob'u·lin
glock'en·spiel'
glom'er·ate
glom'er·a'tion
gloom'i·ly
gloom'i·ness
gloom'y
glo'ri·fi·ca'tion
glo'ri·fi'er
glo'ri·fy'
glo'ri·ous
glo'ry
glos'sa·ry
gloss'er
gloss'i·ness
glos·si'tis
gloss'y
glot'tal
glot'tis
glov'er
glow'er
glow'ing
glow'worm'
glox·in'i·a
glu'cose
glu'co·side'
glue'pot'
glue'y
glu'ing
glum'ly
glu'ta·mine'
glu·te'al

glu'ten
glu'te·nous
glu·te'us
glu'ti·nous
glut'ted
glut'ton
glut'ton·ous
gly·cer'ic
glyc'er·ide'
glyc'er·in
gly'cine
gly'co·gen
gly'col
gly'co·ne'o·gen'e·sis
gly'co·pro'te·in
glyph·ic
gly·phog'ra·phy
glyp'tic
glyp·tog'ra·phy
gnarl'y
gnash'ing
gnath'ic
gnaw'ing
gno'mic
gnom'ish
gno'mon
gno'sis
gnos'tic
Gnos'ti·cism
goad'ing
goal'ie
goal'keep'er
goat·ee'
goat'herd'
goat'ish

goat'skin'
gob'ble
gob'ble·dy·gook'
gob'bler
gob'bling
gob'let
go'cart'
god'child'
god'damned'
god'daugh'ter
god'dess
god'fa'ther
god'for·sak'en
god'head
god'hood
god'less
god'li·ness
god'ly
god'moth'er
god'par'ent
god'send'
god'son
goe'thite
gof'fer·ing
gog'gle
go'ing
goi'ter
goi'trous
gold'brick'
gold'dig'ger
gold'en
gold'en·rod'
gold'finch'
gold'fish'
gold'i·locks'

gold'smith'
go'lem
golf'er
gol'iard
Go·li'ath
gol'ly
gom·pho'sis
gon'ad
gon'ad·al
gon'do·la
gon'do·lier'
gon'er
go·nid'i·um
go'ni·om'e·ter
go'ni·on'
gon'o·coc'cus
gon'or·rhe'a
gon'or·rhe'al
goo'ber
good'by'
good'ly
good'ness
good'will'
good'y
goo'ey
goof'i·ness
goof'y
goo'gol
goose'ber'ry
goose'neck'
goos'y
go'pher
gor'geous
gor'get
Gor'gon

gor'gon·zo'la
go·ril'la
gor'i·ness
gor'mand·ize'
gor'y
gos'hawk'
gos'ling
gos'pel
gos'pel·er
gos'pel·ler
gos'sa·mer
gos'sip
gos'sip·ing
gos'sip·y
Goth'am
Goth'ic
Göt'ter·däm'mer·ung
gou'da
goug'er
goug'ing
gou'lash
gour'mand
gour'man·dise'
gour·met'
gout'i·ness
gout'y
gov'ern
gov'ern·a·ble
gov'ern·ance
gov'ern·ess
gov'ern·ment
gov'ern·men'tal
gov'er·nor
gov'er·nor·ship'
goy'ish

grab·ble
grace'ful
grace'less
Grac'es
grac'ile
gra'cious
grack'le
gra'date
gra'dat·ed
gra·da'tion
grad'er
gra'di·ent
gra'din
grad'u·al
grad'u·ate
grad'u·a'tion
gra'dus
graf·fi'ti
graf·fi'to
graft'ed
graft'ing
gra'ham
grain'field'
grain'y
gral'la·to'ri·al
gra'ma
gra·min'e·ous
gram'i·niv'o·rous
gram'mar
gram·mar'i·an
gram·mat'i·cal
gram·mat'i·cal·ly
gram'o·phone'
gran'a·ry
gran'dam

grand'aunt'
grand'child'
grand'dad'
grand'daugh'ter
gran·dee'
gran'deur
grand'fath'er
gran·dil'o·quence
gran·dil'o·quent
gran'di·ose'
gran'di·os'i·ty
grand'ma
grand'moth'er
grand'neph'ew
grand'niece'
grand'pa
grand'par'ent
grand'sire'
grand'son'
grand'stand'
grand'un'cle
grang'er
grang'er·ize'
gra·nif'er·ous
gran'ite
gra·niv'o·rous
gran'ny
gran'o·lith'ic
grant·ee'
grant'ing
grant'or
gran'u·lar
gran'u·late
gran'u·la'tion
gran'u·la'tor

gran'ule
gran'u·lite'
gran'u·lose'
grape'fruit'
grap'er·y
grape'stone'
grape'vine'
graph'ic
graph'ics
graph'ite
graph·ol'o·gy
grap'nel
grap'ple
grap'pled
grap'pling
grasp'ing
grass'cut'ter
grass'hop'per
grass'i·ness
grass'land
grass'y
grate'ful
grat'er
grat'i·fi·ca'tion
grat'i·fi'er
grat'i·fy'
gra'tin
grat'ing
gra'tis
grat'i·tude'
gra·tu'i·tous
gra·tu'i·ty
grat'u·late'
grat'u·la·to'ry
gra·va'men

grave'dig'ger
grav'el
grav'el·ly
grave'ly
grav'en
grave'ness
grav'er
grave'stone'
grav'id
grav'i·met'ric
gra·vim'e·try
grav'ing
grav'i·tate'
grav'i·ta'tion
grav'i·ta'tion·al
grav'i·ty
gra·vure'
gra'vy
gray'beard'
gray'ish
gra'zier
graz'ing
greas'er
greas'i·ly
greas'i·ness
greas'y
great'coat'
great'ly
Gre'cian
greed'i·ly
greed'i·ness
greed'y
green'back'
green'bri'er
green'er·y

green'gro'cer
green'horn'
green'house'
green'ing
green'ish
green'ness
Green'wich
greet'ed
greet'ing
gre·gar'i·ous
Gre·go'ri·an
grei'sen
grem'lin
gre·nade'
gren'a·dier'
gren'a·dine'
grey'hound'
grid'der
grid'dle
grid'dle·cake'
grid'i'ron
griev'ance
griev'ing
griev'ous
grif'fin
grif'fon
grift'er
gril'lage
grill'ing
grill'room'
grill'work'
gri·mace'
gri·mal'kin
grim'i·ness
grim'y

grind'er
grind'stone'
grin'go
grip'er
grip'ing
grip'per
grip'ping
grip'y
gri·saille'
gri·sette'
gris'li·ness
gris'ly
gris'tle
gris'tly
grist'mill'
grit'ti·ly
grit'ti·ness
grit'ty
griz'zled
griz'zly
gro'cer
gro'cer·y
grog'gi·ly
grog'gi·ness
grog'gy
grog'shop'
Gro'li·er
grom'met
groom'ing
grop'ing
gros'beak'
gros'grain'
gross'ness
gro·tesque'
gro·tes'quer·ie

grot'to
grouch'i·ness
grouch'y
ground'age
ground'er
ground'hog'
ground'less
ground'ling
ground'sel
ground'work'
grous'er
grous'ing
grov'el
grov'eled
grov'elled
grow'er
grow'ing
growl'er
growl'ing
grown'up'
grub'ber
grub'bing
grub'by
grub'stake'
grudg'ing·ly
gru'el
gru'el·ing
gru'el·ling
grue'some
gruff'ly
grum'ble
grum'bler
grum'bling
gru'mose
grump'i·ly

grump'i·ness
grump'y
Grun'dy·sim
grunt'er
grunt'ing
gua·na'co
gua'nine
gua'no
guar'an·tee'
guar'an·tor
guar'an·ty
guard'ed
guard'house'
guard'i·an
guard'i·an·ship'
guard'rail'
guards'man
gua'va
gu'ber·na·to'ri·al
gudg'eon
guer'don
guern'sey
guer·ril'la
guess'work'
guf·faw'
guid'ance
guide'book'
guid'ed
guid'ing
gui'don
guild'hall'
guile'ful
guile'less
guil'lo·tine'
guilt'i·ly

guilt'i·ness
guilt'less
guilt'y
guin'ea
gui·tar'
gui·tar'ist
gul'let
gul'li·bil'i·ty
gul'li·ble
gul'li·bly
Gul'li·ver
gul'ly
gum'bo
gum'boil'
gum'drop'
gum·ma
gum'mi·ness
gum'my
gum'shoe'
gun'boat'
gun'fire'
gun'man
gun'nel

gun'ner
gun'ner·y
gun'ning
gun'ny
gun'pow'der
gun'run'ning
gun'smith'
gun'wale
gup'py
gur'gle
gur'gling
gush'er
gush'ing
gush'y
gus'set
gus'to
gust'y
gut'less
guts'y
gut'ter
gut'ter·snipe'
gut'tur·al

guz'zle
gym·na'si·um
gym'nast
gym·nas'tics
gym'no·sperm'
gyn'arch·y
gyn'e·coc'ra·cy
gyn'e·co·log'ic
gyn'e·col'o·gist
gyn'e·col'o·gy
gyp'sum
gyp'sy
gy'ral
gy'rate
gy·ra'tion
gyr'fal'con
gy'ro·com'pass
gy'ro·pi'lot
gy'ro·scope'
gy'ro·scop'ic
gy'ro·stat'ics
gy'rus

H

ha′be·as cor′pus
hab′er·dash′er
hab′er·dash′er·y
ha·bil′i·ment
ha·bil′i·tate′
hab′it
hab′it·a·ble
hab′it·ant
hab′i·tat
hab′i·ta′tion
hab′it·ed
ha·bit′u·al
ha·bit′u·al·ly
ha·bit′u·ate′
hab′i·tude′
ha·bit′u·é′
ha·chure′
ha·cien′da
hack′a·more′
hack′ing
hack′le
hack′man
hack′ney
hack′saw′
had′dock
Ha′des
hadj′i
haf′ni·um
hag′gard
hag′gis
hag′gle

′hag′gling
hag′i·oc′ra·cy
hag′i·og′ra·pher
hag′i·og′ra·phy
hag′i·ol′o·gy
hag′rid′den
hai′ku
hail′stone′
hail′storm′
hair′ball′
hair′breadth′
hair′brush′
hair′cut′
hair′dress′er
hair′i·ness
hair′less
hair′split′ting
hair′y
Hai′tian
ha·la′tion
hal′berd
hal′berd·ier′
hal′cy·on
half′back′
half′heart′ed
half′pace′
half′way′
hal′i·but
hal′ide
hal′ite
hal′i·to′sis

hal′i·tus
hal·lel′
hal′le·lu′iah
Hal′ley
hall′mark′
hal·loo′
hal′low
hal′lowed
Hal′low·een′
hal·lu′ci·nate′
hal·lu′ci·na′tion
hal·lu′ci·na·to′ry
hal·lu′ci·no·gen
hal·lu′ci·no·gen′ic
hal′lux
hall′way′
ha′lo
hal′o·gen
hal′oid
hal′o·phyte′
hal′ter
ha·lutz′
hal′vah
hal′yard
ham′a·dry′ad
Ham′ble·to′ni·an
ham′burg
ham′burg′er
Ham′il·to′ni·an
Ham·it′ic
ham′let

ham'mer
ham'mered
ham'mer·head'
ham'mock
ham'my
ham'per
ham'ster
ham'string'
ham'u·lus
hand'bag'
hand'ball'
hand'bar'row
hand'bill'
hand'breadth'
hand'car'
hand'clasp'
hand'cuff'
hand'ed
hand'ful'
hand'hold'
hand'i·cap'
hand'i·capped'
hand'i·cap'per
hand'i·craft'
hand'i·ly
hand'i·ness
hand'i·work'
hand'ker·chief'
han'dle
hand'ler
hand'made'
hand'out'
hand'rail'
hand'sel
hand'some

hand'som·er
hand'spring'
hand'work'
hand'writ'ing
hand'writ'ten
hand'y
hang'ar
hang'er
hang'ing
hang'man
hang'nail'
hang'o'ver
hank'er
hank'er·ing
Han'o·ve'ri·an
Han'sen
han'som
Ha'nuk·kah'
hap'haz'ard
hap'haz'ard·ly
haph'ta·rah'
hap'less
hap'loid
hap·lo'sis
hap'ly
hap'pen
hap'pen·ing
hap'pen·stance'
hap'pi·ly
hap'pi·ness
hap'py
ha·rangue'
ha·rangued'
ha·rangu'ing
har'ass, har·ass'

har'ass·ment,
  ha·rass'ment
har'bin·ger
har'bor
har'bor·age
har'bour
hard'en
hard'en·er
hard'en·ing
hard'head'ed
hard'heart'ed
har'di·hood'
har'di·ly
har'di·ness
hard'ly
hard'ness
hard'ship
hard'tack'
hard'top'
hard'ware'
har'dy
hare'bell'
hare'brained'
ha'reem
hare'lip'
ha'rem
har'i·cot'
hark'en
hark'ened
har'le·quin
har'le·quin·ade'
har'lot
har'lot·ry
har'mat·tan'
harm'ful

harm′less
har·mon′ic
har·mon′i·ca
har·mon′i·cal·ly
har·mon′ics
har·mo′ni·ous
har·mo′ni·um
har′mo·nize′
har′mo·ny
har′ness
har′nessed
harp′ing
harp′ist
har·poon′
harp′si·chord′
har′py
har′que·bus
har′ri·dan
har′ri·er
har′row
har′ry
har′ry·ing
harsh′ly
harsh′ness
har·tal′
har′te·beest′
harts′horn′
har·us′pex
har′vest
har′vest·er
har′vest·man
hash′eesh
hash′ish
Ha·sid′ic
Has′i·dim

has′let
has′sle
has′sled
has′sling
has′sock
has′tate
has′ten
hast′i·ly
hast′i·ness
hast′y
hat′band′
hat′box′
hatch′el
hatch′er·y
hatch′et
hatch′ing
hatch′ment
hatch′way′
hate′ful
hat′pin′
hat′rack′
ha′tred
hat′ter
hau′berk
haugh′ti·ly
haugh′ti·ness
haugh′ty
haul′age
haunt′ed
haunt′ing
haus·tel′lum
haus·to′ri·um
haut′boy′
hau·teur′
have′lock

ha′ven
hav′er·sack′
hav′oc
Ha·wai′ian
hawk′er
hawk′ing
hawk′weed′
haw′ser
haw′thorn′
hay′cock′
hay′field′
hay′fork′
hay′loft′
hay′mak′er
hay′mow′
hay′rack′
hay′rick′
hay′ride′
hay′seed′
hay′stack′
hay′wire′
haz′ard
haz′ard·ous
ha′zel
ha′zel·nut′
ha′zi·ly
ha′zi·ness
ha′zy
head′ache′
head′board′
head′cheese′
head′dress′
head′ed
head′er
head′first′

head'fore'most'
head'gear'
head'i·ness
head'ing
head'land'
head'less
head'light'
head'line'
head'lin'er
head'long'
head'mas'ter
head'mis'tress
head'phone'
head'piece'
head'quar'ters
head'rest'
head'set'
head'stand'
head'stone'
head'strong'
head'wait'er
head'wa'ters
head'way'
head'y
heal'er
heal'ing
health'ful
health'i·ly
health'i·ness
health'y
heap'ing
hear'ing
hear'en
hear'say'
heart'ache'

heart'beat'
heart'break'ing
heart'bro'ken
heart'burn'
heart'ed
heart'en
heart'felt'
hearth'stone'
heart'i·ly
heart'i·ness
heart'land'
heart'less
heart'sick'
heart'worm'
heart'y
heat'ed·ly
heat'er
heath'ber'ry
hea'then
hea'then·dom
hea'then·ish
hea'then·ism
heath'er
heath'er·y
heath'y
heat'stroke'
heav'en
heav'en·li·ness
heav'en·ly
heav'en·ward
heav'er
heav'i·ly
heav'i·ness
heav'y
heav'y·weight'

heb'e·tate'
heb'e·tude'
He·bra'ic
He'bra·ism
He'bra·ist
He'brew
hec'a·tomb'
heck'le
heck'ler
hec'tare
hec'tic
hec'to·gram'
hec'to·graph'
hec'to·li'ter
hec'tor
hec'to·stere'
hed'dle
hedge'hog'
hedge'hop'
hedg'er
hedge'row'
hedg'ing
he·don'ic
he·don'ics
he'don·ism
he'don·ist
he'do·nis'tic
he'do·nis'ti·cal·ly
heed'ful
heed'less
hee'haw'
heel'er
heel'ing
heel'piece'
heel'plate'

heel'post'
heel'tap'
heft'y
He·ge'li·an
He·ge'li·an·ism
heg'e·mon'ic
he·gem'o·ny
he·gi'ra
he·gu'men
heif'er
height'en
hei'nous
heir'dom
heir'ess
heir'loom'
he·li'a·cal
he·li·an'thus
hel'i·cal
hel'i·coid'
hel'i·cop'ter
he'li·o·cen'tric
he'li·o·chrome'
he'li·o·graph'
he'li·og'ra·phy
he'li·o'gra·vure'
he'li·ol'a·try
he'li·o·scope'
he'li·o·trope'
he'li·ot'ro·pism
he'li·o·type'
hel'i·port'
he'li·um
he'lix
hell'bent'
hell'cat'

hel'le·bore'
hel'le·bo're·in
hel·leb'o·rin
Hel·len'ic
Hel'len·ism
Hel'len·is'tic
Hel'len·ize'
hell'er
hell'hound'
hell'ion
hell'ish
hel·lo'
hel'met
hel'met·ed
hel'minth
hel'min·thi'a·sis
hel·min'thic
helms'man
hel'ot
hel'ot·ism
hol'ot·ry
help'er
help'ful
help'ing
help'less
help'mate'
help'meet'
hel'ter·skel'ter
Hel·ve'tian
Hel·vet'ic
he'ma·chrome'
hem'ag·ogue'
he'mal
hem'a·te'in
he'ma·ther'mal

he·mat'ic
hem'a·tin'ic
hem'a·tite'
hem'at·o·cyst'
he'ma·to'ma
hem'a·tose'
he'ma·to'sis
hem'a·to·ther'mal
hem'a·to·zo'on
hem'i·al'gi·a
hem'i·cy'cle
hem'i·dem'i·sem'i·
    qua'ver
hem'i·he'dral
hem'i·hy'drate
hem'i·mor'phic
he'min
hem'i·ple'gi·a
hem'i·pleg'ic
he·mip'ter·ous
hem'i·sphere'
hem'i·spher'ic
hem'i·stich'
hem'lock
he'mo·glo'bin
he'moid
he'mo·leu'co·cyte'
he'mo·ly'sin
he·mol'y·sis
he'mo·lyt'ic
he'mo·phil'i·a
he'mo·phil'i·ac'
he'mo·phil'ic
hem'or·rhage
hem'or·rhoid'

hem'or·rhoi'dal
he·mo'sta·sis
he'mo·stat'
hemp'en
hemp'seed'
hem'stitch'
hen'bane'
hence'forth'
hence'for'ward
hench'man
hen'coop'
hen·dec'a·gon'
hen·dec'a·he'dron
hen'dec·a·syl'la·ble
hen·di'a·dys
hen'e·quen
hen'na
hen'ner·y
hen'pecked'
hep'a·rin
hep'a·tec'to·my
he·pat'ic
hep'a·ti'tis
hep'ta·chord'
hep'ta·gon'
hep'ta·he'dron
hep·tam'e·ter
hep'tarch·y
hep'ta·va'lent
her'ald
he·ral'dic
her'ald·ry
her·ba'ceous
herb'age
herb'al

herb'al·ist
her·bar'i·um
her'bi·cid'al
her'bi·cide'
her'biv·ore'
her·biv'o·rous
her·cu'le·an
her'dic
herds'man
here'a·bout'
here·af'ter
here·by'
he·red'i·ta·ble
her'e·dit'a·ment
he·red'i·tar'i·ly
he·red'i·tar'i·ness
he·red'i·tar'y
he·red'i·ty
Her'e·ford
here·in'
here'in·af'ter
here'in·be·fore'
here·in'to
here·of'
here·on'
he·re'si·arch'
her'e·sy
her'e·tic
he·ret'i·cal
here·to'
here'to·fore'
here·up·on'
here·with'
her'it·a·bil'i·ty
her'it·a·ble

her'it·age
her'i·tance
her'i·tor
her'ma
her·maph'rod·ism
her·maph'ro·dite'
her·me·neu'tic
her·met'ic
her·met'i·cal
her·met'i·cal·ly
her'mit
her'mit·age
her·mit'ic
her'ni·a
her'ni·al
her·ni·ot'o·my
he'ro
he·ro'ic
her'o·in
her'o·ine
her'o·ism
her'on
her'pes
her'pes la'bi·a'lis
her'pes sim'plex
her'pes zos'ter
her·pet'ic
her·pe·tol'o·gist
her·pe·tol'o·gy
her'ring
her'ring·bone'
her·self'
Hertz'i·an
hes'i·tan·cy
hes'i·tant

hes'i·tate'
hes'i·tat'ing·ly
hes'i·ta'tion
Hes·pe'ri·an
hes·per'i·din
Hes'sian
hess'ite
he·tae'ra
het'er·o·cer'cal
het'er·o·chro'mo·
 some'
het'er·o·clite'
het'er·o·cy'clic
het'er·o·dox'
het'er·o·dox'y
het'er·o·dyne'
het'er·o·ga·mete'
het'er·og'a·mous
het'er·o·ge·ne'i·ty
het'er·o·ge'ne·ous
het'er·o·gen'e·sis
het'er·og'o·ny
het'er·og'y·nous
het'er·ol'o·gous
het'er·o·mor'phic
het'er·on'o·mous
het'er·o·nym'
het'er·o·sex'u·al
het'er·o·sex'u·al'i·ty
het'er·o·tax'i·a
het'er·o·to'pi·a
het'er·o·zy'gote
heu'land·ite'
heu·ris'tic
hex'a·chlo'ro·phene'

hex'ad
hex'a·em'er·on
hex'a·gon'
hex·ag'o·nal
hex'a·gram'
hex·a·he'dron
hex·a·hy'drate
hex·am'er·ous
hex·am'e·ter
hex'ane
hex'a·pod'
hex'a·stich'
hex'one
hex'ose
hey'day'
hi·a'tus
hi·ba'chi
hi'ber·nac'u·lum
hi·ber'nal
hi'ber·nate'
hi'ber·na'tion
hi·bis'cus
hic'cough
hic'cup
hic ja'cet
hick'ey
hick'o·ry
hi·dal'go
hid'den
hid'den·ite'
hide'bound'
hid'e·ous
hid'e·ous·ly
hid'ing
hi·dro'sis

hi·drot'ic
hi'er·arch'
hi'er·ar'chic
hi'er·ar'chi·cal
hi'er·arch'y
hi'er·at'ic
hi'er·oc'ra·cy
hi'er·o·glyph'
hi'er·o·glyph'ic
hi'er·ol'o·gy
hi'er·o·phant'
hig'gle
hig'gler
high'ball'
high'born'
high'boy'
high'brow'
high'er
high'fa·lu'tin
high'hand'ed
high'jack'
high'land
high'land·er
high'light'
high'ly
high'ness
high'road'
high'way'
high'way'man
hi'jack'
hi'jack'er
hik'er
hi·lar'i·ous
hi·lar'i·ty
hill'bill'y

hill'i·ness
hill'ock
hill'side'
hill'top'
hill'y
hi'lum
Hi'ma·la'yan
him·self'
hin'der
hind'gut'
hind'most'
hind'quar'ter
hin'drance
hind'sight'
Hin'du
Hin'du·ism
Hin'du·sta'ni
hing'ing
hin'ny
hin'ter·land'
hint'ing
hip'bone'
hip'pie
hip'po·cam'pal
hip'po·cam'pus
Hip'po·crat'ic
hip'po·drome'
hip'po·griff'
hip'po·pot'a·mus
hip'py
hip'shot'
hip'ster
hir'cine
hire'ling
hir·sute', hir'sute

His·pan'ic
his'pid
his·pid'i·ty
his'ta·mine'
his'ti·dine'
his·to·log'i·cal
his·tol'o·gy
his·tol'y·sis
his'tone
his·to'ri·an
his·tor'ic
his·tor'i·cal
his·tor'i·cal·ly
his·to·ric'i·ty
his·to'ri·og'ra·pher
his·to'ri·og'ra·phy
his'to·ry
his'tri·on'ic
his'tri·on'i·cal·ly
his'tri·on'ics
hitch'hike'
hitch'hik'er
hith'er
hith'er·to'
hith'er·ward
hit'ter
hoard'ing
hoar'frost'
hoar'hound'
hoar'i·ness
hoars'en
hoar'y
Hob'bism
hob'ble
hob'ble·de·hoy'

hob'by
hob'by·horse'
hob'gob'lin
hob'nail'
hob'nob'
ho'bo
hock'ey
hock'shop'
ho'cus
hodge'podge'
Hodg'kin
hod'man
hoe'cake'
hoe'down'
ho'gan
hog'back'
hog'ger·y
hog'gish
hogs'head'
hog'tie'
hog'wash'
hoi pol·loi'
hoist'ed
ho'key·po'key
ho'kum
hold'all'
hold'back'
hold'en
hold'er
hold'ing
hold'out'
hold'o'ver
hold'up'
hole'y
hol'i·day'

hol'i·ly
ho'li·ness
hol'land
hol'lan·daise'
Hol'land·er
hol'ler
hol·lo'
hol·loa'
hol'low
hol'ly
hol'ly·hock'
Hol'ly·wood'
hol'mic
hol'mi·um
hol'o·blas'tic
hol'o·caine'
hol'o·caust'
Hol'o·cene'
hol'o·graph'
hol'o·he'dral
Hol'stein
hol'ster
ho'ly
ho'ly·tide'
hom'age
hom'bre
hom'burg
home'com'ing
home'land'
home'less
home'li·ness
home'ly
home'made'
home'mak'er
ho'me·o·path'

ho'me·o·path'ic
ho'me·op'a·thy
ho'me·o·ther'a·py
ho'me·o·typ'ic
ho'mer
Ho·mer'ic
home'room'
home'sick'
home'stead'
home'stead'er
home'stretch'
home'ward
home'work'
home'y
hom'i·cid'al
hom'i·cide'
hom'i·let'ic
hom'i·let'ics
hom'i·list
hom'i·ly
hom'i·nid
hom'i·ny
ho'mo·cen'tric
ho'mo·chro'mat'ic
ho'mo·e·rot'ic
ho'mo·er'o·tism
ho·mog'a·mous
ho·mog'a·my
ho'mo·ge·ne'i·ty
ho'mo·ge'ne·ous
ho'mo·gen·ize'
ho·mog'e·nous
ho·mog'e·ny
hom'o·graph'
ho·mol'o·gate'

ho·mol'o·gous
ho·mol'o·gy
ho·mol'o·sine'
ho'mo·mor'phism
ho'mo·mor'phy
hom'o·nym'
ho'mo·nym'ic
hom'o·phone'
hom'o·phon'ic
ho·moph'o·ny
Ho'mo sa'pi·ens
ho'mo·sex'u·al
ho'mo·sex'u·al'i·ty
ho'mo·tax'is
ho'mo·zy'gote
ho·mun'cu·lus
hon'est
hon'est·ly
hon'es·ty
hon'ey
hon'ey·bee'
hon'ey·comb'
hon'ey·dew'
hon'eyed
hon'ey·moon'
hon'ey·moon'er
hon'ey·suck'le
hon'ied
honk'er
honk'ing
hon'or
hon'or·a·ble
hon'or·a·bly
hon'o·ra'ri·um
hon'or·ar'y

hon'or·if'ic
hon'our
hood'ed
hood'lum
hoo'doo'
hood'wink'
hoo'ey
hoof'beat'
hoof'er
hook'ah
hook'er
hook'nose'
hook'up'
hook'worm'
hoo'li·gan
hoo'li·gan·ism
hoop'er
hoop'la
hoo'poe
hoo·ray'
hoose'gow
Hoo'sier
hoot'en·an'ny
Hoo'ver·ville
hope'ful
hope'ful·ly
hope'less
hop'head'
hop'per
hop'scotch'
ho'ral
ho'ra·ry
hore'hound'
hor·i'zon
hor'i·zon'tal

hor'i·zon'tal·ly
hor·mo'nal
hor'mone
horn'beam'
horn'bill'
horn'blende'
horn'book'
hor'net
horn'pipe'
horn'swog'gle
horn'swog'gling
horn'y
ho'ro·loge'
hor'o·log'i·cal
ho·rol'o·gist
ho·rol'o·gy
hor'o·scope'
ho·ros'co·py
hor·ren'dous
hor'ri·ble
hor'ri·bly
hor'rid
hor·rif'ic
hor'ri·fy'
hor·rip'i·la'tion
hor'ror
horse'back'
horse'flesh'
horse'fly'
horse'hair'
horse'man
horse'play'
horse'rad'ish
horse'shoe'
horse'whip'

horse'wom'an
hors'y
hor'ta·to'ry
hor'ti·cul'tur·al
hor'ti·cul'ture
hor'ti·cul'tur·ist
ho·san'na
ho'sier
ho'sier·y
hos'pice
hos'pi·ta·ble,
   hos·pi'ta·ble
hos'pi·tal
hos·pi·tal'i·ty
hos·pi·tal·i·za'tion
hos'pi·tal·ize'
hos'tage
hos'tel
hos'tel·er
hos'tel·ry
host'ess
hos'tile
hos·til'i·ty
hos'tler
hot'bed'
hotch'potch'
ho·tel'
hot'foot'
hot'head'ed
hot'house'
hot'ly
hour'glass'
hou'ri
hour'ly
house'boat'

house′break′ing
house′bro′ken
house′dress′
house′hold′
house′hold′er
house′keep′er
hou′sel
house′maid′
house′moth′er
house′top′
house′warm′ing
house′wife′
house′wif′er·y
house′work′
hous′ing
hov′el
hov′er
hov′er·craft′
how′dah
how′dy
how·ev′er
how′itz·er
howl′er
howl′ing
how′so·ev′er
hoy′den
hoy′den·ish
hua·ra′ches
hub′ble
hub′bub
hub′by
hu′bris
huck′a·buck′
huck′le
huck′le·ber′ry

huck′le·bone′
huck′ster
hud′dle
Hud′son
huff′i·ly
huff′i·ness
huff′ish
huff′y
huge′ly
hug′ger·mug′ger
Hu′gue·not′
hu′la
hulk′ing
hulk′y
hul′la·ba·loo′
hul·lo′
hu′man
hu·mane′
hu′man·ism
hu′man·ist
hu′man·is′ti·cal·ly
hu·man′i·tar′i·an
hu·man′i·tar′i·an·
    ism
hu·man′i·ty
hu′man·ize′
hu′man·kind′
hu′man·ly
hu′man·oid′
hum′ble
hum′ble·bee′
hum′bly
hum′bug′
hum′ding′er
hum′drum′

hu′mer·al
hu′mer·us
hu′mid
hu·mid′i·fi·ca′tion
hu·mid′i·fy′
hu·mid′i·ty
hu′mi·dor′
hu·mil′i·ate′
hu·mil′i·a′tion
hu·mil′i·ty
hum′mer
hum′ming
hum′ming·bird′
hum′mock
hu′mor
hu′mor·esque′
hu′mor·ist
hu′mor·ous
hu′mour
hump′back′
hump′backed′
hu′mus
Hu′nan′
hunch′back′
hunch′backed′
hun′dred
hun′dred·fold′
hun′dredth
Hun·gar′i·an
hun′ger
hun′gri·ly
hun′gry
hunk′y
hunt′er
hunt′ing

hunt′ress
hunts′man
hur′dle
hur′dler
hurl′ing
hur·rah′
hur·ray′
hur′ri·cane′
hur′ried
hur′ry
hurt′ful
hur′tle
hurt′less
hur′tling
hus′band
hus′band·ry
hush′a·by′
husk′i·ness
   (hoarseness)
hus′ki·ness (large-
   ness)
husk′y (hoarse)
hus′ky (large)
hus·sar′
hus′sy
hust′ings
hus′tle
hus′tler
huz·za′
hy′a·cinth′
hy′a·cin′thine
hy′a·lin
hy′a·line
hy′a·lite′
hy′a·lo·plasm

hy′brid
hy′brid·ism
hy′brid·i·za′tion
hy′brid·ize′
hyd′no·car′pic
hy′dra
hy·drac′id
hy′dra·gogue′
hy·dran′ge·a
hy′drant
hy·dras′tine
hy′drate
hy′drat·ed
hy·dra′tion
hy·drau′lic
hy·drau′lics
hy′dra·zine′
hy′dra·zo′ate
hy′dra·zo′ic
hy′dri·od′ic
hy′dro·bro′mic
hy′dro·cele′
hy′dro·ceph′a·lus
hy′dro·chlo′ric
hy′dro·chlo′ride
hy′dro·cy·an′ic
hy′dro·dy·nam′ic
hy′dro·e·lec′tric
hy′dro·e·lec′tric′i·ty
hy′dro·foil′
hy′dro·gen
hy′dro·gen·ate′
hy·drog′en·ous
hy·drog′ra·phy
hy′droid

hy·drol′o·gy
hy·drol′y·sis
hy·dro·me·chan′ics
hy·drom′e·ter
hy·drom′e·try
hy·dron′ics
hy·drop′a·thy
hy′dro·pho′bi·a
hy′dro·pho′bic
hy′dro·pon′ics
hy′dro·sphere′
hy′dro·stat′
hy′dro·stat′ic
hy′dro·sul′fide
hy′dro·sul′fite
hy′dro·ther′a·peu′tics
hy′dro·ther′a·py
hy′dro·ther′mal
hy′dro·tho′rax
hy′dro·trop′ic
hy·drot′ro·pism
hy′drous
hy·drox′ide
hy·e′na
hy′e·tog′ra·phy
hy′e·to·log′i·cal
hy′e·tol′o·gy
hy′giene
hy·gien′ic
hy·gien·ist
hy·grom′e·ter
hy′gro·met′ric
hy′men
hy′me·ne′al
hy′me·nop′ter·ous

hym'nal
hym'nist
hym'no·dy
hym·nol'o·gy
hy'oid
hy·os·cy'a·mine'
hy·pae'thral
hy'per·ac·id'i·ty
hy'per·a·cu'si·a
hy'per·al·ge'si·a
hy·per'bo·la
hy·per'bo·le
hy·per·bol'ic
hy·per·bo're·an
hy·per·crit'i·cal
hy·per·e'mi·a
hy·per·ki·ne'sis
hy·per·ki·net'ic
hy·per·me·tro'pi·a
hy·per·pi·tu'i·ta·rism
hy·per·pla'si·a
hy·per·py·rex'i·a
hy·per·sen'si·tive
hy·per·son'ic
hy·per·ten'sion
hy·per·ten'sive

hy'per·thy'roid
hy'phen
hy'phen·ate'
hy'phen·a'tion
hyp·nol'o·gy
hyp·no'sis
hyp·no·ther'a·py
hyp·not'ic
hyp·no·tism
hyp·no·tist
hyp·no·tize'
hy'po·blast'
hy'po·chon'dri·a
hy'po·chon'dri·ac'
hy·poc'ri·sy
hyp'o·crite
hyp'o·crit'i·cal
hy'po·cy'cloid
hy'po·der'ma
hy'po·der'mic
hy'po·der'mi·cal·ly
hy'po·der'mis
hy'po·gas'tric
hy'po·gas'tri·um
hy'po·ge'al
hyp'o·gene'
hy·poph'y·sis

hy'po·pi·tu'i·ta·rism
hy'po·pla'si·a
hy·pos'ta·sis
hy'po·stat'ic
hy·pos'ta·tize'
hy·po'tax·is
hy·pot'e·nuse'
hy·poth'ec
hy·poth'e·cate'
hy·poth'e·ca'tion
hy'po·ther'mal
hy'po·ther'mi·a
hy·poth'e·sis
hy·poth'e·size'
hy'po·thet'i·cal
hy'po·thy'roid
hy'po·thy'roid·ism
hyp·sog'ra·phy
hyp·som'e·try
hys'sop
hys'ter·ec'to·my
hys·ter·e'sis
hys·te'ri·a
hys·ter'ic
hys·ter'i·cal
hys·ter·ot'o·my

I

i'amb
i·am'bic
i·at'ric
i·a·trol'o·gy
I·be'ri·an
i'bex
i·bi'dem
i'bis
I·car'i·an
ice'berg'
ice'blink'
ice'boat'
ice'bound'
ice'break'er
ice'cap'
ice'house'
Ice·lan'dic
ich·nog'ra·phy
ich·nol'o·gy
ich'thy·og'ra·phy
ich'thy·oid'
ich'thy·ol'o·gist
ich'thy·ol'o·gy
ich'thy·o·saur'
ich'thy·o·sau'rus
ich'thy·o'sis
i'ci·cle
i'ci·ly
i'ci·ness
ic'ing
i'con

i·con'ic
i·con'o·clam
i·con'o·clast'
i'con·o·graph'ic
i'co·nog'ra·phy
i'co·nol'o·gy
i·con'o·scope'
i'co·sa·he'dron
i'co·si·tet'ra·he'dron
ic·ter'ic
ic'ter·us
ic'tus
i'cy
I'da·ho'an
i·de'a
i·de'al, i·deal'
i·de'al·ism
i·de'al·ist
i'de·al·is'tic
i·de'al·i'ty
i·de'al·i·za'tion
i·de'al·ize'
i·de'al·ly
i'de·a'tion
i'de·a'tion·al
i'dée' fixe'
i'dem
i·den'ti·cal
i·den'ti·fi'a·ble
i·den'ti·fi·ca'tion
i·den'ti·fi'er

i·den'ti·fy'
i·den'ti·ty
id'e·o·gram'
id'e·o·graph'ic
id'e·og'ra·phy
id'e·o·log'i·cal
id'e·ol'o·gist
id'e·ol'o·gy
id'e·o·mo'tor
id'i·o·blast'
id'i·o·cy
id'i·o·graph'
id'i·om
id'i·o·mat'ic
id'i·o·mat'i·cal·ly
id'i·o·mor'phic
idc'i·o·path'ic
id'i·op'a·thy
id'i·o·syn'cra·sy
id'i·o·syn·crat'ic
id'i·ot
id'i·ot'ic
id'i·ot'i·cal·ly
i'dle
i'dle·ness
i'dler
i'dly
i'dol
i·dol'a·ter
i·dol'a·tress
i·dol'a·trous

i·dol'a·try
i'dol·i·za'tion
i'dol·ize'
i'dyl
i'dyll
i·dyl'lic
i·dyl'li·cal·ly
ig'loo
ig'ne·ous
ig'nes'cent
ig'nis fat'u·us
ig·nite'
ig·nit'er
ig·ni'tion
ig·ni'tron
ig·no'ble
ig·no'bly
ig'no·min'i·ous
ig'no·min'y
ig'no·ra'mus
ig'no·rance
ig'no·rant
ig·nore'
ig·nor'ing
i·gua'na
i·guan'o·don'
ih·ram'
i'kon
il'e·ac'
il'e·i'tis
il'e·os'to·my
il'e·um
il'e·us
i'lex
il'i·ac

il'i·um
il·la'tion
il'la·tive
il·le'gal
il'le·gal'i·ty
il·leg'i·ble
il·leg'i·bly
il'le·git'i·ma·cy
il'le·git'i·mate
il·lib'er·al
il·lib'er·al'i·ty
il·lic'it
il·lim'it·a·ble
Il'li·nois'an
il·lit'er·a·cy
il·lit'er·ate
ill'ness
il·log'i·cal
il·lu'mi·na·ble
il·lu'mi·nate'
il·lu'mi·na'tion
il·lu'mine
il·lu'sion
il·lu'sion·ism
il·lu'sion·ist
il·lu'sive
il·lu'so·ry
il'lus·trate'
il'lus·tra'tion
il·lus'tra·tive
il·lus'tra·tor
il·lus'tri·ous
il'men·ite'
im'age
im'age·ry

im·ag'i·na·ble
im·ag'i·na·bly
im·ag'i·nar'y
im·ag'i·na'tion
im·ag'i·na·tive
im·ag'ine
im·ag'ined
im'ag·ism
im'ag·ist
im'ag·is'tic
i·ma'go
i·mam'
im·bal'ance
im'be·cile
im'be·cil'ic
im'be·cil'i·ty
im·bibe'
im'bri·cate'
im'bri·ca'tion
im·bro'glio
im·brue'
im·bue'
im·bu'ing
im·ide
im'i·ta·ble
im'i·tate'
im'i·ta'tion
im'i·ta'tive
im'i·ta'tor
im·mac'u·late
im·ma'nence
im·ma'nent
im'ma·te'ri·al
im'ma·te'ri·al·ism
im'ma·te'ri·al'i·ty

im'ma·ture'
im'ma·tur'i·ty
im·meas'ur·a·bil'i·ty
im·meas'ur·a·ble
im·me'di·a·cy
im·me'di·ate
im·me'di·ate·ly
im·med'i·ca·ble
im·me·mo'ri·al
im·mense'
im·men'si·ty
im·merge'
im·merse'
im·mersed'
im·mer'sion
im'mi·grant
im'mi·grate'
im'mi·gra'tion
im'mi·nence
im'mi·nent
im·mis'ci·ble
im·mit'a·ga·ble
im·mo'bile
im·mo·bil'i·ty
im·mo'bi·li·za'tion
im·mo'bi·lize'
im·mod'er·ate
im·mod'est
im'mo·late'
im'mo·la'tion
im·mor'al
im'mo·ral'i·ty
im·mor'tal
im·mor'tal'i·ty
im·mor'tal·ize'

im·mov'a·ble
im·mune'
im·mu'ni·ty
im'mu·ni·za'tion
im'mu·nize'
im'mu·nol'o·gy
im·mure'
im·mure'ment
im·mu'ta·bil'i·ty
im·mu'ta·ble
im·mut'ab·ly
im'pact, im·pact'
im·pact'ed
im·pac'tion
im·pair'
im·pair'ment
im·pale'
im·pal'pa·bil'i·ty
im·pal'pa·ble
im·pa·na'tion
im·par'a·dise'
im·part'
im·par'tial
im·par'ti·al'i·ty
im·part'i·ble
im·pass'a·ble
im'passe
im·pas·si·bil'i·ty
im·pas'si·ble
im·pas'sioned
im·pas'sive
im·pas·siv'i·ty
im·pas'to
im·pa'tience
im·pa'tient

im·peach'
im·peach'a·ble
im·peach'ment
im·pec'ca·bil'i·ty
im·pec'ca·ble
im·pec'cant
im'pe·cu'ni·ous
im·ped'ance
im·pede'
im·ped'i·ment
im·ped'i·men'ta
im·pel'
im·pend'
im·pend'ing
im·pen'e·tra·ble
im·pen'i·tent
im·pen'nate
im·per'a·tive
im'per·cep'ti·ble
im'per·cep'ti·bly
im·per'fect
im'per·fec'tion
im·per'fo·rate
im·pe'ri·al
im·pe'ri·al·ism
im·pe'ri·al·ist
im·pe'ri·al·is'tic
im·per'il
im·pe'ri·ous
im·per'ish·a·ble
im·pe'ri·um
im·per'ma·nent
im·per'me·a·ble
im·per'son·al
im'per·son·al'i·ty

im·per'son·al·ly
im·per'son·ate'
im·per'son·a'tion
im·per'son·a'tor
im·per'ti·nence
im·per'ti·nent
im'per·turb'a·ble
im'per·tur·ba'tion
im·per'vi·ous
im'pe·tig'i·nous
im'pe·ti'go
im'pet·u·os'i·ty
im·pet'u·ous
im'pe·tus
im·pi'e·ty
im·pinge'
im·ping'ing
im·pi·ous
imp'ish
im'pla·ca·bil'i·ty
im·pla'ca·ble
im·plant'
im'plan·ta'tion
im·plant'ed
im'ple·ment
im'ple·men'tal
im'pli·cate'
im'pli·ca'tion
im·plic'it
im·plied'
im·pli'ed·ly
im·plore'
im·plor'ing
im·ply'
im'po·lite'

im·pon'der·a·ble
im·port', im'port
im·por'tance
im·por'tant
im'por·ta'tion
im·por'tu·nate
im'por·tune'
im'por·tun'ing
im'por·tu'ni·ty
im·pose'
im·pos'ing
im'po·si'tion
im·pos'si·bil'i·ty
im·pos'si·ble
im·pos'tor
im·pos'ture
im'po·tence
im'po·tent
im·pound'
im·pound'ing
im·pov'er·ish
im·pow'er
im'prac·ti·ca·bil'i·ty
im·prac'ti·ca·ble
im·prac'ti·cal
im'prac·ti·cal'i·ty
im'pre·cate'
im'pre·ca'tion
im'pre·ca·to'ry
im'preg·na·bil'i·ty
im·preg'na·ble
im·preg'nate
im'preg·na'tion
im'pre·sa'ri·o'
im·press', im'press

im·pres'sion
im·pres'sion·a·ble
im·pres'sion·ism
im·pres'sion·ist
im·pres'sion·is'tic
im·pres'sive
im·press'ment
im'prest
im'pri·ma'tur
im·pri'mis
im·print', im'print
im·pris'on
im·prob'a·bil'i·ty
im·prob'a·ble
im·promp'tu
im·prop'er
im'pro·pri'e·ty
im·prove'
im·prove'ment
im·prov'ing
im·prov'i·dence
im·prov'i·dent
im·pro·vi·sa'tion
im·prov'i·sa·to'ri·al
im'pro·vise'
im'pro·vis'ing
im·pru'dence
im·pru'dent
im'pu·dence
im'pu·den·cy
im'pu·dent
im·pugn'
im'pug·na'tion
im'pulse
im·pul'sion

im·pul'sive
im·pu'ni·ty
im·pure'
im·pu'ri·ty
im·put'a·ble
im·pu·ta'tion
im·put'a·tive
im·pute'
in·a·bil'i·ty
in ab·sen'ti·a
in·ac·ces·si·bil'i·ty
in·ac·ces'si·ble
in·ac'cu·ra·cy
in·ac'cu·rate
in·ac'tion
in·ac'ti·vate'
in·ac'tive
in·ac·tiv'i·ty
in·ad'e·qua·cy
in·ad'e·quate
in·ad·mis·si·bil'i·ty
in·ad·mis'si·ble
in·ad·ver'tence
in·ad·ver'tent
in·ad·vis'a·ble
in·al'ien·a·ble
in·al'ter·a·ble
in·al'ter·a·bly
in·am'o·ra·ta
in·am'o·ra'to
in·ane'
in·an'i·mate
in·a·ni'tion
in·an'i·ty
in·ap·pli'ca·ble

in·ap·pro'pri·ate
in·ar·tic'u·late
in·at·ten'tion
in·at·ten·tive
in·au'di·ble
in·au'gu·ral
in·au'gu·rate'
in·au'gu·ra'tion
in·aus·pi'cious
in'born'
in'bred'
in'breed'ing
in·cal·cu·la·bil'i·ty
in·cal'cu·la·ble
in cam'er·a
In'can
in·can·desce'
in·can·des'cence
in·can·des'cent
in·can·ta'tion
in·ca·pa·bil'i·ty
in·ca'pa·ble
in·ca·pac'i·tate'
in·ca·pac'i·ta'tion
in·ca·pac'i·ty
in·car'cer·ate'
in·car'cer·a'tion
in·car'na·dine'
in·car'nate
in·car'nat·ed
in·car·na'tion
in·cau'tious
in·cen'di·a·rism
in·cen'di·ar'y
in'cense,

in·cense'
in·cen'tive
in·cept'
in·cep'tion
in·cep'tive
in·cer'ti·tude'
in·ces'sant
in'cest
in·ces'tu·ous
in·cho'ate
in·cho'ate·ly
inch'worm'
in'ci·dence
in'ci·dent
in·ci·den'tal·ly
in·cin'er·ate'
in·cin'er·a'tion
in·cin'er·a'tor
in·cip'i·ence
in·cip'i·ent
in·cise'
in·ci'sion
in·ci'sive
in·ci'sor
in·cite'
in·cite'ment
in·cit'ing
in·ci·vil'i·ty
in·clem'en·cy
in·clem'ent
in·clin'a·ble
in·cli·na'tion
in·cline'
in·clined'
in·cli·nom'e·ter

in·close'
in·clo'sure
in·clude'
in·clud'ed
in·clud'ing
in·clu'sion
in·clu'sive
in'co·er'ci·ble
in·cog'i·tant
in·cog'ni·to'
in'co·her'ence
in'co·her'ent
in'com·bus'ti·ble
in'come
in'com'ing
in'com·men'su·ra·
   bil'i·ty
in'com·men'su·ra·ble
in'com·men'su·rate
in'com·mode'
in'com·mo'di·ous
in'com·mu'ni·ca·ble
in'com·mu'ni·ca'do
in'com·mu'ni·ca'tive
in'com·pa·ra·bil'i·ty
im·com'pa·ra·ble
in·com'pa·ra·bly
in'com·pa'ti·bil'i·ty
in'com·pat'i·ble
in·com'pe·tence
in·com'pe·tent
in'com·plete'
in'com·plete'ly
in'com·ple'tion
in'com·pli'ance

in'com·pli'ant
in'com·pre·hen'si·
   bil'i·ty
in'com·pre·hen'si·ble
in'com·pre·hen'sive
in'com·press'i·ble
in'com·put'a·ble
in'con·ceiv'a·ble
in'con·ceiv'a·bly
in'con·clu'sive
in'con·den'sa·ble
in'con·den'si·ble
in·con'dite
in·con'gru·ent
in'con·gru'i·ty
in·con'gru·ous
in'con·se·quent'
in'con·se·quen'tial
in'con·sid'er·a·ble
in'con·sid'er·ate
in'con·sid'er·a'tion
in'con·sist'en·cy
in'con·sis'tent
in'con·sol'a·ble
in·con'so·nance
in·con'so·nant
in'con·spic'u·ous
in·con'stan·cy
in·con'stant
in'con·test'a·ble
in·con'ti·nence
in·con'ti·nent
in'con·tro·vert'i·ble
in'con·ven'ience
in'con·ven'ient

in'con·ven'ient·ly
in'con·vert'i·ble
in·cor'po·ra·ble
in·cor'po·rate'
in·cor'po·rat'ed
in·cor'po·ra'tion
in·cor'po·ra'tor
in'cor·po're·al
in'cor·rect'
in'cor·ri·gi·bil'i·ty
in·cor'ri·gi·ble
in'cor·rupt'
in'cor·rupt'i·ble
in·crease',
   in'crease
in·creas'ing·ly
in·cred'i·ble
in·cred'i·bly
in'cre·du'li·ty
in·cred'u·lous
in'cre·ment
in'cre·men'tal
in·cre'tion
in·crim'i·nate'
in·crim'i·na'tion
in·crim'i·na·to'ry
in·crust'
in'crus·ta'tion
in'cu·bate'
in'cu·ba'tion
in'cu·ba'tor
in'cu·bus
in·cul'cate
in'cul·ca'tion
in·cum'ben·cy

in·cum′bent
in′cu·nab′u·la
in·cur′
in′cur·a·bil′i·ty
in·cur′a·ble
in·cur′i·ous
in·curred′
in·cur′rent
in·cur′sion
in·cur′sive
in′cus
in′da·mine′
in·debt′ed
in·debt′ed·ness
in·de·cen′cy
in·de′cent
in′de·ci′pher·a·ble
in′de·ci′sion
in′de·ci′sive
in′de·clin′a·ble
in·dec′o·rous
in·de·co′rum
in·deed′
in′de·fat′i·ga·ble
in′de·fen′si·ble
in′de·fen′si·bly
in′de·fin′a·ble
in·def′i·nite
in·del′i·ble
in·del′i·ca·cy
in·del′i·cate
in·dem′ni·fi·ca′tion
in·dem′ni·fi′er
in·dem′ni·fy′
in·dem′ni·tor

in·dem′ni·ty
in·dent′
in′den·ta′tion
in·den′tion
in·den′ture
in·den′tured
in′de·pend′ence
in′de·pend′ent
in′des·crib′a·bil′i·ty
in′des·crib′a·ble
in′de·struct′i·bil′i·ty
in′de·struct′i·ble
in′de·ter′mi·na·cy
in′de·ter′mi·nate
in′de·ter′min·ism
in′dex
In′di·an
In′di·an′i·an
in′di·can′
in′di·cant
in′di·cate′
in′di·ca′tion
in·dic′a·tive
in′di·ca′tor
in·di′ci·a
in·dict′
in·dict′a·ble
in·dic′tion
in·dict′ment
in′dif′fer·ence
in′dif′fer·ent
in′di·gence
in′di·gene′
in·dig′e·nous
in′di·gent

in′di·gest′i·ble
in′di·ges′tion
in·dig′nant
in′dig·na′tion
in·dig′ni·ty
in′di·go′
in′di·rect′
in′di·rec′tion
in′dis·cern′i·ble
in′dis·creet′
in′dis·crete′
in′dis·cre′tion
in′dis·crim′i·nate
in′dis·crim′i·na′tion
in′dis·pen′sa·ble
in′dis·pose′
in′dis·posed′
in′dis·po·si′tion
in′dis·pu′ta·ble
in·dis′sol′u·ble
in·dis·tinct′
in′dis·tinc′tive
in′dis·tin′guish·a·ble
in′di·um
in′di·vid′u·al
in′di·vid′u·al·ism
in′di·vid′u·al·ist
in′di·vid′u·al·is′tic
in′di·vid′u·al′i·ty
in′di·vid′u·al·ize′
in′di·vid′u·al·ly
in′di·vid′u·ate′
in′di·vid′u·a′tion
in′di·vis′i·ble
In′do·chi·nese′

in·doc'tri·nate'
in·doc'tri·na'tion
in'dole
in'do·lence
in'do·lent
in·dom'i·ta·ble
In'do·ne'sian
in'door'
in'do·phe'nol
in·du'bi·ta·ble
in·du'bi·ta·bly
in·duce'
in·duce'ment
in·duc'i·ble
in·duc'ing
in·duct'
in·duct'ance
in·duct'ee'
in·duc'tile
in·duc'tion
in·duc'tive
in·duc'tor
in·due'
in·dulge'
in·dul'gence
in·dul'gent
in·dulg'ing
in'du·line'
in'du·rate'
in'du·ra'tion
in·du'si·ate
in·du'si·um
in·dus'tri·al
in·dus'tri·al·ism
in·dus'tri·al·ist

in·dus'tri·al·i·za'tion
in·dus'tri·al·ize'
in·dus'tri·ous
in'dus·try
in·e'bri·ant
in·e'bri·at'ed
in·e'bri·a'tion
in·ed'i·bil'i·ty
in·ed'i·ble
in·ef'fa·bil'i·ty
in·ef'fa·ble
in'ef·face'a·bly
in'ef·fec'tive
in'ef·fec'tu·al
in'ef·fi·ca'cious
in·ef'fi·ca·cy
in·ef'fi'cien·cy
in·ef'fi'cient
in'e·las'tic
in·el'e·gance
in·el'e·gant
in·el'i·gi·bil'i·ty
in·el'i·gi·ble
in·el'o·quence
in·el'o·quent
in'e·luc'ta·ble
in·ept'
in·ept'i·tude'
in'e·qual'i·ty
in·eq'ui·ta·ble
in·eq'ui·ty
in'e·rad'i·ca·ble
in·er'ra·bly
in·er'rant
in·ert'

in·er'tia
in·er'tial
in'es·cap'a·ble
in'es·sen'tial
in·es'ti·ma·ble
in·ev'i·ta·bil'i·ty
in·ev'i·ta·ble
in'ex·act'
in'ex·cus'a·ble
in'ex·haust'i·bil'i·ty
in'ex·haust'i·ble
in·ex'o·ra·ble
in·ex'o·ra·bly
in·ex·pe'di·ent
in'ex·pen'sive
in'ex·pe'ri·ence
in'ex·pe'ri·enced
in'ex·pert'
in·ex'pi·a·ble
in·ex'pli·ca·ble
in'ex·press'i·ble
in'ex·pres'sive
in'ex·tin·guish'a·ble
in ex·tre'mis
in·ex'tri·ca·bil'i·ty
in·ex'tri·ca·bly
in·fal'li·bil'i·ty
in·fal'li·ble
in·fal'li·bly
in'fa·mous
in'fa·my
in'fan·cy
in'fant
in·fan'ta
in·fan'ti·cide'

in'fan·tile'
in'fan·ti·lism
in'fan·try
in'fan·try·man
in·farct'
in·fat'u·ate'
in·fat'u·at'ed
in·fat'u·a'tion
in·fea·si·bil'i·tɟ
in·fea·si·ble
in·fect'
in·fec'tion
in·fec'tious
in·fe·lic'i·tous
in·fe·lic'i·ty
in·fer'
in'fer·ence
in'fer·en'tial
in·fe'ri·or
in·fe'ri·or'i·ty
in·fer'nal
in·fer'no
in·fer'tile
in'fer·til'i·ty
in·fest'
in'fes·ta'tion
in'fi·del
in'fi·del'i·ty
in'field'
in'field'er
in'fil·trate',
   in·fil'trate
in'fil·tra'tion
in'fi·nite
in'fi·nite·ly

in'fin·i·tes'i·mal
in·fin'i·tive
in·fin'i·tude'
in·fin'i·ty
in·firm'
in·fir'ma·ry
in·fir'mi·ty
in·fix'
in·flame'
in·flam'ma·bil'i·ty
in·flam'ma·ble
in'flam·ma'tion
in·flam'ma·to'ry
in·flat'a·ble
in·flate'
in·flat'ed
in·fla'tion
in·fla'tion·ar'y
in·flect'
in·flec'tion
in·flec'tive
in·flex'i·bil'i·ty
in·flex'i·ble
in·flict'
in·flic'tion
in'flo·res'cence
in'flo·res'cent
in'flow'
in'flu·ence
in'flu·ent
in'flu·en'tial
in'flu·en'za
in'flux'
in·fold'
in·form'

in·for'mal
in'for·mal'i·ty
in·form'ant
in'for·ma'tion
in·form'a·tive
in·formed'
in·form'er
in'fra·cos'tal
in·fract'
in·frac'tion
in·fran'gi·ble
in'fra·red'
in'fra·struc'ture
in·fre'quen·cy
in·fre'quent
in·fringe'
in·fringe'ment
in·fring'ing
in'fun·dib'u·lum
in·fu'ri·ate'
in·fu'ri·at'ed
in·fus'cate
in·fuse'
in·fu'si·ble
in·fu'sion
in·gen'ious
in·gé·nue'
in·ge·nu'i·ty
in·gen'u·ous
in·gest'
in·ges'tion
in·ges'tive
in'gle
in·glo'ri·ous
in'got

in·grain'
in·grained'
in'grate
in·gra'ti·ate'
in·grat'i·tude'
in'gra·ves'cent
in·gre'di·ent
in'gress
in·gres'sion
in·gres'sive
in'grow'ing
in'grown'
in'gui·nal
in·gur'gi·tate'
in·hab'it
in·hab'it·a·bil'i·ty
in·hab'it·a·ble
in·hab'i·tant
in·hab'it·ed
in·hal'ant
in'ha·la'tion
in·hale'
in·hal'er
in'har·mo'ni·ous
in·here'
in·her'ence
in·her'ent
in·her'ent·ly
in·her'it
in·her'it·a·bil'i·ty
in·her'it·ance
in·her'i·tor
in·he'sion
in·hib'it
in'hi·bi'tion

in·hib'i·tor
in·hib'i·to'ry
in'hos·pi'ta·ble
in'hos·pi'ta·bly
in'hos·pi·tal'i·ty
in·hu'man
in'hu·mane'
in'hu·man'i·ty
in'hu·ma'tion
in·im'i·cal
in·im'i·ta·ble
in'i·on
in·iq'ui·tous
in·iq'ui·ty
in·i'tial
in·i'tial·ly
in·i'ti·ate'
in·i'ti·a'tion
in·i'ti·a·tive
in·i'ti·a'tor
in·ject'
in·jec'tion
in·jec'tor
in'ju·di'cious
in·junc'tion
in'jure
in·ju'ri·ous
in'ju·ry
in·jus'tice
ink'er
ink'horn'
ink'i·ness
in'kle
ink'ling
ink'well'

ink'y
in'laid'
in'land
in·lay'
in'let
in'li·er
in lo'co pa·ren'tis
in'mate
in me'di·as res
in me·mo'ri·am
in'most'
in'nards
in'nate, in·nate'
in'ner
in'ner·most'
in'ner·vate'
in'ner·va'tion
in'ning
in'no·cence
in'no·cent
in·noc'u·ous
in'no·vate'
in'no·va'tion
in'no·va'tive
in'no·va'tor
in'nu·en'do
in·nu'mer·a·ble
in·nu'mer·a·bly
in'ob·serv'ance
in'ob·serv'ant
in·oc'u·la·ble
in·oc'u·late'
in·oc'u·la'tion
in·oc'u·la'tor
in·oc'u·lum

in'of·fen'sive
in'of·fi'cious
in·op'er·a·ble
in·op'er·a'tive
in·op'por·tune'
in·or'di·na·cy
in·or'di·nate
in·or'di·nate·ly
in'or·gan'ic
in'or·gan'i·cal·ly
in·os'cu·late'
in·os'cu·la'tion
in·o'si·tol'
in'pa'tient
in per·pe'tu·um
in per·so'nam
in'phase'
in'put'
in'quest
in·qui'e·tude'
in·quire'
in'quir·y, in·quir'y
in'qui·si'tion
in'qui·si'tion·al
in·qui'si·tive
in·qui'si·tor
in·qui'si·to'ri·al
in'road'
in'rush'
in·sane'
in·san'i·tar'y
in·san'i·ty
in·sa'ti·a·bil'i·ty
in·sa'ti·a·ble
in·scribe'

in·scrip'tion
in·scru'ta·ble
in·scru'ta·bly
in'sect
in·sec·tar'i·um
in·sec'ti·cide'
in·sec'ti·val
in·sec'ti·vore'
in·sec·tiv'o·rous
in·sec·tol'o·gy
in·se·cure'
in·se·cu'ri·ty
in·sem'i·nate'
in·sem'i·na'tion
in·sen'sate
in·sen'si·bil'i·ty
in·sen'si·ble
in·sen'si·bly
in·sen'si·tive
in·sen'ti·ent
in·sep'a·ra·ble
in·sert', in'sert
in·sert'ed
in·sert'ing
in·ser'tion
in'set'
in'shore'
in'side'
in·sid'er
in·sid'i·ous
in'sight'
in·sig'ni·a
in'sig·ni'fi·cance
in'sig·ni'fi·can·cy
in'sig·ni'fi·cant

in'sin·cere'
in'sin·cer'i·ty
in·sin'u·ate'
in·sin'u·a'tion
in·sip'id
in'si·pid'i·ty
in·sip'i·ence
in·sist'
in·sist'ence
in·sist'ent
in si'tu
in'so·bri'e·ty
in'so·far'
in'so·late'
in'so·lat'ing
in'so·la'tion
in'sole'
in'so·lence
in'so·lent
in·sol·u·bil'i·ty
in·sol'u·ble
in·sol'ven·cy
in·sol'vent
in·som'ni·a
in·som'ni·ac'
in'so·much'
in·sou'ci·ance
in·sou'ci·ant
in·spect'
in·spect'ing
in·spec'tion
in·spec'tor
in·spec·to'ri·al
in'spir·a'tion
in'spir·a'tion·al

in·spire'
in·spir'ing
in·spir'it
in·sta·bil'i·ty
in·sta'ble
in·stall'
in·stal·la'tion
in·stall'ment
in'stance
in'stant
in·stan·tan'e·ous
in'stant·ly
in·star'
in·state'
in·stau·ra'tion
in·stead'
in·step'
in'sti·gate'
in'sti·gat'ing
in'sti·ga'tion
in'sti·ga'tor
in·still'
in·still'ing
in·still'ment
in'stinct
in·stinc'tive
in·stinc'tu·al
in'sti·tute'
in'sti·tu'tion
in'sti·tu'tion·al
in'sti·tu'tion·al·ize'
in'sti·tu'tion·ar'y
in'sti·tu'tive
in·struct'
in·struc'tion

in·struc'tion·al
in·struc'tive
in'stru·ment
in'stru·men'tal
in'stru·men'tal·ism
in'stru·men·tal'i·ty
in'stru·men·ta'tion
in'sub·or'di·nate
in'sub·or'di·na'tion
in'sub·stan'tial
in'sub·stan'ti·al'i·ty
in·suf'fer·a·ble
in'suf·fi'cien·cy
in'suf·fi'cient
in'suf'flate
in'suf·fla'tion
in'su·lar
in'su·lar'i·ty
in'su·late'
in'su·la'tion
in'su·la'tor
in'su·lin
in'sult, in·sult'
in·sult'ing
in·su'per·a·ble
in'sup·port'a·ble
in·sur'a·bil'i·ty
in·sur'a·ble
in·sur'ance
in·sur'ant
in·sure'
in·sured'
in·sur'er
in·sur'gence
in·sur'gen·cy

in·sur'gent
in·sur'ing
in'sur·mount'a·ble
in'sur·rec'tion
in'sur·rec'tion·ar'y
in'sus·cep'ti·bil'i·ty
in'sus·cep'ti·ble
in'swept'
in·tact'
in·tagl'io
in·take'
in·tan'gi·bil'i·ty
in·tan'gi·ble
in·tan'gi·bly
in·tar'si·a
in'te·ger
in'te·gral
in'te·grand'
in'te·grant
in'te·grate'
in'te·gra'tion
in'te·gra'tive
in'te·gra'tor
in·teg'ri·ty
in·teg'u·ment
in'tel·lect'
in'tel·lec'tion
in'tel·lec'tu·al
in'tel·lec'tu·al·ism
in'tel·lec'tu·al'i·ty
in'tel·lec'tu·al·ize'
in·tel'li·gence
in·tel'li·genc·er
in·tel'li·gent
in·tel'li·gent'si·a

in·tel'li·gi·bil'i·ty
in·tel'li·gi·ble
in·tel'li·gi·bly
in·tem'per·ance
in·tem'per·ate
in·tend'
in·tend'ance
in·tend'ant
in·tend'ed
in·tend'ment
in·tense'
in·tense'ly
in·ten'si·fi·ca'tion
in·ten'si·fi·er
in·ten'si·fy'
in·ten'si·ty
in·ten'sive
in·tent'
in·ten'tion
in·ten'tion·al
in·ten'tion·al·ly
in·ten'tioned
in·ter'
in'ter·act'
in'ter·ac'tion
in'ter·ac'tive
in'ter·bor'ough
in'ter·breed'
in·ter'ca·lar'y
in'ter·cede'
in'ter·cel'lu·lar
in'ter·cept'
in'ter·cep'tion
in'ter·cep'tive
in'ter·cep'tor

in'ter·ces'sion
in'ter·change'
in'ter·change'a·ble
in·ter·clav'i·cle
in·ter·col·le'gi·ate
in'ter·com'
in'ter·con·nect'
in'ter·con·nec'tion
in'ter·con'ti·nen'tal
in'ter·cos'tal
in'ter·course'
in'ter·de·part'men'tal
in'ter·de·pend'ence
in'ter·de·pend'ent
in'ter·dict'
in'ter·dic'tion
in'ter·dic'to·ry
in'ter·est
in'ter·est·ed
in'ter·est·ing
in'ter·face'
in'ter·fa'cial
in'ter·fere'
in'ter·fer'ence
in'ter·fuse'
in'ter·im
in·te'ri·or
in'ter·ject'
in'ter·jec'tion
in'ter·jec'tion·al
in'ter·knit'
in'ter·lace'
in'ter·lay'
in'ter·line'
in'ter·lin'e·al

in'ter·lin'e·ar
in'ter·lin'ing
in'ter·lock'
in'ter·lo·cu'tion
in'ter·loc'u·tor
in'ter·loc'u·to'ry
in'ter·lope'
in'ter·lop'er
in'ter·lude'
in'ter·mar'riage
in'ter·mar'ry
in'ter·me'di·a·cy
in'ter·me'di·ar'y
in'ter·me'di·ate
in'ter·me'di·a'tor
in·ter'ment
in'ter·mez'zo
in·ter'mi·na·ble
in'ter·min'gle
in'ter·mis'sion
in'ter·mit'
in'ter·mit'tence
in'ter·mit'tent
in'ter·mon'tane
in'tern, in·tern'
in·ter'nal
in'ter·na'tion·al
in'ter·na'tion·al·ly
in'tern·ee'
in·tern'ment
in'ter·pel'late
in'ter·plan'e·tar'y
in'ter·play'
in·ter'po·late'
in·ter'po·la'tion

in·ter·pose'
in·ter'pret
in·ter'pre·ta'tion
in·ter'pret·er
in·ter'pre·tive
in'ter·ra'cial
in'ter·re·late'
in'ter·re·lat'ed
in'ter·re·la'tion
in·ter'ro·gate'
in·ter'ro·ga'tion
in'ter·rog'a·tive
in'ter·rog'a·to'ry
in'ter·rupt'
in'ter·rup'tion
in'ter·sect'
in'ter·sec'tion
in'ter·sperse'
in'ter·spers'ing
in'ter·sper'sion
in'ter·state'
in·ter·stel'lar
in·ter'stice
in·ter'stic·es
in'ter·sti'tial
in'ter·twine'
in'ter·ur'ban
in'ter·val
in'ter·vene'
in'ter·ven'ing
in'ter·ven'tion
in'ter·view'
in·tes'ta·cy
in·tes'tate
in·tes'ti·nal

in·tes'tine
in'ti·ma·cy
in'ti·mate
in'ti·ma'tion
in·tim'i·date'
in·tim'i·da'tion
in·tol'er·a·ble
in·tol'er·ant
in'to·na'tion
in·tone'
in·tox'i·cant
in·tox'i·cat'ing
in·tox'i·ca'tion
in·trac'ta·ble
in'tra·mu'ral
in·tran'si·gent
in·tran'si·tive
in'tra·state'
in'tra·ve'nous
in·trep'id
in'tre·pid'i·ty
in·trep'id·ly
in'tri·ca·cy
in'tri·cate
in·trigue'
in·tri'guing
in·trin'sic
in·trin'si·cal·ly
in'tro·duce'
in'tro·duc'tion
in'tro·duc'to·ry
in·tro'it
in'tro·jec'tion
in'tro·spect'
in'tro·spec'tion

in'tro·spec'tive
in'tro·ver'sion
in'tro·vert'
in·trude'
in·tru'sion
in·tru'sive
in·trust'
in·tu'it
in·tu·i'tion
in·tu'i·tive
in'un·date'
in'un·da'tion
in·ure'
in·ur'ing
in·vade'
in·va·lid,
  in·val'id
in·val'i·date'
in·val'i·da'tion
in·val'id·ism
in·val'u·a·ble
in·var'
in·var'i·a·ble
in·var'i·ant
in·va'sion
in·va'sive
in·vec'tive
in·veigh'
in·vei'gle
in·vent'
in·ven'tion
in·ven'tive
in·ven'tor
in'ven·to'ry
in·verse'

in·ver'sion
in·vert'
in·vert'ase
in·vert'ed
in·vert'er
in·vest'
in·ves'ti·gate'
in·ves'ti·ga'tion
in·ves'ti·ga'tive
in·ves'ti·ture'
in·vest'ment
in·ves'tor
in·vet'er·ate
in·vid'i·ous
in·vig'or·ate'
in·vig'or·a'tion
in·vin'ci·bil'i·ty
in·vin'ci·ble
in·vi'o·la·bil'i·ty
in·vi'o·la·ble
in·vi'o·late
in'vis·i·bil'i·ty
in·vis'i·ble
in·vis'i·bly
in'vi·ta'tion
in·vite'
in·vit'ing
in'vo·ca'tion
in'voice
in·voke'
in'vo·lu'cre
in·vol'un·tar'i·ly
in·vol'un·tar'y
in'vo·lute'
in'vo·lut'ed

in'vo·lu'tion
in·volve'
in·volve'ment
in·vul'ner·a·bil'i·ty
in·vul'ner·a·ble
in'ward
in'ward·ly
in'ward·ness
in'wrought'
i'o·date'
i·od'ic
i'o·dide'
i'o·dine'
i'o·dize'
i'o·dol'
i'o·lite'
i'on
I·o'ni·an
I·on'ic
i'on·i·za'tion
i'on·ize'
i·on'o·sphere'
I'o·wan
ip'e·cac'
ip'so fac'to
I·ra'ni·an
I·ra'qi
i·ras'ci·ble
i·rate'
ire'ful
i·ren'ics
ir'i·des'cence
ir'i·des'cent
i·rid'i·um
i'ris

I'rish
irk'some
i'ron
i'ron·bound'
i'ron·clad'
i'ron·hand'ed
i·ron'ic
i·ron'i·cal
i'ron·mon'ger
i'ron·stone'
i'ron·work'er
i'ro·ny
ir·ra'di·ate'
ir·ra'di·a'tion
ir·ra'tion·al
ir·ra'tion·al'i·ty
ir·rec'on·cil'a·bil'i·ty
ir'rec·on·cil'a·ble
ir're·cov'er·a·ble
ir're·deem'a·ble
Ir're·den'tist
ir're·duc'i·ble
ir·ref'ra·ga·ble
ir·ref'u·ta·ble
ir·reg'u·lar
ir·reg'u·lar'i·ty
ir·rel'e·vance
ir·rel'e·vant
ir're·li'gious
ir're·me'di·a·ble
ir're·mov'a·bly
ir·rep'a·ra·ble
ir're·place'a·ble
ir're·press'i·ble
ir're·proach'a·bly

ir·re·sist′i·ble
ir·res′o·lute′
ir′re·solv′a·ble
ir′re·spec′tive
ir′re·spon′si·bil′i·ty
ir′re·spon′si·ble
ir′re·spon′sive
ir′re·triev′a·ble
ir′re·vers′i·ble
ir·rev′o·ca·ble
ir′ri·gate′
ir′ri·ga′tion
ir′ri·ta·bil′i·ty
ir′ri·ta·ble
ir′ri·tant
ir′ri·tate′
ir′ri·tat′ed
ir′ri·ta′tion
ir·rup′tion
ir·rup′tive
i′sa·gog′ic
I·sa′iah
Is·car′i·ot
is·chi·at′ic
is′chi·um
i′sin·glass′
Is′lam
Is·lam′ic
is′land
is′land·er
is′let
i′so·ag·glu′ti·na′tion
i′so·bar′

i′so·cheim′
i′so·chro·mat′ic
i·soch′ro·nal
i′so·cli′nal
i′so·cline′
i′so·dy·nam′ic
i′so·ga′mete
i·sog′a·my
i·sog′e·nous
i·sog′e·ny
i′so·ge′o·therm′
i′so·gloss′
i′so·gon′
i·sog′o·nal
i·so·gon′ic
i′so·la·ble
i′so·late′
i′so·la′tion
i′so·la′tion·ism
i·sol′o·gous
i′so·mag·net′ic
i′so·mer
i·som′er·ous
i′so·met′ric
i·som′e·try
i′so·mor′phic
i′so·mor′phism
i′so·pleth′
i′so·pod′
i′so·pro′pyl
i·sos′ce·les′
i′so·seis′mal

i·sos′ta·sy
i·so·stat′ic
i′so·therm′
i′so·ton′ic
i′so·tope′
i′so·top′ic
i′so·trop′ic
Is·ra·el′i
Is′ra·el·ite′
is′su·a·ble
is′su·ance
is′sue
isth′mus
I·tal′ian
I·tal′ian·ate′
i·tal′ic
i·tal′i·cize′
i′tem
i′tem·ize′
it′er·ance
it′er·ate′
it′er·a′tion
it′er·a′tive
i·tin′er·an·cy
i·tin′er·ant
i·tin′er·ar′y
i·tin′er·ate
it·self′
i′vied
i′vo·ry
i′vo·ry·type′
i′vy

J

jab'ber
ja·bot'
ja'cinth
jack'al
jack'a·napes'
jack'ass'
jack'boot'
jack'et
jack'knife'
jack'pot'
jack'screw'
jack'straw'
Jac'o·bin
Jac'o·bite
jac'o·net'
jac·quard'
jac·ta'tion
jac'ti·ta'tion
jad'ed
jag'ged
jag'uar
jail'bird'
jail'er
jail'or
ja·lop'y
ja'lou·sie'
Ja·mai'can
jam'bo·ree'
jan'gle
jan'gling
jan'i·tor

Jan'sen·ism
Jan'u·ar'y
Jap'a·nese'
ja·pon'i·ca
jar'di·niere'
jar'gon
jar'o·vize'
jas'mine
jas'per
jaun'dice
jaun'diced
jaun'ti·ness
jaun'ty
Jav'a·nese'
jave'lin
jaw'bone'
jaw'break'er
jay'hawk'er
jay'walk'
jay'walk'er
jazz'y
jeal'ous
jeal'ous·ly
jeal'ous·y
jeer'ing
Je·ho'vah
je·june'
je·ju'num
jel'lied
jel'li·fy'
jel'ly

jel'ly·bean'
jel'ly·fish'
jel'ly·roll'
jen'net
jen'ny
jeop'ard·ize'
jeop'ard·y
jer·bo'a
jer'e·mi'ad
jerk'i·ly
jer'kin
jerk'i·ness
jerk'wa'ter
jerk'y
jer'ry
jer'sey
Je·ru'sa·lem
jest'er
jest'ing
Jes'u·it
Jes'u·it'i·cal
jet'black'
jet'sam
jet'ti·son
jet'ty
jew'el
jew'el·er
jew'el·ler
jew'el·ry
Jew'ish
Jew'ry

153

jez'e·bel
jif'fy
jig'ger
jig'gle
jig'gling
jig'saw'
ji·had'
jilt'ed
jilt'ing
jim'my
jim'son
jin'gle
jin'gling
jin'gly
jin'go
jin'go·ism
jin'go·is'tic
jin·ni'
jin·rik'i·sha
jinx'ing
jit'ney
jit'ter
jit'ter·bug'
jit'ter·y
job'ber
jock'ey
jock'o
jock'strap'
jo·cose'
jo·cos'i·ty
joc'u·lar
joc'u·lar'i·ty
joc'und
jodh'purs
jog'gle

john'ny·cake'
John·so'ni·an
join'der
join'er
join'er·y
joint'ed
joint'er
joint'ly
join'ture
jok'er
jol'li·er
jol'li·ty
jol'ly
jon'gleur
jon'quil
jo'rum
jos'tle
jounc'ing
jour'nal
jour'nal·ese'
jour'nal·ism
jour'nal·ist
jour'nal·is'ti·cal·ly
jour'ney
jour'ney·man
joust'ing
jo'vi·al
jo'vi·al'i·ty
jowl'y
joy'ful
joy'less
joy'ous
ju'bi·lance
ju'bi·lant
ju'bi·late'

ju'bi·la'tion
ju'bi·lee'
Ju·da'ic
Ju·da·ism
Ju·de'an
judg'es
judg'ing
judg'ment
ju'di·ca·ble
ju'di·ca·to'ry
ju'di·ca·ture
ju·di'cial
ju·di'ci·ar'y
ju·di'cious
ju'do
ju'gal
jug'ger·naut'
jug'gle
jug'gler
jug'gler·y
jug'u·lar
ju'gu·late'
juic'i·ness
juic'y
ju·jit'su
ju'ju
ju'jube
ju'lep
Jul'ian
ju·li·enne'
Ju·ly'
jum'ble
jum'bo
jump'er
jump'i·ness

jump'ing
jump'suit'
jump'y
jun'co
junc'tion
junc'ture
jun'gle
jung'ly
jun'ior
ju'ni·per
jun'ket
junk'yard'
Ju'no·esque'
jun'ta

Ju'pi·ter
ju'ral
ju'rant
ju'rat
ju'ra·to'ry
ju·rid'i·cal
ju'ris·dic'tion
ju'ris·pru'dence
ju'rist
ju·ris'ti·cal·ly
ju'ror
ju'ry
jus'sive

jus'tice
jus·ti'ci·a·ble
jus·ti'ci·ar'y
jus'ti·fi'a·ble
jus'ti·fi·ca'tion
jus'ti·fi'er
jus'ti·fy'
just'ly
ju've·nes'cent
ju've·nile
ju've·nil'i·a
jux'ta·pose'
jux'ta·po·si'tion

K

ka·bobs'
kad'dish
kaf'fir
kail'yard'
ka'i·nite'
kai'ser
ka'ke·mo'no
ka'la·a·zar'
ka·lei'do·scope'
ka·lei'do·scop'ic
kale'yard'
ka'mi·ka'ze
kan'ga·roo'
Kan'san
kan·tar'
Kant'i·an
ka'o·lin
ka'pok
kap'pa
ka·put'
kar'at
ka·ra'te
kar'ma
ka·tab'a·sis
ka'ty·did'
kay'ak
kay'o'
ka·zoo'
keel'haul'
keel'son
keen'er

keep'er
keep'ing
keep'sake'
ke'loid
kel'pie
Kel'vin
ken'nel
ken'ning
ke'no
ke·no'sis
Ken·tuck'i·an
ker'a·tin
ker'a·ti'tis
ker'a·toid'
ker'a·to·plas'ty
ker'a·tose'
ker'a·to'sis
ker'chief
ker'mis
ker'nel
ker'o·sene'
ker'sey
ketch'up
ke'tene
ke'to·gen'e·sis
ke'tone
ke·to'sis
ket'tle
ket'tle·drum'
kev'el
key'board'

key'hole'
key'note'
key'not'er
key'stone'
kha'ki
kib·butz'
kib'itz
kib'itz·er
kib'lah
ki'bosh
kick'back'
kick'off'
kid'der
kid'nap
kid'nap·per
kid'ney
kid'skin'
kil'erg'
kill'er
kill'ing
ki'lo
kil'o·cal'o·rie
kil'o·cy'cle
kil'o·gram'
kil'o·li'ter
kil'o·met'ric
kil'o·watt'
kil'ter
ki·mo'no
kin'der·gar'ten
kind'heart'ed

kin'dle
kin'dling
kind'ly
kind'ness
kin'dred
kin·e·mat'ics
kin'e·scope'
kin·es·the'si·a
kin·es·thet'ic
ki·net'ic
kin'folk'
king'dom
king'fish'
king'fish'er
king'li·ness
king'pin'
king'ship
kin'ka·jou'
kink'i·ness
kink'y
kins'folk'
kin'ship
ki·osk'
kip'per
kir'tle
kis'met
kiss'er
kiss'ing
kitch'en
kitch'en·ette'
kitch'en·ware'
kit'ten
kit'ten·ish
kit'ty

ki'wi
klea'gle
klep'to·ma'ni·a
klep'to·ma'ni·ac'
klys'tron
knack'er
knap'sack'
knav'er·y
knav'ish
knead'ed
knee'cap'
kneel'ing
knee'pad'
knick'ers
knight'hood
knit'ting
knob'by
knob'ker'rie
knock'a·bout'
knock'down'
knock'er
knock'kneed'
knock'out'
knot'hole'
knot'ted
knot'ti·ness
knot'ty
know'a·ble
know'ing
know'ing·ly
knowl'edge
knowl'edge·a·ble
knuck'le

knuck'le·bone'
ko·a'la
ko'bold
ko'di·ak
kohl'ra'bi
koi·ne'
ko'la
ko·lin'sky
kook'y
ko'peck
ko'pek
Ko·ran'
Ko·re'an
ko·ru'na
ko'sher
kow'tow'
kra'ken
krieg'spiel'
kro'na
kro'ne
kryp'ton
ku'chen
ku'dos
ku'du
ku·lak'
kum'quat
kunz'ite
Kurd'ish
Ku·wait'i
ky'ack
ky'an·ize'
ky'mo·graph'
ky·pho'sis

L

lab′da·num
lab′e·fac′tion
la′bel
la·bel′lum
la′bi·a
la′bi·al
la′bi·al·ize′
la′bi·a ma·jo′ra
la′bi·a mi·no′ra
la′bi·ate′
la′bile
la′bi·o·den′tal
la′bi·o·na′sal
la′bi·o·ve′lar
la′bi·um
la′bor
lab′o·ra·to′ry
la′bored
la′bor·er
la·bo′ri·ous
la′bor·ite′
Lab′ra·dor′
la′bret
la′brum
lab′y·rinth′
lab′y·rin′thine
lac′co·lith
lac′er·ate′
lac′er·a′tion
la′cer·til′i·an
lace′work′

lach′es
lach′ry·mal
lach′ry·ma′tor
lach′ry·mose′
lac′i·ness
lac′ing
la·cin′i·ate′
lack′a·dai′si·cal
lack′ey
lack′lus′ter
la·con′ic
la·con′i·cal·ly
lac′quer
la·crosse′
lac′tam
lac′ta·ry
lac′tase
lac′tate
lac·ta′tion
lac′te·al
lac·tes′cence
lac′tic
lac′to·ba·cil′lus
lac·tom′e·ter
lac′to·scope′
lac′tose
la·cu′na
la·cus′trine
lac′y
lad′der
lad′en

lad′ing
La·di′no
la′dle
la′dle·ful′
la′dling
la·drone′
la′dy
la′dy·bird′
la′dy·bug′
la′dy·fin′ger
la′dy·like′
la′dy·ship′
lag′an
la′ger
lag′gard
lag′ger
lag′ging
la·gniappe′
lag′o·morph′
la·goon′
la′ic
la′i·cize′
lais′sez faire
la′i·ty
lak′y
la′ma
La·marck′ism
la′ma·ser′y
lam·bast′
lam·baste′
lam·bast′ing

158

lamb'da
lamb'doid
lam'ben·cy
lam'bent
lam'bert
lamb'kin
lam'bre·quin
lamb'skin'
la·mé'
la'medh
la·mel'la
lam'el·late'
la·ment'
lam·en'ta·ble
lam·en'ta·bly
lam·en·ta'tion
la·ment'ed
la'mi·a
lam'i·na
lam'i·nate'
lam'i·na'tion
lam'pas
lamp'black'
lam'per
lam'pi·on
lam·poon'
lam·poon'er·y
lam·poon'ist
lamp'post'
lam'prey
lan'ce·o·late
lanc'er
lan'cet
lan'ci·nate'
lan'dau

land'ed
land'fall'
land'hold'er
land'ing
land'la'dy
land'locked'
land'lord'
land'lub'ber
land'own'ing
land'scape'
land'scap'ist
land'slide'
lands'man
land'ward
lang'lauf'
lan'guage
lan'guet
lan'guid
lan'guish
lan'guished
lan'guish·ing
lan'guish·ment
lan'guor
lan'guor·ous
lan'iard
la'ni·ar'y
lan'i·tal
lank'i·ness
lank'y
lan'ner
lan'ner·et'
lan'o·lin
lans'downe
lan'tern
lan'tha·nide'

lan'tha·num
la·nu'gi·nous
la·nu'go
lan'yard
lap'a·rot'o·my
la·pel'
lap'ful'
lap'i·dar'y
lap'i·date'
la·pid'i·fi·ca'tion
la·pid'i·fy'
la·pil'lus
lap'in
lap'is laz'u·li'
lap'per
lap'strake'
lap'wing'
lar'board
lar'ce·nous
lar'ce·ny
lar·da'ceous
lard'er
lar'don
la'res
large'ly
lar'gess
lar'gesse
larg'ish
lar'go
lar'i·at
lark'spur'
lar'ri·gan
lar'va
lar'val
la·ryn'gal

la·ryn'ge·al
la'ryn·gi'tis
lar'yn·got'o·my
lar'ynx
la·sa'gna
las'car
las·civ'i·ous
la'ser
lash'ing
las'sie
las'si·tude'
las'so
last'ing
latch'key'
la·teen'
late'ly
la'ten·cy
la'tent
lat'er
lat'er·al
lat'er·al·ly
lat'er·ite'
la·tes'cent
lat'est
la'tex
lath'er
lath'er·y
lath'ing
lath'work'
Lat'in
Lat'in·ate'
Lat'in·ism
La·tin'i·ty
Lat'in·ize'
lat'ish

lat'i·tude'
lat'i·tu'di·nal
lat'i·tu'di·nar'i·an
la·tri'a
la·trine'
lat'ten
lat'ter
lat'ter·most'
lat'tice
lat'tice·work'
lat'tic·ing
laud'a·ble
laud'a·bly
laud'a·num
lau·da'tion
laud'a·to'ry
laugh'a·ble
laugh'a·bly
laugh'ing
laugh'ing·stock'
laugh'ter
laun'der
laun'dress
laun'dry
lau·ra'ceous
lau're·ate
lau'rel
Lau·ren'ti·an
la'va
la·va'bo
lav'age
lav'a·to'ry
lav'en·der
la'ver
lav'ish

law'book'
law'break'er
law'ful
law'giv'er
law'less
law'mak'er
law·ren'ci·um
law'suit'
law'yer
lax·a'tion
lax'a·tive
lay'er
lay'er·age
lay'er·ing
lay·ette'
lay'man
lay'off'
lay'out'
lay'o'ver
lay'per'son
la'zar
laz'a·ret'to
laz'u·lite'
la'zy
leach'ing
leach'y
lead'en
lead'er
lead'er·ship'
lead'in'
lead'ing
leaf'i·ness
leaf'let
leaf'stalk'
leaf'y

lea'guer
leak'age
leak'i·ness
leak'ing
leak'y
lean'ing
leap'frog'
learn'ed
learn'ing
leas'a·ble
lease'hold'
lease'hold'er
leas'ing
leath'er
leath'er·ette'
leath'er·i·ness
leath'ern
leath'er·neck'
leath'er·y
leav'en
leav'en·ing
leav'ing
Leb'a·nese'
lech'er
lech'er·ous
lech'er·y
lec'i·thin
lec'tern
lec'tion
lec'tion·ar'y
lec'tor
lec'ture
lec'tur·er
ledg'er
lee'board'

leer'y
lee'ward
lee'way'
left'ist
left'o'ver
left'y
leg'a·cy
le'gal
le'gal·ism
le'gal·is'tic
le·gal'i·ty
le'gal·i·za'tion
le'gal·ize'
le'gal·ly
leg'ate
leg'a·tee'
le·ga'tion
le·ga'to
leg'end
leg'end·ar'y
leg'er·de·main'
leg'ged
leg'ging
leg'gy
leg'horn'
leg'i·bil'i·ty
leg'i·ble
leg'i·bly
le'gion
le'gion·ar'y
le'gion·naire'
leg'is·late'
leg'is·la'tive
leg'is·la'tor
leg'is·la'ture

le·git'
le·git'i·ma·cy
le·git'i·mate'
le·git'i·mize'
leg'ume, le·gume'
le·gu'mi·nous
leish'man·i'a·sis
lei'sure
lei'sured
lei'sure·ly
leit'mo·tif'
leit'mo·tiv'
lem'ma
lem'ming
lem·nis'cus
lem'on
lem·pi'ra
le'mur
lend'er
lend'ing
length'en
length'i·ly
length'i·ness
length'wise'
length'y
le'ni·en·cy
le'ni·ent
Len'in·ism
le'nis
len'i·ty
len·tic'u·lar
len·tic'u·lat'ed
len·ti'go
len'til
len'to

Le'o·nid
le'o·nine'
leo'pard
leo'pard·ess
le'o·tard'
lep'er
lep'i·dop'ter·ous
lep'o·rid
lep're·chaun'
lep'ro·sa'ri·um
lep'ro·sy
lep·rous
les'bi·an
les'bi·an·ism
lese maj'es·ty
le'sion
les·see'
less'en
less'er
les'son
les'sor
let'down'
le'thal
le·thar'gic
le·thar'gi·cal·ly
leth'ar·gy
let'ter
let'tered
let'ter·head'
let'ter·ing
let'ter·press'
let'tuce
let'up'
leu'cine
leu'cite

leu'co·cyte'
leu'co·cy'to·sis
leu'co·der'ma
leu·co'ma
leu'co·plast'
leu·ke'mi·a
leu'ko·pe'ni·a
le·vant'er
le·va'tor
lev·ee'
lev'el
lev'el·er
lev'el·ing
lev'er
lev'er·age
le·vi'a·than
lev'i·er
lev'i·gate'
lev'i·rate'
lev'is
lev'i·tate'
lev'i·ta'tion
lev'i·ty
le'vo·ro·ta'tion
le'vo·ro'ta·to'ry
lev'u·lin
lev'u·lose'
lev'y
lewd'ness
lew'is
lew'is·ite'
lex'i·cal
lex'i·cog'ra·pher
lex'i·co·graph'i·cal
lex'i·cog'ra·phy

lex'i·con
Ley'den
li'a·bil'i·ty
li'a·ble
li'ai·son'
li·a'na
li'ar
li·ba'tion
li'bel
li'bel·ant
li'bel·ee'
li'bel·er
li'bel·lant
li'bel·lee'
li'bel·ler
li'bel·lous
li'bel·ous
li'ber
lib'er·al
lib'er·al·ism
lib'er·al·i·ty
lib'er·al·ize'
lib'er·ate'
lib'er·a'tion
lib'er·a'tor
lib'er·tar'i·an
lib'er·tine'
lib'er·tin·ism
lib'er·ty
li·bid'i·nal
li·bid'i·nous
li·bi'do
li'bra
li·brar'i·an
li'brar'y

li′brate
li·bra′tion
li·bret′tist
li·bret′to
li′cense
li′cen·see′
li′cen·ser
li′cen·sor
li·cen′ti·ate
li·cen′tious
li′chen
li′chen·ous
lic′it
lick′ing
lic′o·rice
lid′ded
Lie′der·kranz′
li′en·ec′to·my
li′en·ter′y
lieu·ten′an·cy
lieu·ten′ant
life′blood′
life′boat′
life′guard′
life′less
life′like′
life′long′
lif′er
life′sav′ing
life′time′
life′work′
lift′off′
lig′a·ment
li′gate
li·ga′tion

lig′a·ture
light′en
light′er
light′head′ed
light′house′
light′ing
light′ly
light′ness
light′ning
light′weight′
lig′ni·fy′
lig′nin
lig′nite
lig′no·cel′lu·lose′
lig′ule
lig′ure
lik′a·ble
like′a·ble
like′li·hood′
like′ly
lik′en
like′ness
like′wise′
lik′ing
li′lac
lil′i·a′ceous
Lil′li·pu′tian
lil′y
li′ma
lim′bate
lim′ber
lim′bo
Lim′burg·er
lim′bus
lime′ade′

lime′kiln′
lime′light′
li′men
lim′er·ick
lime′stone′
lim′ey
li·mic′o·line′
lim′i·nal
lim′it
lim′i·ta′tion
lim′it·ed
lim′it·ing
lim′it·less
lim·nol′o·gy
Li′moges′
lim′o·nene′
li′mo·nite′
lim′ou·sine′
limp′et
lim′pid
lim·pid′i·ty
lin′age
linch′pin′
lin′den
lin′e·age
lin′e·al
lin′e·al·ly
lin′e·a·ment
lin′e·ar
lin′e·ate′
lin′e·a′tion
line′back′er
line′man
lin′en
lin′er

lines'man
lin'gam
lin'ger
lin'ge·rie'
lin'go
lin'gua fran'ca
lin'gual
lin'guist
lin·guis'tic
lin·guis'ti·cal·ly
lin·guis'tics
lin'i·ment
lin'ing
link'age
link'ing
link'work'
Lin·nae'an
lin'net
li·no'le·um
lin'o·type'
lin'o·typ'er
lin'seed
lin'sey
lin'tel
lint'er
lint'free'
lint'y
li'on
li'on·ness
li'on·i·za'tion
li'on·ize'
lip'a·roid'
li'pase
lip'ide
lip'o·lyt'ic

lip'per
lip'stick'
li'quate
liq'ue·fac'tion
liq'ui·fi'er
liq'ui·fy'
li:·ques'cent
liq'uid
liq'ui·date'
liq'ui·da'tion
liq'ui·da'tor
li·quid'i·ty
liq'uor
li'ra
lis'some
lis'ten
lis'ten·er
lis'ten·ing
list'er
list'ing
list'less
lit'a·ny
li'tchi'
li'ter
lit'er·a·cy
lit'er·al
lit'er·al·ism
lit'er·al'i·ty
lit'er·al·ly
lit'er·ar'i·ness
lit'er·ar'y
lit'er·ate
lit'e·ra'ti
lit'er·a·ture
lith'arge

li·the'mi·a
lithe'some
lith'i·a
lith'ic
lith'i·um
lith'o·graph'
li·thog'ra·pher
li·thog'ra·phy
lith'oid
lith'o·phyte'
li·thot'o·my
li·thot'ri·ty
lit'i·ga·ble
lit'i·gant
lit'i·gate'
lit'i·ga'tion
li·ti'gious
lit'mus
li'to·tes'
li'tre
lit'ter
lit'té·ra·teur'
lit'ter·bug'
lit'ter·ing
lit'tle
lit'tle·neck'
lit'to·ral
li·tur'gic
li·tur'gi·cal
lit'ur·gist
lit'ur·gy
liv'a·ble
live'a·ble
live'li·hood'
live'li·ness

live'long'
live'ly
liv'en
liv'er
liv'er·ish
liv'er·wort'
liv'er·wurst'
liv'er·y
live'stock'
liv'id
liv'ing
li'vre
liz'ard
lla'ma
lla'no
load'ed
load'ing
load'star'
load'stone'
loaf'er
loaf'ing
loam'y
loath'ing
loath'some
lo'bar
lo'bate
lo·ba'tion
lob'by
lob'by·ist
lo·bec'to·my
lo·be'li·a
lo·bot'o·my
lob'ster
lob'u·lar
lob'ule

lo'cal
lo·cale'
lo'cal·ism
lo·cal'i·ty
lo'cal·i·za'tion
lo'cal·ly
lo'cate
lo·ca'tion
loc'a·tive
lo'chi·a
lo'ci
lock'age
lock'er
lock'et
lock'jaw'
lock'out'
lock'smith'
lock'up'
lo'co
lo'co·mo'tion
lo'co·mo'tive
lo'co·mo'tor
lo'co·weed'
loc'u·lar
loc'u·lus
lo'cus
lo'cus clas'si·cus
lo'cust
lo'cu'tion
loc'u·to'ry
lode'star'
lode'stone'
lodg'er
lodg'ing
lodg'ment

lo'ess
loft'er
loft'i·ly
loft'i·ness
loft'y
lo'gan·ber'ry
log'a·rithm
log'a·rith'mic
log'a·rith'mi·cal·ly
log'book'
log'ger
log'ger·heads'
log'gia
log'ging
log'i·a
log'ic
log'i·cal
log'i·cal'i·ty
lo·gis'tic
lo·gis'tics
log'o·gram'
log'o·griph'
lo·gom'a·chy
log'o·type'
log'roll'ing
lo'gy
loin'cloth'
loi'ter
lol'la·pa·loo'za
lo'ment
lone'li·ness
lone'ly
lone'some
lon·gev'i·ty
lon·ge'vous

long'hair'
long'hand'
long'horn'
long'ing
lon'gi·tude'
lon'gi·tu'di·nal
long'shore'man
loo'fah
look'er
look'ing
look'out'
loon'y
loop'er
loop'hole'
loop'ing
loos'en
loos'en·ing
lop'er
lop'ing
lo'pho·branch'
lop'ping
lop'sid'ed
lo·qua'cious
lo·quac'i·ty
lo'quat
lord'ing
lord'li·ness
lord'ly
lor·do'sis
lor·dot'ic
lord'ship
Lor'e·lei'
lor·gnette'
lo·ri'ca
lor'i·cate'

lor'ry
los'er
los'ing
lo'tion
lot'ter·y
lot'to
lo'tus
loud'mouthed'
Lou·i·si·an'an
loung'er
loung'ing
lous'i·ness
lous'y
lout'ish
lou'ver
lov'a·ble
lov'a·bly
love'a·ble
love'a·bly
love'less
love'li·ness
love'lorn
love'ly
lov'er
lov'ing
low'born'
low'boy'
low'er
low'er·ing
low'land
low'land·er
low'li·ness
low'ly
lox'o·drom'ic
loy'al

loy'al·ist
loy'al·ty
loz'enge
lu·au'
lub'ber
lub'ber·ly
lu'bri·cant
lu'bri·cate'
lu'bri·ca'tion
lu'bri·ca'tor
lu·bric'i·ty
lu'bri·cous
lu'cent
lu·cerne'
lu'cid
lu'ci·da
lu·cid'i·ty
Lu'ci·fer
lu·cif'er·in
lu'cite
luck'i·ly
luck'i·ness
luck'less
luck'y
lu'cra·tive
lu'cre
lu'cu·brate'
lu'cu·bra'tion
Lud'dite
lu'di·crous
lu'es
lu·et'ic
lug'gage
lug'ger
lug'sail

lu·gu'bri·ous
luke'warm'
lull'a·by'
lum·ba'go
lum'bar
lum'ber
lum'ber·ing
lum'ber·jack'
lum'ber·man
lum'ber·yard'
lum'bri·ca'lis
lum'bri·coid'
lu'men
lu'mi·nar'y
lu'mi·nesce'
lu'mi·nes'cence
lu'mi·nes'cent
lu'mi·nos'i·ty
lu'mi·nous
lum'mox
lump'er
lump'ing
lump'ish
lump'y
lu'na·cy
lu'nar
lu'nate
lu'na·tic
lu·na'tion
lunch'eon
lunch'eon·ette'
lunch'room'
lu·nette'

lung'er
lung'ing
lu'ni·so'lar
lu'ni·ti'dal
lunk'head'
lu'nule
lu'pine
lu'pu·lin
lu'pus
lurch'er
lurch'ing
lu'rid
lur'ing
lurk'ing
lus'cious
lush'ly
lus'ter
lus'ter·ware'
lust'ful
lust'i·ly
lust'i·ness
lus'tral
lus'trate
lus·tra'tion
lus'tre
lus'trous
lus'trum
lust'y
lu'ta·nist
lu'te·nist
lu'te·o·lin
lu'te·ous
lu·te'ti·um

Lu'ther·an
lu'thern
lux'ate
lux·a'tion
lux·u'ri·ance
lux·u'ri·ant
lux·u'ri·ate'
lux·u'ri·ous
lux'u·ry
ly'can·thrope'
ly·can'thro·py
ly'cée'
ly·ce'um
lydd'ite
Lyd'i·an
ly'ing
lym·phat'ic
lym'pho·cyte'
lymph'oid
lyn·ce'an
lynch'ing
ly'on·naise'
lyr'ic
lyr'i·cal
lyr'i·cism
lyr'i·cist
lyr'ist
ly·sim'e·ter
ly'sin
ly'sine
ly'sis
ly'sol
lys'so·pho'bi·a

M

ma·ca′bre
mac·ad′am
mac·ad′am·ize′
ma·caque′
mac′a·ro′ni
mac′a·ron′ic
mac′a·roon′
ma·caw′
ma′cé·doine′
Mac′e·do′ni·an
mac′er
mac′er·ate′
mac′er·a′tion
ma·che′te
Mach′i·a·vel′i·an
Mach′i·a·vel′li·an
ma·chic′o·la′tion
mach′i·nate′
mach′i·na′tions
ma·chine′
ma·chin′er·y
ma·chin′ist
ma·chree′
mack′er·el
mack′i·naw′
mack′in·tosh′
mack′le
ma′cle
mac′ra·mé′
mac′ro·ce·phal′ic
mac′ro·ceph′a·lous

mac′ro·ceph′a·ly
mac′ro·cosm
mac′ro·cos′mic
mac′ro·cyte′
mac′ro·ga′mete
ma′cron
ma′cro·phys′ics
mac′ro·scop·ic
ma·cru′ral
ma·cru′ran
mac′u·la
mac′u·late′
mac′u·la′tion
mac′ule
mad′am
mad′ame,
  ma′dame′
mad′cap′
mad′den
mad′der
mad′ding
ma·deir′a
ma′de·moi·selle′
mad′house′
mad′ly
mad′man
mad′ness
ma·don′na
ma′dras
mad′ri·gal
mad′ri·gal·ist

ma·du′ro
mad′wom′an
mael′strom
mae′nad
mae·nad′ic
ma·es′tro
ma′fi·a
mag′a·zine′
mag′da·le′ne′
Mag′da·le′ni·an
ma·gen′ta
mag′got
mag′got·y
ma′gi
ma′gi·an
mag′ic
mag′i·cal
ma·gi′cian
Ma′gi·not′
mag′is·te′ri·al
mag′is·tra·cy
mag′is·tral
mag′is·trate′
mag′ma
mag·mat′ic
mag′na cum lau′de
mag′na·nim′i·ty
mag·nan′i·mous
mag′nate
mag·ne′sia
mag′ne·site′

mag·ne′si·um
mag′net
mag·net′ic
mag·net′i·cal·ly
mag′net·ism
mag′net·ite′
mag′net·ize′
mag·ne′to
mag·ne·tom′e·ter
mag·ne·tron′
mag·ni·fi·ca′tion
mag·nif′i·cence
mag·nif′i·cent
mag·nif′i·co′
mag′ni·fi′er
mag′ni·fy′
mag′ni·fy′ing
mag·nil′o·quence
mag·nil′o·quent
mag′ni·tude′
mag·no′li·a
mag′num
mag′num o′pus
Mag′nus
mag′pie′
mag′uey
ma′gus
ma′ha·ra′jah
ma′ha·ra′ni
ma·hat′ma
mah′jong′
ma·hog′a·ny
ma·hout′
maid′en
maid′en·hair′

maid′en·head′
maid′en·hood′
maid′en·ly
maid′ser′vant
ma·ieu′tic
mai′gre
mail′bag′
mail′box′
mail′er
mail′lot′
mail′man′
maim′ing
main′land
main′line′
main′ly
main′mast
main′sail
main′spring′
main′stay′
main·tain′
main·tain′ing
main′te·nance
mai·son′
maî′tre d′hô·tel′
ma·jes′tic
maj′es·ty
ma·jol′i·ca
ma′jor
ma′jor·do′mo
ma·jor′i·ty
ma·jus′cu·lar
ma·jus′cule
mak′er
make′weight′
mak′ing

ma·la′ceous
mal′a·chite′
mal′a·cos′tra·can
mal′ad·just′ed
mal′ad·just′ment
mal′a·droit′
mal′a·dy
ma·laise′
ma′la·mute′
mal′an·ders
mal′a·pert′
mal′a·prop·ism
mal′ap·ro·pos′
ma′lar
ma·lar′i·a
ma·lar′i·al
ma·lar′key
ma·lar′ky
mal′ate
mal′a·thi′on
Ma·lay′an
Ma·lay′sian
mal′con·tent′
mal′e·dict′
mal′e·dic′tion
mal′e·dic′to·ry
mal′e·fac′tion
mal′e·fac′tor
mal′e·fac′tress
ma·lef′ic
ma·le′ic
ma·lev′o·lence
ma·lev′o·lent
mal·fea′sance
mal·fea′sant

mal'for·ma'tion
mal·formed'
mal·func'tion
mal'ic
mal'ice
ma·li'cious
ma·lign'
ma·lig'nan·cy
ma·lig'nant
ma·lign'ing
ma·lig'ni·ty
ma·lines'
ma·lin'ger
ma·lin'ger·er
mal'kin
mal'lard
mal'le·a·bil'i·ty
mal'le·a·ble
mal'le·ate'
mal'let
mal'le·us
mal'low
malm'sey
mal'nu·tri'tion
mal'oc·clu'sion
mal·o'dor·ous
ma·lo'nic
mal·prac'tice
malt'ase
Mal'tese'
mal'tha
Mal·thu'sian
malt'ose
mal·treat'
mal·treat'ment

malt'y
mal'ver·sa'tion
ma'ma
mam'ba
mam'bo
mam'ma
mam'mal
mam·ma'li·an
mam'ma·ry
mam·mil'la
mam'mon
mam'moth
mam'my
ma'na
man'a·cle
man'age
man'age·a·bil'i·ty
man'age·a·ble
man'aged
man'age·ment
man'ag·er
man'a·ge'ri·al
man'ag·ing
ma·ña'na
man'a·tee'
man'ci·ple
man·da'mus
man'da·rin
man'date
man'da·to'ry
man'di·ble
man·dib'u·lar
man·do·lin'
man'drake
man'drel

man'dril
man'drill
ma·nège'
ma·neu'ver
ma·neu'ver·a·bil'i·ty
ma·neu'ver·a·ble
man'ga·nate'
man'ga·nese'
man·gan'ic
man'ga·nite'
man'ger
man'gi·ness
man'gle
man'gler
man'gling
man'go
man'grove
man'gy
man'han'dle
man'han'dling
man'hole'
man'hood
ma'ni·a
ma'ni·ac'
ma·ni'a·cal
man'ic
Man'i·che'an
Man'i·che'ism
man'i·cure'
man'i·cur'ist
man'i·fest'
man'i·fes·ta'tion
man'i·fest'ed
man'i·fes'to
man'i·fold'

man'i·kin
ma·nil'a
man'i·oc'
man'i·ple
ma·nip'u·late'
ma·nip'u·la'tion
ma·nip'u·la'tive
ma·nip'u·la'tor
man'kind'
man'like'
man'li·ness
man'ly
man'na
man'ne·quin
man'ner
man'nered
man'ner·ism
man'ner·li·ness
man'ner·ly
man'nish
man'ni·tol'
ma·nom'e·ter
man'or
ma·no'ri·al
man·qué'
man'sard
man'ser'vant
man'sion
man'slaugh'ter
man'ta
man'teau
man'tel
man'tel·piece'
man·til'la
man'tis

man'tle
man'u·al
man'u·al·ly
man'u·fac'ture
man'u·fac'tur·er
man'u·mis'sion
man'u·mit'
ma·nure'
man'u·script'
man'y
man'y·plies'
ma'ple
ma·quis'
mar'a·bou'
mar'a·bout'
ma·ra'ca
mar'a·schi'no
ma·ras'mus
mar'a·thon
ma·raud'
ma·raud'er
ma·raud'ing
mar'ble
mar'bled
mar'ble·ize'
mar'bling
mar'ca·site'
mar·cel'
mar·ces'cent
march'er
march'ing
mar'chion·ess
march'land'
march'pane'
Mar'di·gras

ma're
ma're clau'sum
ma're li'be·rum
mar'ga·rin
mar'ga·rine
mar'ga·rite'
mar'gin
mar'gin·al
mar'gi·na'li·a
mar'gin·ate'
mar'gin·a'tion
mar'grave
Mar'i·an
mar'i·gold'
ma'ri·hua'na
ma'ri·jua'na
ma·rim'ba
ma·ri'na
mar'i·nade'
mar'i·nate'
ma·rine'
mar'i·ner
mar'i·o·nette'
mar'i·tal
mar'i·time'
mar'jo·ram
mark'down'
mark'ed·ly
mark'er
mar'ket
mar'ket·a·bil'i·ty
mar'ket·a·ble
mark'ing
mark'ka
marks'man

marks'man·ship'
mark'up'
mar·la'ceous
mar'lin
mar'line
mar'ling
marl'y
mar'ma·lade'
mar·mo're·al
mar·mo·set'
mar'mot
ma·roon'
mar·quee'
mar'que·try
mar'quis
mar·quise'
mar'riage
mar'riage·a·bil'i·ty
mar'riage·a·ble
mar'ried
mar'ron
mar'row
mar'ry
mar'ry·ing
mar'shal
mar'shal·cy
marsh'i·ness
marsh'mal'low
marsh'y
mar·su'pi·al
mar·su'pi·um
mar'ten
mar'tial
Mar'tian
mar'tin

mar'ti·net'
mar'tin·gale'
mar·ti'ni
mar'tyr
mar'tyr·dom
mar'tyr·ize'
mar'tyr·ol'o·gy
mar'tyr·y
mar'vel
mar'vel·lous
mar'vel·ous
Marx'ism
Marx'ist
mas·ca'ra
mas'cot
mas'cu·line
mas'cu·lin'i·ty
mas'cu·lin·ize'
ma'ser
mash'er
mash'ie
mash'y
mas'jid
mask'er
mask'ing
mas'och·ism
mas'och·ist
mas'och·is'tic
ma'son
ma·son'ic
ma'son·ite'
ma'son·ry
mas'quer·ade'
mas'sa·cre
mas'sa·cred

mas·sage'
mas·sag'er
mas·sag'ing
mas·sé'
mas·se'ter
mas·seur'
mas·seuse'
mas'si·cot'
mas'sif
mas'sive
mas'ta·ba
mas·tec'to·my
mas'ter
mas'ter·ful
mas'ter·li·ness
mas'ter·ly
mas'ter·mind'
mas'ter·piece'
mas'ter·work'
mas'ter·y
mast'head'
mas'tic
mas'ti·cate'
mas'ti·ca'tion
mas'ti·ca'tor
mas'tiff
mas·ti'tis
mas'to·don'
mas'toid
mas'tur·bate'
mas'tur·ba'tion
mas'tur·ba'tor
ma·su'ri·um
mat'a·dor'
match'board'

match′box′
match′less
match′mak′er
match′mak′ing
match′wood′
ma′ter
ma′ter·fa·mil′i·as
ma·te′ri·al
ma·te′ri·al·ism
ma·te′ri·al·ist
ma·te′ri·al·is′tic
ma·te′ri·al′i·ty
ma·te′ri·al·ize′
ma·te′ri·al·ly
ma·te′ri·el′
ma·ter′nal
ma·ter′ni·ty
mate′y
math′e·mat′i·cal
math′e·mat′i·cal·ly
math′e·ma·ti′cian
math′e·mat′ics
mat′in
mat′i·nee′
mat′ing
ma′tri·arch′
ma′tri·ar′chal
ma′tri·arch′y
ma′tri·cide′
ma·tric′u·lant
ma·tric′u·late′
ma·tric′u·la′tion
ma′tri·lin′e·al
mat′ri·mo′ni·al
mat′ri·mo′ny

ma′trix
ma′tron
ma′tron·li·ness
ma′tron·ly
mat′ted
mat′ter
mat′ting
mat′tock
mat′tress
mat′u·rate′
mat′u·ra′tion
ma·ture′
ma·tured′
ma·tu′ri·ty
ma·tu′ti·nal
matz′oth
maud′lin
maul′er
maul′stick′
maun′der
Maun′dy
mau′ser
mau·so·le′um
mav′er·ick
maw′kish
max·il′la
max·il′lar·y
max′im
max′i·mal
max′im·ite′
max′i·mize′
max′i·mum
Ma′yan
may′be
may′hem

may′on·naise′
may′or
may′or·al·ty
ma′zer
ma·zur′ka
ma′zy
maz′zard
maz′el tov′
mead′ow
mea′ger
mea′ger·ly
meal′i·ness
meal′time′
meal′y
me·an′der
me·an′dered
mean′ing
mean′ing·ful
mean′time′
mea′sles
mea′sly
meas·ur·a·bil′i·ty
meas·ur·a·ble
meas′ure
meas·ure·ment
meat′y
me·chan′ic
me·chan′i·cal·ly
mech′a·nism
mech′a·nis′tic
mech′a·ni·za′tion
mech′a·nize
med′al
me·dal′lion
med′dle

med'dler
me'di·a
me'di·an
me'di·ate'
me'di·a'tion
me'di·a'tor
med'ic
med'i·cal
med'i·cal·ly
me·dic'a·ment
med'i·cate'
med'i·cat'ing
med'i·ca'tion
me·dic'i·nal
me·di'e·val
me·di'e·val·ism
me'di·o'cre
me'di·oc'ri·ty
med'i·tate'
med'i·ta'tion
med'i·ta'tive
med'i·ta'tor
Med'i·ter·ra'ne·an
me'di·um
med'lar
med'ley
me·dul'la
me·dul'la
   ob'lon·ga'ta
me·du'sa
meer'schaum
meet'ing
meet'ing·house'
meg'a·cy'cle
meg'a·lith'

meg'a·lo·car'di·a
meg'a·lo·ma'ni·a
meg'a·phone'
meg'a·ton'
me'grim
mei·o'sis
mei·ot'ic
mel'an·cho'li·a
mel'an·chol'ic
mel'an·chol'y
mé'lange'
mel'a·nin
mel'a·no'ma
me·lee', me'lee
mel'ic
mel'io·rate'
mel'io·ra'tion
mel'io·ra'tive
mel'io·rism
mel·lif'lu·ence
mel·lif'lu·ent
mel·lif'lu·ous
mel'low
me·lo'de·on
me·lo'di·a
me·lod'ic
me·lod'i·cal·ly
me·lo'di·ous
mel'o·dra'ma
mel'o·dra·mat'ic
mel'o·dy
mel'on
melt'age
melt'ing
mel'ton

mem'ber
mem'ber·ship'
mem'brane
mem'bra·nous
me·men'to
mem'oir
mem'o·ra·bil'i·a
mem'o·ra·ble
mem·o·ran'dum
me·mo'ri·al
mem'o·ri·za'tion
mem'o·rize'
mem'o·ry
men'ace
men'ac·ing
mé·nage'
me·nag'er·ie
men·da'cious
men·dac'i·ty
men·de·le'vi·um
Men·de'li·an
men'di·can·cy
men'di·cant
men'hir
me'ni·al
me·nin'ges
men'in·gi'tis
me·nin'go·coc'cus
me·nis'cus
me·nol'o·gy
men'o·pause'
men'or·rha'gi·a
men'sal
men'ses
men'stru·al

men'stru·ate'
men'stru·a'tion
men'sur·a·bil'i·ty
men'sur·a·ble
men'su·ra'tion
men'tal
men·tal'i·ty
men'tal·ly
men'thol
men'tho·lat'ed
men'tion
men'tioned
men'tor
Me'phis·to·phe·li'an
me·phi'tis
mer'can·tile
mer'can·til·ism
mer'ce·nar'y
mer'cer·ize'
mer'chan·dise'
mer'chant
mer'ci·ful
mer'ci·less
mer·cu'ri·al
mer·cu'ric
mer·cu'ro·chrome'
mer'cu·ry
mer'cy
mere'ly
mer'e·tri'cious
mer'ger
me·rid'i·an
me·rid'i·o·nal
me·ringue'
me·ri'no

mer'it
mer'it·ed
mer'i·to'ri·ous
mer'lin
mer'maid'
mer'man'
mer'o·blas'tic
mer'ri·ly
mer'ri·ment
mer'ry
mer'ry·mak'er
mer·thi'o·late'
me'sa
mes·cal'
mes'ca·line'
mes·dames'
mes·de·moi·selles'
mes'en·ceph'a·lon'
mes'en·ter'y
mesh'ing
mesh'work'
me'si·al
mes'mer·ism
mer'mer·ize'
mes'o·ce·phal'ic
mes'o·ceph'a·lon
mes'o·mor'phic
mes'on
mes'o·tron'
mes·quite',
   mes'quite
mes'sage
mes'sa·line'
mes'sen·ger
Mes·si'ah

mes·si·an'ic
mes·sieurs'
mess'i·ness
mess'y
mes·ti'zo
met'a·bol'ic
me·tab'o·lism
met'a·car'pus
met'al
me'tal·ing
me·tal'lic
met'al·lur'gi·cal
met'al·lur'gist
met'al·lur'gy
met'al·work'ing
met'a·mor'phic
met'a·mor'phism
met'a·mor'phose'
met'a·mor·pho'sis
met'a·phor
met'a·phor'i·cal
met'a·phys'i·cal
met'a·phy·si'cian
met'a·phys'ics
met'a·tar'sal
met'a·tar'sus
me·tath'e·sis
met'a·zo'an
met'ed
met'em·pir'ics
met'em·psy·cho'sis
me'te·or
me'te·or'ic
me'te·or·ite'
me'te·or·oid'

me·te·or·o·log′i·cal
me′te·or·ol′o·gist
me′te·or·ol′o·gy
me′ter
me′ter·age
meth′a·don′
meth′ane
meth′a·nol′
me·thi′o·nine′
meth′od
me·thod′i·cal
Meth′od·ism
Meth′od·ist
meth′od·ize′
meth′od·ol′o·gy
Me·thu′se·lah
meth′yl
meth′yl·ene
me·tic′u·lous
mé·tier′
met′o·nym
met′o·nym′ic
me·ton′y·my
met′ra·zol′
me′tre
met′ric
met′ri·cal·ly
me·tri′cian
met′rics
me·trol′o·gy
met′ro·nome′
me·tro·nym′ic
me·trop′o·lis
met′ro·pol′i·tan
met′tle

met′tle·some
Mex′i·can
mez′za·nine′
mez′zo
mez′zo·tint′
mi·as′ma
mi·as′mal
mi′ca
mick′ey
mi′cra
mi′crobe
mi·cro′bi·al
mi·cro′bic
mi′cro·bi·ol′o·gy
mi′cro·ceph′a·lous
mi′cro·ceph′a·ly
mi′cro·cosm
mi′cro·cos′mic
mi′cro·cyte′
mi′cro·far′ad
mi′cro·film′
mi·crog′ra·phy
mi·crom′e·ter
mi′cron
mi′cro·or′gan·ism
mi′cro·phone′
mi′cro·phyte′
mi′cro·scope′
mi′cro·scop′ic
mi·cros′co·py
mi′cro·some′
mi·crot′o·my
mi′cro·wave′
mic′tu·rate′
mic′tu·ri′tion

mid′brain′
mid′con′ti·nent
mid′day′
mid′den
mid′dle
mid′dle·man′
mid′dle·weight′
mid′dling
mid′dy
midg′et
mid′i′ron
mid′land
mid′most′
mid′night′
mid′riff
mid′ship′
mid′stream′
mid′sum′mer
mid′term′
mid′way′
mid′wife′
mid′wife′ry
mid′year′
might′i·ly
might′i·ness
might′y
mi′gnon
mi′gnon·ette′
mi′graine
mi′grant
mi′grate
mi·gra′tion
mi′gra·to′ry
mi·ka′do
mil′age

mil'dew'
mild'ly
mild'ness
mile'age
mile'stone'
mil'i·a'ri·a
mil'i·ar'y
mi·lieu'
mil'i·tan·cy
mil'i·tant
mil'i·tar'i·ly
mil'i·tar·ism
mil'i·tar·ist
mil'i·ta·ris'tic
mil'i·ta·ri·za'tion
mil'i·tar·ize'
mil'i·tar'y
mil'i·tate'
mi·li'tia
mil'i·um
milk'er
milk'i·ness
milk'ing
milk'maid'
milk'man'
milk'weed'
milk'y
mill'board'
mil'le·nar'i·an
mil'le·nar'y
mil·len'ni·al
mil·len'ni·um
mil'le·pede'
mill'er
mil·les'i·mal

mil'let
mil'li·bar'
mil'li·far'ad
mil'li·gram'
mil'li·li'ter
mil'li·me'ter
mil'li·mi'cron
mill'ine'
mill'i·ner
mill'i·ner'y
mill'ing
mil'lion
mil'lion·aire'
mil'lionth
mill'race'
mill'run'
mill'stone'
mill'stream'
milque'toast'
milt'er
Mil·ton'ic
mim'e·o·graph'
mi·me'sis
mi·met'ic
mim'ic
mim'ic·ry
mi·mo'sa
mi'na
min'a·ret'
min'a·to'ry
mince'meat'
minc'ing
mind'ed
mind'ful
mind'less

min'er
min'er·al
min'er·al·ize'
min'er·al·iz'er
min'er·a·log'i·cal
min'er·al·o·gist
min'er·al·o·gy
mi'ne·stro'ne
min'gle
min'gling
min'i·a·ture
min'i·a·tur·ize'
min'im
min'i·mal
min'i·mi·za'tion
min'i·mize'
min'i·miz'er
min'i·mum
min'ing
min'ion
min'i·skirt'
min'is·ter
min'is·te'ri·al
min'is·trant
min'is·tra'tion
min'is·try
min'i·track'
min'i·ver
min'ne·sing'er
min'now
mi'nor
mi·nor'i·ty
min'o·taur'
min'ster
min'strel

min'strel·sy
mint'age
min'u·end'
min'u·et'
mi'nus
mi·nus'cule
min'ute,
    mi·nute'
min·ute'ly
min'ute·man'
mi·nute'ness
mi·nu'ti·ae'
mi·o'sis
mi·ot'ic
mir'a·cle
mi·rac'u·lous
mi·rage'
mir'ror
mir'rored
mirth'ful
mirth'less
mir'y
mis'ad·ven'ture
mis·al·li'ance
mis'an·thrope'
mis'an·throp'ic
mis·an'thro·py
mis'ap·pre·hend'
mis'ap·pre·hen'sion
mis'ap·pro'pri·a'tion
mis·be·got'ten
mis·be·hav'ior
mis·cal·cu·la'tion
mis·car'riage
mis·car'ry

mis'ce·ge·na'tion
mis·cel·la'ne·ous
mis·cel·la'ny
mis·chance'
mis·chief
mis·chie·vous
mis·ci·ble
mis·con·cep'tion
mis·con'duct,
    mis'con·duct'
mis·con·strue'
mis·cre·ance
mis·cre·ant
mis·de·mean'or
mis·di·rect'
mi'ser
mis'er·a·ble
mi'ser·ly
mis'er·y
mis·fea'sance
mis·fea'sor
mis'fit'
mis·for'tune
mis·giv'ing
mis·guid'ed
mis·han'dle
mis'hap'
mish'mash'
mis·in·formed'
mis·in·for·ma'tion
mis·in·ter'pret
mis·lay'
mis·lead'ing
mis·man'age
mis·match'

mis·no'mer
mi·sog'y·nist
mi·sog'y·ny
mi·sol'o·gy
mis·place'
mis·plead'ing
mis·print',
    mis'print
mis·pri'sion
mis·prize'
mis'pro·nounce'
mis'pro·nun·ci·
    a'tion
mis·quote'
mis·read'
mis·read'ing
mis'rep·re·sent'
mis'rep·re·sen·
    ta'tion
mis·rule'
mis'sal
mis·shap'en
mis'sile
miss'ing
mis'sion
mis'sion·ar'y
Mis'sis·sip'pi·an
mis'sive
Mis·sour'i·an
mis·spell'
mis·spelled'
mis·step'
miss'y
mis·tak'a·ble
mis·take'

mis·tak'en
mis·tak'en·ly
mis'ter
mis'ti·ness
mis'tle·toe'
mis·took'
mis'tral
mis·trans·la'tion
mis·treat'
mis'tress
mis·tri'al
mis·trust'
mis·trust'ful
mist'y
mis'un·der·stand'
mis'un·der·stood'
mis·use'
mi'ter
mit'i·gate'
mit'i·ga'tion
mit'i·ga'tive
mit'i·ga'tor
mi'tis
mi·to'sis
mi·tot'ic
mi'tre
mit'ten
mit'ti·mus
mitz'vah
mix'er
mix'ture
miz'zen
mne·mon'ics
mob'cap'
mo'bile

mo·bil'i·ty
mo·bil·i·za'tion
mo'bil·ize'
mob'ster
moc'ca·sin
mo'cha
mock'er·y
mock'ing·bird'
mod'al
mo·dal'i·ty
mod'el
mod'el·er
mod'el·ing
mod'el·ler
mod'el·ling
mod'er·ate,
   mod'er·ate'
mod'er·a'tion
mod'e·ra'to
mod'er·a'tor
mod'ern
mod'ern·ism
mod'ern·ist
mo·der'ni·ty
mod'ern·ize'
mod'est
mod'es·ty
mod'i·cum
mod'i·fi'a·ble
mod'i·fi·ca'tion
mod'i·fi'er
mod'i·fy'
mo·di'o·lus
mod'ish
mo·diste'

mod'u·lar
mod'u·late'
mod'u·la'tion
mod'u·la'tor
mod'ule
mod'u·lus
mo'dus o·pe·ran'di
mo'dus vi·ven'di
mo·fette'
mo'gul
mo'hair
Mo·ham'med
moi'e·ty
moi·ré'
mois'ten
mois'tened
mois'ture
mo'lal
mo'lar
mo·las'ses
mold'board'
mold'er
mold'i·ness
mold'ing
mold'y
mo·lec'u·lar
mol'e·cule'
mole'hill'
mole'skin'
mo·lest'
mo'les·ta'tion
mol·les'cent
mol'li·fi·ca'tion
mol'li·fi'er
mol'li·fy'

mol'lusk
mol'ly
mol'ly·cod'dle
mo'loch
mo'lo·tov
mol'ten
mo'ly
mo'ment
mo'men·tar'i·ly
mo'men·tar'i·ness
mo'men·tar'y
mo·men'tous
mo·men'tum
mon'ad
mon'ad·ism
mo·nad'nock
mo·nan'drous
mo·nan'dry
mo·nan'thous
mon'arch
mo·nar'chal
mo·nar'chic
mon'arch·ist
mon'arch·y
mon'as·te'ri·al
mon'as·ter'y
mon'a·tom'ic
mon·au'ral
Mon'day'
mon'e·tar'y
mon'e·ti·za'tion
mon'e·tize'
mon'ey
mon'ey·bag'
mon'ey·chang'er

mon'eyed
mon'ger
Mon·go'li·an
Mon'gol·ism
mon'goose
mon'grel
mon'ies
mon'i·ker
mon'ism
mo·nis'tic
mo·ni'tion
mon'i·tor
mon'i·to'ry
monk'er·y
monk'key
mon'key·shines'
monk'ish
mon'o·ac'id
mon'o·car'pic
mon'o·chord'
mon'o·chro·mat'ic
mon'o·chrome'
mon'o·cle
mon'o·cli'nal
mon'o·cline'
mo·noc'u·lar
mon'o·cul'ture
mon'o·cyte'
mon'o·dy
mo·nog'a·mous
mo·nog'a·my
mon'o·gen'e·sis
mon'o·gram'
mon'o·graph'
mo·nog'y·ny

mon'o·lith'
mon'o·lith'ic
mon'o·logue'
mon'o·ma'ni·a
mon'o·ma'ni·a·cal
mon'o·met'al·lism
mo·no'mi·al
mon'o·nu'cle·o'sis
mon'o·phon'ic
mo·noph'o·ny
mon'o·plane'
mo·nop'o·list
mo·nop'o·li·za'tion
mo·nop'o·lize'
mo·nop'o·ly
mon'o·rail'
mon'o·syl·lab'ic
mon'o·syl'la·ble
mon'o·the·ism
mon'o·the·is'tic
mon'o·tone'
mo·not'o·nous
mo·not'o·ny
mon'o·type'
mon·ox'ide
mon·sieur'
mon·si'gnor
mon·soon'
mon'ster
mon·stros'i·ty
mon'strous
mon·tage'
Mon·tan'an
mon'te
month'ly

mon'u·ment
mon'u·men'tal
mon'zo·nite'
mood'i·ly
mood'i·ness
mood'y
moon'beam'
moon'light'
moon'light'ing
moon'shine'
moon'shin'er
moon'stone'
moor'age
moor'ing
Moor'ish
mop'ing
mop'ish
mop'pet
mo·raine'
mor'al
mo·rale'
mor'al·ist
mor'al·is'tic
mo·ral'i·ty
mor'al·i·za'tion
mor'al·ly
mo·rass'
mor'a·to'ri·um
mor'a·to'ry
mo'ray
mor'bid
mor·bid'i·ty
mor'dan·cy
mor'dant
mor'dent

more·o'ver
mor'ga·nat'ic
mor'gan·ite'
mor'i·bund
morn'ing
mo'ron
mo·ron'ic
mo·rose'
mor'pheme
mor'phine
mor·pho·gen'e·sis
mor·phol'o·gy
mor·pho'sis
mor'ris
mor'row
mor'sel
mor'tal
mor·tal'i·ty
mor'tal·ly
mor'tar
mor'tar·board'
mort'gage
mort'ga·gee'
mort'ga·gor
mor·ti'cian
mor'ti·fi·ca'tion
mor'ti·fi'er
mor'ti·fy'
mor'tise
mort'main
mor'tu·ar'y
mo·sa'ic
mo·selle'
mo'sey
mos·qui'to

mos'sy
most'ly
mo·tel'
mo·tet'
moth'er
moth'er·hood'
moth'er·land'
moth'er·li·ness
moth'er·ly
mo·tif'
mo'tile
mo·til'i·ty
mo'tion
mo'tion·less
mo'ti·vate'
mo'ti·va'tion
mo'ti·va'tion·al
mo'tive
mot'ley
mo'tor
mo'tor·boat'
mo'tor·cade'
mo'tor·cy'cle
mo'tored
mo'tor·ist
mo'tor·ize'
mot'tled
mot'to
mou·lage'
mou·lin'
moun'tain
moun'te·bank'
mount'ed
mount'ing
mourn'er

mourn'ful
mourn'ing
mous'er
mouse'trap'
mous'ing
mous'y
mouth'ful
mouth'piece'
mouth'y
mou'ton'
mov'a·ble
move'ment
mov'er
mov'ie
mov'ing
mow'er
mow'ing
mox'a
mu'cic
mu'ci·lage
mu'ci·lag'i·nous
mu'cin
muck'er
muck'rake'
muck'rak'er
muck'rak'ing
muck'y
mu·co'sa
mu·cos'i·ty
mu'cous
mu'cus
mud'der
mud'di·ness
mud'dle
mud'dled

mud'dy
mud'guard'
mud'sling'ing
mu·ez'zin
muf'fin
muf'fle
muf'fler
muf'ti
mug'ger
mug'gi·ness
mug'gy
mug'wump'
mu·lat'to
mul'ber·ry
mu'le·teer'
mul'lish
mul'lah
mull'er
mul'let
mul'ley
mul'li·gan
mul'li·ga·taw'ny
mul'lion
mul'lock
mul'ti·far'i·ous
mul'ti·form'
mul'ti·lat'er·al
mul'tip'a·ra
mul'tip'a·rous
mul'ti·ple
mul'ti·plex
mul'ti·pli·cand'
mul'ti·pli·ca'tion
mul'ti·plic'i·ty
mul'ti·pli·er

mul'ti·ply'
mul'ti·tude'
mul'ti·tu·di'nous
mul'ti·va'lence
mum'ble
mum'ble·ty·peg'
mum'bo jum'bo
mum'mer
mum'mer·y
mum'mi·fi·ca'tion
mum'mi·fy'
mum'my
mun'dane
mun'go
mu·nic'i·pal
mu·nic'i·pal'i·ty
mu·nif'i·cence
mu·nif'i·cent
mu'ni·ment
mu·ni'tions
mu'ral
mur'der
mur'der·er
mur'der·ess
mur'der·ous
mu'ri·at'ic
mu'rine
murk'y
mur'mur
mur'rain
mur'rey
mus'ca·dine
mus'ca·rine
mus'cat
mus'ca·tel'

mus'cid
mus'cle
mus'co·va'do
mus'co·vite'
mus'cu·lar
mus'cu·lar'i·ty
mus'cu·la·ture
mu·sette'
mu·se'um
mush'room
mush'y
mu'sic
mu'si·cal
mu'si·cale'
mu·si'cian
mu'si·col'o·gist
mu'si·col'o·gy
mus'ing
mus'keg
mus'ket
mus'ket·eer'
mus'ket·ry
musk'mel'on
musk'rat'
musk'y
mus'sel
mus·tache'
mus·ta'chio
mus'tang
mus'tard

mus'te·line'
mus'ter
mus'ti·ness
mus'ty
mu·ta·bil'i·ty
mu'ta·ble
mu'tant
mu'tate
mu·ta'tion
mu'ti·late'
mu'ti·la'tion
mu'ti·la'tor
mu'ti·neer'
mu'ti·nous
mu'ti·ny
mut'ism
mut'ter
mut'ter·ing
mut'ton
mu'tu·al
mu'tu·al'i·ty
mu'tu·al·ism
muz'zle
my·as·the'ni·a
my·ce'li·um
my·col'o·gy
my·co'sis
my·cot'ic
my·e·len·ceph'a·lon'
my'e·lin

my'e·li'tis
my'na
my'nah
my'o·car'di·um
my·ol'o·gy
my·o'ma
my·o'pi·a
my'o·sin
my·o'sis
myr'i·ad
myr'me·col'o·gy
Myr'mi·don'
myr'tle
my·self'
mys'ta·gogue'
mys·te'ri·ous
mys'ter·y
mys'tic
mys'ti·cal
mys'ti·cism
mys'ti·fi·ca'tion
mys'ti·fy'
mys·tique'
myth'ic
myth'i·cal
myth'o·log'i·cal
my·thol'o·gize'
my·thol'o·gy
myth'o·ma'ni·a
myth'o·poe'ic

N

na'bob
na·celle'
na'cre
na'cre·ous
nag'ging
nai'ad
nail'brush'
nail'set'
na·ive'
na·ïve'té'
na'ked
nam'a·ble
name'a·ble
name'less
name'sake'
nan·keen'
nan'ny
na'palm
na'per·y
naph'tha
naph'tha·lene'
nap'kin
na·po'le·on
nap'per
nap'py
na·prap'a·thy
nar'ce·ine'
nar·cis'sism
nar·cis'sist
nar·cis·sis'tic
nar'co·lep'sy

nar·co'sis
nar·cot'ic
nar'co·tism
nar'co·tize'
na'res
nar'i·al
nar·rate', nar·rate'
nar·ra'tion
nar'ra·tive
nar'ra·tor
nar'row
nar'thex
nar'whal
nar'y
na'sal
na·sal'i·ty
na'sal·ize'
nas'cen·cy
nas'cent
na'si·al
na'si·on'
nas'tic
nas'ti·ly
nas'ti·ness
na·stur'tium
nas'ty
na'tal
na'tant
na·ta'tion
na·ta·to'ri·um
na'tes

na'tion
na'tion·al
na'tion·al·ism
na'tion·al·ist
na'tion·al·is'tic
na'tion·al'i·ty
na'tion·al·ize'
na'tion·al·ly
na'tive
na'tiv·ism
na·tiv'i·ty
nat'ti·ly
nat'ty
nat'u·ral
nat'u·ral·ism
nat'u·ral·is'tic
nat'u·ral·i·za'tion
nat'u·ral·ize'
nat'u·ral·ly
na'ture
naught'i·ly
naugh'ti·ness
naugh'ty
nau'se·a
nau'se·ate'
nau'seous
nau'ti·cal
nau'ti·lus
na'val
na'vel
nav'i·cert'

184

nav'i·ga·bil'i·ty
nav'i·ga·ble
nav'i·gate'
nav'i·ga'tion
nav'i·ga'tor
na'vy
Naz'a·rene'
Naz'a·rite'
Na'zi
Ne·an'der·thal'
Ne'a·pol'i·tan
near'by'
near'ly
near'sight'ed
neat'herd'
Ne·bras'kan
neb'u·la
neb'u·lar
neb'u·lize'
neb'u·los'i·ty
neb'u·lous
nec'es·sar'i·ly
nec'es·sar'y
ne·ces'si·tate'
ne·ces'si·ty
neck'band'
neck'cloth'
neck'ing
neck'lace
neck'tie'
nec'ro·bi'o·sis
ne·crol'a·try
ne·crol'o·gy
nec'ro·man'cer
nec'ro·man'cy

nec'ro·phil'i·a
nec'ro·pho'bi·a
ne·crop'o·lis
nec'rop·sy
ne·cro'sis
nec'tar
nec'tar·ine'
need'i·ness
nee'dle
need'less
nee'dle·work'
need'y
ne·far'i·ous
ne·gate'
ne·ga'tion
neg'a·tive
neg'a·tiv·ism
neg'a·tiv·is'tic
neg'a·tiv'i·ty
neg·lect'
neg·lect'ed
neg·lect'ful
neg'li·gee'
neg'li·gence
neg'li·gent
neg'li·gi·ble
ne·go'ti·a·bil'i·ty
ne·go'ti·a·ble
ne·go'ti·ate'
ne·go'ti·a'tion
ne·go'ti·a'tor
né'gri·tude'
Ne'gro
ne'groid
ne'gus

neigh'bor
neigh'bor·hood
neigh'bor·li·ness
neigh'bor·ly
nei'ther
nek'ton
nel'son
Nem'bu·tal'
nem'e·sis
Ne'o·cene'
ne'o·class'sic
ne'o·clas·si·cal
ne'o·dym'i·um
ne'o·lith'ic
ne·ol'o·gism
ne·ol'o·gize'
ne'o·my'cin
ne'on
ne'o·phyte'
ne'o·plasm
Ne'o·pla'to·nism
ne'o·prene'
ne'o·ter'ic
Ne'o·zo'ic
Nep'a·lese'
ne·pen'the
neph'ew
ne·phol'o·gy
ne·phral'gi·a
ne·phrid'i·um
neph'rism
ne·phri'tis
ne·phro'sis
nep'o·tism
nep·tu'ni·um

ner'o·li
ner·va'tion
nerve'less
nerv'ine
nerv'ous
nerv'y
nes'ci·ence
nes'ci·ent
nes'tle
nest'ling
neth'er
Neth'er·land'er
neth'er·most'
net'ting
net'tle
net'tled
net'work'
neu'ral
neu·ral'gia
neu·ral'gic
neu·ras·the'ni·a
neu·ri'tis
neu·rog'li·a
neu·ro·log'i·cal
neu·rol'o·gy
neu'ron
neu·ro·pa·thol'o·gy
neu·ro'sis
neu·ro·sur'ger·y
neu·rot'ic
neu'ter
neu'tral
neu'tral·list
neu·tral'i·ty
neu'tral·ize'

neu·tri'no
neu·tro·dyne'
neu'tron
Ne·vad'an
né'vé'
nev'er
nev'er·more'
nev'er·the·less'
ne'vus
new'born'
new'com'er
new'el
new'fan'gled
new'ly
new'ly·wed'
news'boy'
news'cast'
news'cast'er
news'let'ter
news'pa'per
news'print'
news'reel'
news'stand'
news'wor'thy
news'y
New·to'ni·an
nex'us
ni'a·cin
nib'ble
nib'bling
nib'lick
Nic'a·ra'guan
nice'ly
ni'ce·ty
nick'el

nick'el·o'de·on
nick'er
nick'name'
nic'o·tine'
nic'o·tin'ic
nic'ti·tate'
nid'i·fy'
ni'dus
ni·el'lo
nif'ty
nig'gard
nig'gard·li·ness
nig'gard·ly
night'cap'
night'gown'
night'in·gale'
night'ly
night'mare'
night'mar'ish
night'shade'
night'shirt'
night'time'
ni·gres'cence
nig'ri·tude'
ni'hil·ism
ni'hil·ist
ni'hil·is'tic
nim'ble
nim'bus
nin'com·poop'
nine'fold'
nine'pins'
nine'teen'
nine'teenth'
nine'ti·eth

nine'ty
nin'ny
ni·o'bi·um
nip'per
nip'ple
nip'py
nir·va'na
ni·sei'
ni'si
ni'si pri'us
ni'trate
ni·tra'tion
ni'tric
ni'tride
ni'tri·fy'
ni'trite
ni'tro
ni'tro·gen
ni·trog'e·nize'
ni·trog'e·nous
ni'tro·glyc'er·in
ni'trous
nit'wit'
niv'e·ous
no·bel'i·um
no·bil'i·ty
no'ble
no'ble·man
no·blesse'
no'ble·wom'an
no'bly
no'bod·y
no'cent
noc·tam'bu·lism
noc'ti·lu'ca

noc'tu·id
noc·tur'nal
noc'turne
noc'u·ous
nod'al
nod'ding
nod'u·lar
nod'ule
no'dus
no·el'
no·e'sis
no·et'ic
nog'gin
no'how'
noise'less
noise'mak'er
nois'i·ly
noi'some
nois'y
nol'le pros'e·qui'
no'lo con·ten'de·re
no'ma
no'mad
no·mad'ic
no'mad·ism
no'men·cla'tor
no'men·cla'ture
nom'i·nal
nom'i·nal·ism
nom'i·nal·ly
nom'i·nate'
nom'i·na'tion
nom'i·na·tive
nom'i·na'tor
nom'i·nee'

no'mism
no·mol'o·gy
nom'o·thet'ic
non'age
non'a·ge·nar'i·an
non'ag·gres'sion
non'a·gon'
non'cha·lance'
non'cha·lant'
non·com'bat·ant
non'com·mit'tal
non'com·pli'ance
non com'pos
    men'tis
non'con·form'i·ty
non'de·script'
non·en'ti·ty
none'such'
non'ex·ist'ence
no·nil'lion
non'in·ter·ven'tion
non'pa·reil'
non·par'ti·san
non·plus'
non·plused'
non·plussed'
non·prof'it
non pro·se'qui·tur
non're·stric'tive
non'sense
non se'qui·tur
non'stop'
non'sup·port'
noo'dle
noon'day'

noon′time′
no′ri·a
nor′mal
nor′mal·cy
nor·mal′i·ty
nor′mal·ize′
nor′mal·ly
nor′ma·tive
north′bound′
north′east′
north′east′er·ly
north′east′ern
north′er
north′er·ly
north′ern
north′en·er
north′ward
north′west′
north′west′ern
north′west′ward
Nor·we′gian
nose′bleed′
nose′piece′
nos′ing
no·sol′o·gy
nos·tal′gi·a
nos·tal′gic
nos·tol′o·gy
nos′tril
nos′trum
nos′y
no·ta·bil′i·ty
no′ta·ble
no′ta·bly
no′ta·rize′

no′ta·ry
no·ta′tion
no·ta′tion·al
note′book′
not′ed
note′wor′thy
noth′ing
noth′ing·ness
no′tice
no′tice·a·ble
no′ti·fi·ca′tion
no′ti·fi′er
no′ti·fy′
no′tion
no′tion·al
no·to·ri′e·ty
no·to′ri·ous
not′with·stand′ing
nou′gat
nou′me·nal
nou′me·nal·ism
nou′me·non
nour′ish
nour′ish·ment
no′va
no·va′tion
nov′el
nov′el·ette′
nov′el·is′tic
nov′el·i·za′tion
no·vel′la
nov′el·ty
No·vem′ber
no·ve′na
no·ver′cal

nov′ice
no·vi′ti·ate
no′vo·cain′
now′a·days′
no′way′
no′where′
nox′ious
noz′zle
nu′ance
nub′bly
nu′bile
nu·bil′i·ty
nu′bi·lous
nu′cle·ar
nu′cle·ate′
nu′cle·a′tion
nu·cle′ic
nu·cle′o·lus
nu′cle·us
nud′ism
nud′ist
nu′di·ty
nu′ga·to′ry
nug′get
nui′sance
nul′li·fi·ca′tion
nul′li·fy′
nul·lip′a·ra
nul′li·ty
num′ber
num′ber·less
nu′mer·a·ble
nu′mer·al
nu′mer·ate′
nu′mer·a′tion

nu'mer·a'tor
nu·mer'i·cal
nu'mer·ol'o·gy
nu'mer·ous
nu'mis·mat'i·cal
nu'mis·mat'ics
nu·mis'ma·tist
num'skull'
nun'ci·o'
nun'ner·y
nup'tial
nurse'maid'
nus'er·y

nurs'ing
nurs'ling
nur'ture
nu·ta'tion
nut'crack'er
nut'meg
nu'tri·a
nu'tri·ent
nu'tri·ment
nu·tri'tion
nu·tri'tion·al
nu·tri'tious

nu'tri·tive
nut'shell'
nut'ti·ness
nut'ty
nuz'zle
nyc'ti·trop'ic
nyc'to·pho'bi·a
ny'lon
nymph'et
nym'pho·ma'ni·a
nym'pho·ma'ni·ac
nys·tag'mus

O

oaf'ish
oak'en
oa'kum
oar'lock'
oars'man
o·a'sis
oat'en
oat'meal'
ob'bli·ga'to
ob'du·ra·cy
ob'du·rate
o'be·ah
o·be'di·ence
o·be'di·ent
o·bei'sance
ob'e·lisk'
ob'e·lus
o·bese'
o·bes'i·ty
o·bey'
ob·fus'cate
ob'fus·ca'tion
o·bi
o·bit'u·ar'y
ob'ject, ob·ject'
ob·jec'ti·fy'
ob·jec'tion
ob·jec'tion·a·ble
ob·jec'tive
ob'jec·tiv'i·ty
ob'ject·less

ob·jec'tor
ob·jur·gate'
ob'late
ob·la'tion
ob'li·gate'
ob'li·ga'tion
ob·lig'a·tor'y
o·blige'
ob'li·gee'
o·blig'ing
o·blique'
ob·liq'ui·ty
ob·lit'er·ate'
ob·lit'er·a'tion
ob·liv'i·on
ob·liv'i·ous
ob'long
ob'lo·quy
ob·nox'ious
o'boe
o'bo·ist
ob·scene'
ob·scen'i·ty
ob·scur'ant·ism
ob·scure'
ob·scu'ri·ty
ob'se·crate'
ob·se'qui·ous
ob'se·quy
ob·serv'a·ble
ob·serv'ance

ob·serv'ant
ob'ser·va'tion
ob·serv'a·to'ry
ob·serve'
ob·serv'er
ob·sess'
ob·ses'sion
ob·ses'sive
ob·sid'i·an
ob'so·les'cence
ob'so·lete'
ob'sta·cle
ob·stet'ric
ob'ste·tri'cian
ob·stet'rics
ob'sti·na·cy
ob'sti·nate
ob·strep'er·ous
ob·struct'
ob·struc'tion
ob·struc'tion·ist
ob'stru·ent
ob·tain'
ob·tain'a·ble
ob·trude'
ob·trud'ing
ob·tru'sion
ob·tru'sive
ob·tuse'
ob·verse', ob'verse
ob·ver'sion

ob·vert'
ob'vi·ate'
ob'vi·ous
oc'a·ri'na
oc·ca'sion
oc·ca'sion·al
oc·ca'sion·al·ly
oc'ci·dent
oc'ci·den'tal
oc'ci·pi·tal
oc'ci·put'
oc·clude'
oc·clu'sion
oc·cult'
oc·cul·ta'tion
oc·cult'ism
oc'cu·pan·cy
oc'cu·pant
oc'cu·pa'tion·al
oc'cu·py
oc·cur'
oc·cur'rence
o'cean
o'ce·an'ic
o'ce·a·nog'ra·pher
o'ce·a·no·graph'ic
o'ce·a·nog'ra·phy
oc·el'lat'ed
o·cel'lus
o'ce·lot'
o'cher
oc'ta·chord'
oc'tad
oc'ta·gon'
oc·tag'o·nal

oc'ta·he'dron
oc'tam'er·ous
oc'tane
oc'tant
oc'tave
oc·ta'vo
oc·tet'
oc·til'lion
Oc·to'ber
oc'to·dec'i·mo'
oc'to·ge·nar'i·an
oc'to·pus
oc'to·roon'
oc'to·syl·lab'ic
oc'u·lar
oc'u·list
odd'i·ty
o·de'um
o'di·ous
o'di·um
o·dom'e·ter
o'don·tal'gi·a
o'don·tol'o·gy
o'dor
o'dor·if'er·ous
o'dor·less
o'dor·ous
od'ys·sey
Oed'i·pal
Oed'i·pus
oe·nol'o·gy
o'fay'
of'fal
off'beat'
of·fend'

of·fen'sive
of'fer
of'fer·ing
of'fer·to'ry
off'hand'
off'hand'ed
of'fice
of'fice·hold'er
of'fi·cer
of·fi'cial
of·fi'cial·dom
of·fi'cial·ly
of·fi'ci·ate'
of·fic'i·nal
of·fi'cious
of'fing
off'print'
off'set'
off'shoot'
off'shore'
off'spring'
of'ten
oft'en·times
o·gee'
o'give
o'gle
o'gling
o'gre
o'gre·ish
O·hi'o·an
ohm'age
oil'cloth'
oil'er
oil'i·ness
oil'skin'

oil'y
oint'ment
o'kay'
O'kla·ho'man
o'kra
old'ish
old'ster
o'le·a'ceous
o'le·ag'i·nous
o'le·an'der
o'le·fin
o·le'ic
o'le·in
o'le·o·mar'ga·rine
ol·fac'tion
ol·fac'to·ry
ol'i·garch'
ol'i·garch'y
o'li·o'
ol'i·va'ceous
ol'i·var'y
ol'ive
ol'i·vine'
ol'la
O·lym'pic
o·ma'sum
om'ber
om'buds·man
o·me'ga
om'e·let
om'e·lette
o'men
om'i·cron'
om'i·nous
o·mis'sion

o·mit'
om'ni·bus'
om'ni·far'i·ous
om·nif'er·ous
om·nip'o·tence
om·nip'o·tent
om'ni·pres'ent
om·nis'cience
om·nis'cient
om·niv'o·rous
o'nan·ism
o'nan·ist
on·col'o·gy
on'com'ing
on·dom'e·ter
o·nei'ro·crit'ic
o·nei'ro·man'cy
one'ness
on'er·ous
one'self'
on'ion
on'look'er
on'ly
on·o·mat'o·poe'ia
on'rush'
on'shore'
on'slaught'
on·tog'e·ny
on·to·log'i·cal
on·tol'o·gy
o'nus
on'ward
on'yx
oo'dles
oo'long

ooz'ing
oo'zy
o·pac'i·ty
o'pal
o'pal·es'cence
o·paque'
o'pen
o'pen·er
o'pen·hand'ed
o'pen·heart'ed
o'pen·ing
o'pen·ness
o'pen·work'
op'er·a
op'er·a·ble
op'er·ant
op'er·ate'
op'er·at'ic
op'er·a'tion
op'er·a'tion·al
op'er·a·tive
op'er·a'tor
o·per'cu·lum
op'er·et'ta
op'er·ose'
o·phid'i·an
oph'i·ol'o·gy
oph'ite
oph·thal'mic
oph'thal·mol'o·gist
oph'thal·mol'o·gy
oph·thal'mo·scope'
o'pi·ate
o·pine'
o·pin'ion

o·pin'ion·at'ed
o'pi·um
o·pos'sum
op·po'nent
op·por·tune'
op·por·tun'ism
op·por·tun·is'tic
op·por·tun'i·ty
op·pos'a·ble
op·pose'
op·posed'
op'po·site
op·po·si'tion
op·press'
op·pres'sion
op·pres'sive
op·pres'sor
op·pro'bri·ous
op·pro'bri·um
op·pugn'
op·pug'nan·cy
op'so·nin
op'ta·tive
op'tic
op'ti·cal
op·ti'cian
op'tics
op'ti·mism
op'ti·mist
op'ti·mis'ti·cal·ly
op'ti·mize'
op'ti·mum
op'tion
op'tion·al
op·tom'e·ter

op·tom'e·trist
op·tom'e·try
op'u·lence
op'u·lent
o'pus
or'a·cle
o·rac'u·lar
o'ral
o'ral·ly
or'ange
or'ange·ade'
or'ange·ry
or'ange·wood'
o·rang'u·tan'
o'rate, o·rate'
o·ra'tion
or'a·tor
or'a·tor'i·cal
or'a·to'ri·o
or'a·to'ry
or·bic'u·lar
or'bit
or'bit·al
or'chard
or'ches·tra
or'ches·trate'
or'ches·tra'tion
or'chid
or'chis
or·dain'
or·dained'
or·deal'
or'der
or'der·ly
or'di·nal

or'di·nance
or'di·nar'i·ly
or'di·nar'i·ness
or'di·nar'y
or'di·nate'
or'di·na'tion
ord'nance
or'dure
o·rec'tic
o·re'ga·no'
Or'e·go'ni·an
or'gan
or'gan·dy
or·gan'ic
or'gan·ism
or'gan·ist
or'gan·i·za'tion
or'gan·ize'
or'gan·iz'er
or'ga·nol'o·gy
or'ga·non'
or'ga·num
or'gasm
or·gas'mic
or'gi·as'tic
or'gy
o'ri·el
or'i·ent
or'i·en'tal
o'ri·en·tate'
o'ri·en·ta'tion
or'i·fice
or'i·gan
or'i·gin
o·rig'i·nal

o·rig'i·nal'i·ty
o·rig'i·nal·ly
o·rig'i·nate'
o·rig'i·na'tor
o'ri·ole
or'i·son
or'lon
or'lop
or'mo·lu'
or'na·ment
or'na·men·ta'tion
or·nate'
or'ner·y
or·nith'ic
or'ni·tho·log'i·cal
or'ni·thol'o·gy
o·rog'e·ny
o·rog'ra·phy
o·rom'e·ter
or'o·met'ric
o'ro·tund'
or'phan
or'phan·age
or'phic
or'pi·ment
or'rer·y
or'ris·root'
or'tho·chro·mat'ic
or'tho·don'ti·a
or'tho·don'tist
or'tho·dox'
or'tho·dox'y
or'tho·gen'e·sis
or·thog'ra·pher
or'tho·graph'ic

or·thog'ra·phy
or'tho·pe'dic
or'tho·pe'dist
or·thop'ter
or·thop'ter·on'
or'tho·scope'
os'cil·late'
os'cil·la'tion
os'cil·la'tor
os·cil'lo·scope'
os'cine
os'cu·lant
os'cu·lar
os'cu·late'
os'cu·la'tion
o'sier
os'mi·um
os·mo'sis
os'na·burg'
os'prey
os'si·cle
os'si·fi·ca'tion
os'si·fy'
os'su·ar'y
os'te·i'tis
os·ten'si·ble
os·ten'si·bly
os'ten·ta'tion
os'ten·ta'tious
os'te·o·path'
os'te·op'a·thy
os'te·o·plas'ty
os'ti·ar'y
os'ti·ole'
ost'ler

os·to'sis
os'tra·cism
os'tra·cize'
os'trich
o·tal'gi·a
oth'er
oth'er·wise'
oth'er·world'li·ness
oth'er·world'ly
o'ti·ose'
o'ti·os'i·ty
o·ti'tis
o·tol'o·gy
o'to·scope'
ot·ta'va ri'ma
ot'ter
ot'to·man
ou'bli·ette'
oui'ja
our·self'
our·selves'
oust'er
oust'ing
out'age
out·bid'
out'board'
out'break'
out'cast'
out'come'
out'crop'
out'cry'
out·dat'ed
out'door'
out'er
out'field'

out'field'er
out'fit
out'go'ing
out'growth'
out'house'
out'ing
out·land'ish
out'law'
out'let
out'line'
out'look'
out'ly'ing
out·mod'ed
out'post'
out'put'
out'rage'
out·ra'geous
ou'trance'
out·reach'
out'rig'ger
out'right'
out'side'
out·sid'er
out'spo'ken
out'stand'ing
out·strip'
out'ward
ou'zel
o·var'i·an
o'va·ry
o'vate
o·va'tion

ov'en
o'ver
o'ver·a·bun'dance
o'ver·alls'
o'ver·bear'ing
o'ver·bur'dened
o'ver·charge'
o'ver·com'pen·sate'
o'ver·de·vel'oped
o'ver·draft'
o'ver·draught'
o'ver·es'ti·mate'
o'ver·flow'
o'ver·hand'
o'ver·haul'
o'ver·lap'
o'ver·looked'
o'ver·night'
o'ver·pow'er·ing
o'ver·pro·duc'tion
o'ver·reach'
o'ver·ride'
o'ver·see'
o'ver·se'er
o'ver·sight'
o'ver·state'ment
o'vert, o·vert'
o'ver·throw'
o'ver·time'
o'ver·ture
o'ver·weight'
o'ver·whelm'ing

o'ver·wrought'
ov'i·duct'
o'vine
o·vip'a·ra
o·vip'a·rous
o'void
o'vo·vi·vip'a·rous
o'vu·late'
o'vu·la'tion
o'vum
ow'ing
owl'et
own'er
own'er·ship'
ox·al'ic
ox'a·lis
ox'blood'
ox'bow'
ox'en
ox'ford
ox'i·da'tion
ox'ide
ox'i·dize'
ox'tail'
ox'y·gen
ox'y·gen·ate'
ox'y·mo'ron
ox'y·to'cin
oys'ter
o'zone
o·zon'ic
o'zo·nize'

P

pace′mak′er
pace′mak′ing
pac′er
pach′y·derm′
pa·cif′ic
pac′i·fi·ca′tion
pac′i·fi′er
pac′i·fism
pac′i·fist
pac′i·fy′
pack′age
pack′er
pack′et
pack′ing
pack′sad′dle
pack′thread′
pad′ded
pad′dle
pad′dler
pad′dling
pad′dock
pad′dy
pad′lock′
pa′dre
pad′u·a·soy′
pae′an
pa′gan
pa′gan·ism
pag′eant
pag′eant·ry
pag′i·nate′

pag′i·na′tion
pa·go′da
pa·gu′ri·an
pah′la·vi′
pail·lasse′
pail·lette′
pain′ful
pain′kill′er
pain′less
pains′tak′ing
paint′brush′
paint′ed
paint′er
paint′ing
pais′ley
pa·ja′mas
Pa′ki·stan′i
pal′ace
pal′a·din
pa·laes′tra
pal′an·quin′
pal′at·a·ble
pal′a·tal
pal′a·tal·i·za′tion
pal′a·tal·ize′
pal′ate
pa·la′tial
pa·lat′i·nate′
pal′a·tine′
pa·lav′er
pa′le·eth·nol′o·gy

pa′le·o·bot′a·ny
pa′le·og′ra·pher
pa′le·og′ra·phy
pa′le·o·lith′ic
pa′le·on·tog′ra·phy
pa′le·on·tol′o·gy
Pa′le·o·zo′ic
pa′le·o·zo′ol·o·gy
Pal′es·tin′i·an
pal′ette
pal′frey
pal′imp·sest′
pal′in·drome′
pal′ing
pal′in·gen′e·sis
pal′i·node′
pal′i·sade′
Pal·la′di·an
pal·la′di·um
pall′bear′er
pal′let
pal′li·ate′
pal′li·a′tive
pal′lid
pal′li·um
pal′lor
pal·ma′ceous
pal′mar
pal′mate
pal·ma′tion
palm′er

196

pal·met'to
palm'is·try
pal·mit'ic
palm'y
pal'o·mi'no
pa·loo'ka
pal'pa·bil'i·ty
pal'pa·ble
pal'pate
pal·pa'tion
pal'pe·bral
pal'pi·tate'
pal'pi·tat'ing
pal'pi·ta'tion
pal'sied
pal'sy
pal'tri·ness
pal'try
pam'pas
pam'pe·an
pam'phlet
pam'phlet·eer'
pan'a·ce'a
pa·nache'
Pan·a·ma'ni·an
pan'cake'
pan'chro·mat'ic
pan'cre·as
pan'cre·at'ic
pan'cre·a·tin
pan'da
pan'dect
pan·dem'ic
pan'de·mo'ni·um
pan'der

pan·der·ing
pan·do'ra
pan·dow'dy
pan·dy
pan'e·gyr'ic
pan'e·gyr'ist
pan'el
pan'el·ing
pab'el·ist
pan'el·ling
pan'e·tel'a
pan·gen'e·sis
pan·han'dle
pan·han'dler
pan'ic
pan'ick·y
pan'nier
pan'o·plied
pan'o·ply
pan'o·ra'ma
pan'o·ram'ic
pan'so·phism
pan'so·phy
pan'sy
pan'ta·loon'
pan'the·ism
pan'the·ist
pan'the·is'tic
pan'the·on
pan'ther
pan'ties
pan'tile'
pan'to·graph'
pan'to·mime'
pan'to·mim'ist

pan'to·scope'
pan'to·then'ic
pan'try
pan'zer
pa'pa
pa'pa·cy
pa·pa'in
pa'pal
pa·pa'ya
pa'per
pa'per·back'
pa'per·weight'
pa·pil'la
pap'il·lar'y
pa·pil·lon'
pap'il·lote'
pa'pist
pa·poose'
pap'pus
pap·ri'ka
pap'ule
pa·py'rus
par'a·ble
pa·rab'o·la
par'a·bol'ic
par'a·bol'i·cal
par'a·chute'
par'a·chut'ist
par'a·clete'
pa·rade'
par'a·digm
par'a·dise'
par'a·dis'i·ac'
par'a·dos'
par'a·dox'

par'a·dox'i·cal
par·af·fin
par'a·gen'e·sis
par'a·gon'
par'a·graph'
par'a·keet'
par·al·lac'tic
par·al·lax'
par·al·lel'
par·al·lel'e·pi'ped
par·al·lel·ism
par·al·lel'o·gram'
pa·ral'o·gize'
pa·ral'y·sis
par'a·lyt'ic
par'a·lyze'
par'a·me'ci·um
par'a·med'ic
pa·ram'e·ter
par'a·mil'i·tar'y
par'a·mount'
par'a·mour'
par'a·noi'a
par'a·noi'ac
par'a·noid'
par'a·pet
par'a·pher·na'li·a
par'a·phrase'
par'a·phras'tic
par'a·ple'gi·a
par'a·pleg'ic
par'a·psy·chol'o·gy
par'a·site'
par'a·sit'ic
par'a·sit'i·cide'

par'a·sit·ism
par'a·sol'
par'a·sym'pa·thet'ic
par'a·syn'the·sis
par'a·tax'is
par'a·troop'er
par'a·vane'
par'boil'
par'buck'le
par'cel
par'ce·ner
par·chee'si
parch'ment
par'don
par'don·a·ble
par'don·er
par'e·gor'ic
pa·ren'chy·ma
par'ent
par'ent·age
pa·ren'tal
per·en'ter·al
pa·ren'the·sis
par'en·thet'i·cal
par'ent·hood'
pa·re'sis
par'es·the'si·a
pa·ret'ic
par ex'cel·lence'
par·fait'
par'get
par·he'li·on
pa·ri'ah
pa·ri'e·tal
par'ing

par'i·pin'nate
par'ish
pa·rish'ion·er
par'i·ty
par'ka
park'ing
park'way'
parl'ance
par'lay
par'ley
par'lia·ment
par'lia·men·tar'i·an
par'lia·men'ta·ry
par'lor
par'lous
par'me·san
pa·ro'chi·al
pa·ro'chi·al·ism
par'o·dy
pa·role'
pa·rol·ee'
par'o·no·ma'si·a
pa·rot'id
par'o·ti'tis
par·ox·ysm
par·ox·ys'mal
par·quet'
par'quet·ry
par'ri·cid'al
par'ri·cide'
par'rot
par'ry
par'ry·ing
par'sec'
par'si·mo'ni·ous

par'si·mo'ny
pars'ley
pars'nip
par'son
par'son·age
par·take'
part'ed
par·terre'
par'the·no·gen'e·sis
par'tial
par'ti·al'i·ty
par'tial·ly
par·tic'i·pance
par·tic'i·pant
par·tic'i·pate'
par·tic'i·pa'tion
par'ti·cip'i·al
par'ti·ci·ple
par'ti·cle
par·tic'u·lar
par·tic'u·lar'i·ty
par·tic'u·lar·ize'
par·tic'u·lar·ly
part'ing
par'ti·san
par'ti·san·ship'
par'tite
par·ti'tion
par'ti·tive
part'ly
part'ner
part'ner·ship'
par·took'
par'tridge
par·tu'ri·ent

par'tu·ri'tion
par'ty
pa·rure'
par·ve·nu'
par'vis
pas'chal
pa'sha
pas·quin·ade'
pass'a·ble
pass'a·bly
pass'a·cagl'ia
pas'sage
pas'sant
pass'book'
pas·sé'
pas'sen·ger
pas'ser·ine'
pass'ing
pas'sion
pas'sion·ate
pas'sion·less
pas'sive
pas·siv'i·ty
pass'key'
Pass'o'ver
pass'port'
pass'word'
pas'ta
paste'board'
pas·tel'
pas'tern
pas'teur·i·za'tion
pas'teur·ize'
pas·tiche'
pas·tille'

pas'time
past'i·ness
pas'tor
pas'to·ral
pas'to·ra'le
pas'to·ral·ist
pas'tor·ate
pas·tra'mi
pas'try
pas'tur·a·ble
pas'tur·age
pas'ture
past'y
patch'i·ness
patch·ou'li
patch'work'
patch'y
pa·tel'la
pa·tel'lar
pat'en
pa'ten·cy
pat'ent
pat'ent·ee'
pa'tent·ly
pat'en·tor
pa'ter
pa'ter·fa·mil'i·as
pa·ter'nal
pa·ter'nal·ism
pa·ter'nal·is'tic
pa·ter'ni·ty
pa·ter'nos'ter
pa·thet'ic
path'find'er
path'less

path'o·gen'e·sis
path'o·ge·net'ic
path'o·log'i·cal
pa·thol'o·gist
pa·thol'o·gy
pa'thos
path'way'
pa'tience
pa'tient
pat'i·na
pa'ti·o'
pa'tri·arch'
pa'tri·ar'chal
pa'tri·ar'chy
pa·tri'cian
pat'ri·ci'dal
pat'ri·cide'
pa'tri·lin'e·al
pat'ri·mo'ny
pa'tri·ot
pa'tri·ot'ic
pa'tri·ot·ism
pa·tris'tic
pa·trol'
pa·trol'man
pa'tron
pa'tron·age
pa'tron·al
pa'tron·ess
pa'tron·ize'
pat'ro·nym'ic
pa·troon'
pat'ten
pat'ter
pat'tern

pat'terned
pat'tern·mak'er
pat'ty
pau'ci·ty
Paul'ine
paunch'y
pau'per
pau'per·ize'
pav'an
pave'ment
pav'er
pa·vil'ion
pav'ing
pawn'bro'ker
pawn'bro'king
pawn'er
pawn'shop'
pay'a·ble
pay·ee'
pay'er
pay'ment
pay·o'la
pay'roll'
peace'a·ble
peace'ful
peace'mak'er
peace'time'
peach'i·ness
peach'y
pea'cock'
pea'fowl'
pea'hen'
peak'ed
pea'nut
pearl'i·ness

pearl'ite
pearl'y
peas'ant
peas'ant·ry
pease'cod'
peat'y
pea'vey
peb'ble
peb'bly
pec'ca·ble
pec'ca·dil'lo
pec'cant
peck'er
peck'ing
pec'tic
pec'tin
pec'ti·na'tion
pec'to·ral
pec'u·late'
pec'u·la'tion
pe·cul'liar
pe·cu'li·ar'i·ty
pe·cu'li·um
pe·cu'ni·ar'y
ped'a·gog'ic
ped'a·gog'i·cal·ly
ped'a·gog·ism
ped'a·gogue'
ped'a·go'gy
ped'al
ped'ant
pe·dan'tic
pe·dan'ti·cal·ly
ped'ant·ry
ped'dle

ped'dler
ped'dling
ped'er·ast'
ped'er·as'ty
ped'es·tal
pe·des'tri·an
pe·des'tri·an·ism
pe'di·at'ric
pe'di·a·tri'cian
pe'di·at'rics
ped'i·cure'
ped'i·form'
ped'i·gree'
ped'i·greed'
ped'i·ment
ped'lar
pe'do·don'ti·a
peel'er
peel'ing
peep'er
peep'hole'
peep'ing
peer'age
peer'less
pee'vish
peg'board'
peign·oir'
pe'jo·ra'tion
pe·jo'ra·tive
Pe'king·ese'
pe'koe
pel'age
pe·lag'ic
pel'i·can
pe·lisse'

pe·lite
pel·la'gra
pel·la'grous
pel'let
pel'li·cle
pel·lu'cid
pe·lo'ta
pelt'ing
pelt'ry
pel'vic
pel'vis
pem'mi·can
pe'nal
pe'nal·i·za'tion
pe'nal·ize'
pen'al·ty
pen'ance
pe·na'tes
pen'chant
pen'cil
pend'ant
pend'en·cy
pend'ent
pend'ing
pen'du·lous
pen·du·lum
pen'e·tra·bil'i·ty
pen'e·tra·ble
pen'e·tra'li·a
pen'e·trate'
pen'e·tra'tion
pen'guin
pen'i·cil'lin
pen·in'su·la
pen·in'su·lar

pe'nis
pen'i·tence
pen'i·tent
pen'i·ten'tial
pen'i·ten'tia·ry
pen'knife'
pen'man·ship'
pen'nant
pen'ni·less
pen'non
Penn'syl·va'ni·an
pen'ny
pe·nol'o·gy
pen'sile
pen'sion
pen'sioned
pen'sion·er
pen'sive
pen'stock'
pen'ta·cle
pen'tad
pen'ta·gon'
pen·tag'o·nal
pen·ta·he'dron
pen·tam'e·ter
pen'tane
Pen'ta·teuch'
pen·tath'lon
pen'ta·ton'ic
Pen'te·cost'
Pen'te·cos'tal
pent'house'
pe'nult
pe·nul'ti·mate
pe·num'bra

pe·nu'ri·ous
pen'u·ry
pe'on
pe'on·age
pe'o·ny
peo'ple
peo'pled
pep'lum
pep'per
pep'per·mint'
pep'per·y
pep'py
pep'sin
pep'tic
per·ad·ven'ture
per·am'bu·late'
per·am'bu·la'tion
per·am'bu·la'tor
per an'num
per·cale'
per cap'i·ta
per·ceiv'a·ble
per·ceive'
per·cent'age
per·cen'tile
per·cep'ti·bil'i·ty
per·cep'ti·ble
per·cep'tion
per·cep'tive
per·chance'
Per'che·ron'
per·cip'i·ence
per·cip'i·ent
per'co·late'
per'co·la'tion

per'co·la'tor
per·cus'sion
per di'em
per·di'tion
per'e·gri·na'tion
per'e·gri·na'tor
per'e·grine
per·emp'to·ri·ly
per·emp'to·ry
per·en'ni·al
per'fect, per·fect'
per·fect'i·bil'i·ty
per·fect'i·ble
per·fec'tion
per'fect·ly
per·fid'i·ous·ness
per'fi·dy
per'fo·rate'
per'fo·ra'tion
per'fo·ra'tor
per·force'
per·form'
per·form'ance
per·form'er
per·form'ing
per·fume',
    per'fume
per·fum'er·y
per·func'to·ri·ly
per·func'to·ry
per·haps'
per'i·car'di·ac'
per'i·car·di'tis
per'i·car'di·um
per'i·ge'al

per'i·gee'
per'i·he'li·on
per'il
per'il·ous
pe·rim'e·ter
per'i·met'ric
per'i·ne'um
pe'ri·od
pe'ri·od'ic
pe'ri·od'i·cal
pe'ri·o·dic'i·ty
per'i·os'te·al
per'i·os'te·um
per'i·pa·tet'ic
pe·riph'er·al
pe·riph'er·y
per'i·phrase'
pe·riph'ra·sis
per'i·phras'tic
per'i·scope'
per'i·scop'ic
per'ish
per'ish·a·ble
per'i·stal'sis
per'i·stal'tic
per'i·style'
per'i·to·ne'al
per'i·to·ne'um
per'i·to·ni'tis
per'i·wig'
per'i·win·kle
per'jure
per'jured
per'ju·ry
perk'i·ness

perk'y
per'ma·nence
per'ma·nent
per'ma·nent·ly
per·man'ga·nate'
per·me·a·bil'i·ty
per·me·a·ble
per·me·ate'
per·me·a'tion
per·me·a'tive
per·mis'si·ble
per·mis'sion
per·mis'sive
per·mit, per·mit'
per·mit'ted
per·mu·ta'tion
per·ni'cious
per·o·ra'tion
per·ox'ide
per·pen·dic'u·lar
per'pe·trate'
per'pe·trat'ing
per'pe·tra'tion
per'pe·tra'tor
per·pet'u·al
per·pet'u·ate'
per·pet'u·a'tion
per'pe·tu'i·ty
per·plex'
per·plex'ing
per·plex'i·ty
per'qui·site
per'se·cute'
per'se·cu'tion
per'se·cu'tor

per'se·ver'ance
per'se·vere'
per'si·flage'
per·sim'mon
per·sist'
per·sist'ence
per·sist'ent
per'son
per·so'na
per'son·a·ble
per'son·age
per'son·al
per'son·al'i·ty
per'son·al·ize'
per'son·al·ly
per·so'na non
   gra'ta
per'son·ate'
per'son·a'tion
per·son'i·fi·ca'tion
per·son'i·fy'
per'son·nel'
per·spec'tive
per'spi·ca'cious
per'spi·cac'i·ty
per'spi·cu'i·ty
per·spic'u·ous
per'spi·ra'tion
per·spire'
per·suade'
per·suad'er
per·sua'sion
per·sua'sive
per·tain'
per·tain'ing

per'ti·na'cious
per'ti·nac'i·ty
per'ti·nence
per'ti·nent
per·turb'
per·tur·ba'tion
per·tus'sis
pe·rus'al
pe·ruse'
per·vade'
per·vad'ing
per·va'sion
per·va'sive
per·verse'
per·ver'sion
per·ver'si·ty
per·vert', per'vert
per·vert'ed
per'vi·ous
pes'ky
pes'sar·y
pes'si·mism
pes'si·mist
pes'si·mis'tic
pes'ter
pes'ti·cide'
pes'ti·lence
pes'ti·lent
pes'ti·len'tial
pes'tle
pet'al
pe·tard'
pe'ter
pe·tite'
pe·ti'tion

pe·ti'tion·er
pet'it point
pe'tits fours
Pe·trar'chan
pet'rel
pet'ri·fac'tion
pet'ri·fy'
pe·trog'ra·phy
pet'rol
pe·tro'le·um
pe·trol'o·gy
pet'rous
pet'ti·coat'
pet'ti·fog'
pet'ti·fog'ger
pet'ti·ly
pet'ti·ness
pet'ty
pet'u·lance
pet'u·lant
pe·tu'ni·a
pe'wee
pew'ter
pha'e·ton
phag'o·cyte'
pha·lan'ger
pha·lan'ges
pha'lanx
phal'lic
phal'lus
phan'tasm
phan·tas'ma·go'ri·a
phan·tas'ma·gor'ic
phan'tom
Phar'aoh

phar'ma·ceu'ti·cal
phar'ma·ceu'tics
phar'ma·cist
phar'ma·co·log'i·
   cal
phar'ma·col'o·gist
phar'ma·col'o·gy
phar'ma·cy
pha·ryn'ge·al
phar'yn·gi'tis
phar'ynx
phas'ing
pheas'ant
phe'no·bar'bi·tal'
phe'nol
phe·nom'e·nal
phe·nom'e·non'
phi'al
Phi Be'ta Kap'pa
phi·lan'der
phi·lan'der·er
phi·lan'der·ing
phil'an·throp'ic
phi·lan'thro·pist
phi·lan'thro·py
phil'a·tel'ic
phi·lat'e·list
phi·lat'e·ly
phil'har·mon'ic
Phi'lis·tine'
phil'o·den'dron
phi·log'y·nist
phi·log'y·ny
phi·lol'o·gist
phi·lol'o·gy

phi·los'o·pher
phil'o·soph'ic
phi·los'o·phize'
phi·los'o·phy
phil'tre
phle·bi'tis
phleg·mat'ic
phlo·gis'ton
pho'bi·a
pho'bic
phoe'be
phoe'nix
pho'neme
pho·ne'mic
pho·net'ic
pho·net'i·cal·ly
pho·net'ics
phon'ic
pho'no·graph'
pho·nog'ra·phy
pho'no·log'i·cal
pho·nol'o·gy
pho'ny
phos'gene
phos'phate
phos'phene
phos'phide
phos'phor
phos'pho·res'cence
phos'pho·res'cent
phos'pho·rous
phos'pho·rus
pho'tic
pho'to·chem'is·try
pho'to·dy·nam'ics

pho'to·e·lec'tric
pho'to·en·grav'ing
pho'to·flash'
pho'to·gen'ic
pho'to·graph'
pho·tog'ra·pher
pho·tog'ra·phy
pho'to·gra·vure'
pho·tom'e·ter
pho'ton
pho'to·play'
pho'to·syn'the·sis
pho'to·syn·thet'ic
pho'to·trop'ic
pho·tot'ro·pism
phras'al
phra'se·ol'o·gy
phras'ing
phra'try
phre·net'ic
phre·nol'o·gist
phre·nol'o·gy
phthal'ic
phthi'sis
phy·lac'ter·y
phy·lax'is
phy·log'e·ny
phy'lum
phys'ic
phys'i·cal
phys'i·cal·ly
phy·si'cian
phys'i·cist
phys'ics
phys'i·og'no·my

phys'i·ol'o·gist
phys'i·ol'o·gy
phy·sique'
piaf'fer
pi'a ma'ter
pi·an'ist, pi'an·ist
pi·an'o
pi·an'o·for'te
pi·as'ter
pi·az'za
pi'ca
pic'a·dor'
pic'a·resque'
pic'a·yune'
pic'ca·lil'li
pic'co·lo'
pick'ax'
pick'er
pick'er·el
pick'et
pick'ing
pick'le
pick'led
pick'up'
pic'nic
pic'nick·ing
pic'to·graph'
pic·tog'ra·phy
pic·to'ri·al
pic'ture
pic'tur·esque'
pidg'in
pie'bald'
piece'meal'
piec'er

piece'work'
pierc'ing
pi'e·tism
pi'e·ty
pi'e·zom'e·try
pif'fle
pi'geon
pi'geon·hole'
pig'gish
pig'gy·back'
pig'head'ed
pig'ment
pig'men·ta'tion
pig'men·ted
pig'nus
pig'skin'
pik'er
pi·las'ter
pil'fer
pil'fer·age
pil'grim
pil'grim·age
pil'ing
pil'lage
pil'lar
pill'box'
pil'lo·ry
pil'low
pil'low·y
pi'lose
pi'lot
pi'lot·age
pi'lot·ed
pi'lot·house'
pi·men'to

pi·mien'to
pimp'ing
pim'ple
pim'pled
pim'ply
pin'a·fore'
pin'ball'
pin'cers
pin'cush'ion
pin'e·al
pine'ap'ple
pin'er·y
pine'sap'
pin'guid
pin'ion
pink'ing
pink'y
pin'nace
pin'na·cle
pin'nate
pin·na'tion
pi'noch'le
pi'noc'le
pin'tle
pin'to
pin'wheel'
pin'y
pi'o·neer'
pi'ous
pip'age
pipe'ful
pip'er
pipe'stem'
pi·pette'
pip'ing

pip'pin
pi'quan·cy
pi'quant
pi'ra·cy
pi·ra'nha
pi'rate
pi·rat'i·cal
pi·rogue'
pir'ou·ette'
pis'ca·ry
pis'ca·to'ri·al
pis'ci·cul'ture
pis'cine
pis'mire'
pis·ta'chi·o'
pis'til
pis'tol
pis'ton
pi'ta
pitch'blende'
pitch'er
pitch'fork'
pit'e·ous
pit'fall'
pith'i·ness
pith'y
pit'i·a·ble
pit'i·ful
pi'ti·less
pit'tance
pit'ted
pi·tu'i·tar'y
pit'y
piv'ot
piv'ot·al

pix'i·lat'ed
piz'za
piz'ze·ri'a
piz'zi·ca'to
pla'ca·ble
plac'ard
pla'cate
pla'cat·ing
pla·ce'bo
place'ment
pla·cen'ta
pla·cen'tal
plac'er
plac'id
plac'ing
plack'et
pla'gal
pla'gi·a·rism
pla'gi·a·rist
pla'gi·a·rize'
pla'guy
plains'man
plain'tiff
plait'ed
plan'er
plan'et
plan'e·tar'i·um
plan'e·tar'y
plan'gent
pla·nim'e·try
plan'i·sphere'
plank'ing
plank'ton
plan'tain
plan'tar

plan·ta'tion
plant'er
plas'ma
plas·mat'ic
plas'ter
plas'tered
plas'ter·ing
plas'tic
plas'ti·cal·ly
pla·teau'
plat'ed
plate'ful
plate'let
plat'en
plat'form'
plat'ing
plat'i·noid'
plat'i·num
plat'i·tude'
plat'i·tu'di·nous
Pla·ton'ic
Pla'ton·ism
pla·toon'
plat'ter
plau'dit
plau·si·bil'i·ty
plau'si·ble
plau'sive
pla'ya
play'back'
play'bill'
play'boy'
play'er
play'ful
play'ground'

play'mate'
play'wright'
pla'za
plead'er
plead'ing
pleas'ance
pleas'ant
pleas'ant·ry
pleas'ing
pleas'ur·a·ble
pleas'ure
ple·be'ian
pleb'i·scite'
plec'trum
pledg'or
Pleis'to·cene'
ple'na·ry
plen'i·po·ten'ti·ar'y
plen'ti·tude'
plen'te·ous
plen'ti·ful
plen'ty
ple'num
pleth'o·ra
pleu'ra
pleu'ri·sy
plex'i·glass'
plex'us
pli'a·ble
pli'an·cy
pli'ant
pli·ca'tion
pli'ers
Pli'o·cene'
plod'der

plod'ding
plo'sive
plot'ter
plot'ting
plov'er
plow'share'
pluck'y
plug'ger
plum'age
plumb'er
plumb'ing
plum'met
plump'er
plum'y
plun'der
plun'der·er
plung'er
plu·per'fect
plu'ral
plu'ral·ism
plu'ral·is'tic
plu·ral'i·ty
plu'ral·ize'
plu·toc'ra·cy
plu'to·crat'
plu·to'ni·um
plu'vi·al
plu'vi·om'e·ter
plu'vi·ous
ply'wood'
pneu'ma
pneu·mat'ic
pneu'mo·coc'cus
pneu·mo'ni·a
poach'er

pock'et
pock'et·book'
pock'et·knife'
pock'mark'
po·des'ta
po·di'a·trist
po·di'a·try
po'di·um
po'em
pop'e·sy
po'et
po'et·as'ter
po·et'ic
po·et'i·cal
po'et·ry
po'go
po·grom'
poign'an·cy
poign'ant
poi'kil·o·ther'mal
poin·set'ti·a
point'ed
point'er
poin'til·lism
point'less
poi'son
poi'son·ous
poke'ber'ry
pok'cr
pok'ey
po'lar
po·lar'i·ty
po'lar·i·za'tion
po'lar·ize'
po'lar·oid'

pole'ax'
pole'cat'
po·lem'i·cal
po·lem'i·cist
po·lem'ics
po·len'ta
po·lice'
po·lice'man
po·lice'wom'an
pol'i·cy
pol'ish
pol'ished
pol'ish·ing
po·lite'
pol'i·tic
po·lit'i·cal
pol'i·ti'cian
po·lit'i·cize'
pol'i·tics
pol'i·ty
pol'ka
pol'lard
pol'len
pol'lex
pol'li·nate'
pol'li·nat'ing
pol'li·na'tion
pol'li·wog'
poll'ster
pol·lute'
pol·lu'tion
pol'o·naise'
po·lo'ni·um
pol·troon'
pol'y·an'drous

pol'y·an'dry
pol'y·eth'yl·ene'
po·lyg'a·mist
po·lyg'a·mous
po·lyg'a·my
pol'y·glot'
pol'y·gon'
po·lyg'o·nal
pol'y·he'dron
pol'y·mer'ic
pol'y·mor'phism
pol'y·mor'phous
pol'y·no'mi·al
pol'yp
pol'y·phon'ic
po·lyph'o·ny
pol'y·syl·lab'ic
pol'y·syl'la·ble
pol'y·tech'nic
pol'y·the'ism
pol'y·u're·thane'
pol'y·vi'nyl
po·made'
pom'e·gran'ate
Pom·er·a'ni·an
pom'mel
pom'pa·dour'
pom·pos'i·ty
pom'pous
pon'cho
pon'der
pon'der·a·ble
pon'der·ous
pon·gee'
pon'iard

pon'tiff
pon·tif'i·cal
pon·tif'i·cate
pon·too
po'ny
po'ny·tail'
poo'dle
pool'room'
poor'house'
poor'ly
pop'corn'
pop'er·y
pop'in·jay'
pop'lar
pop'lin
pop'per
pop'pet
pop'py
pop'u·lace
pop'u·lar
pop'u·lar'i·ty
pop'u·lar'i·za'tion
pop'u·lar·ize'
pop'u·late'
pop'u·la'tion
pop'u·list
pop'u·lous
por'ce·lain
por'cine
por'cu·pine'
por'gy
pork'er
por'no·graph'ic
por·nog'ra·phy
po·ros'i·ty

po'rous
por'phy·ry
por'poise
por'ridge
por'rin·ger
port'a·ble
por'tage
por'tal
port·cul'lis
por·tend'
por·tend'ing
por'tent
por'ter
por'ter·age
por'ter·house'
port·fo'li·o'
port'hole'
por'ti·co'
por'tion
port'li·ness
port'ly
port·man'teau
por'trait
por'trai·ture
por·tray'
por·tray'al
por'tu·lac'a
po·seur'
pos'it
po·si'tion
pos'i·tive
pos'i·tiv·is'tic
pos'i·tron'
pos'se
pos·sess'

pos·ses'sion
pos·ses'sive
pos·ses'sor
pos'set
pos·si·bil'i·ty
pos'si·ble
pos'sum
post'age
post'al
post'date'
post'er
pos·te'ri·or
pos·ter'i·ty
pos'tern
post'grad'u·ate
post'hu·mous
pos·til'ion
pos·til'lion
poist'im·pres'sion·ism
post'li·min'i·um
post'man
post'mark'
post'mas'ter
post'me·rid'i·an
post'op'er·a'tive
post·pone'
post'script'
pos'tu·late'
pos'tu·la'tion
pos'ture
pos'tur·ing
post'war'
po'sy
po'ta·ble
po'tash'

po·tas'si·um
po·ta'tion
po·ta'to
pot'bel'lied
po'ten·cy
po'tent
po'ten·tate'
po·ten'tial
po·ten'ti·al'i·ty
poth'er
pot'hold'er
pot'hole'
po'tion
pot'luck'
pot'pour·ri'
pot'sherd'
pot'tage
pot'ted
pot'ter
pot'ter·y
pou·lard'
poul'ter·er
poul'tice
poul'try
pound'age
pound'cake'
pound'er
pov'er·ty
pow'der
pow'der·y
pow'er
pow'er·ful
pow'er·house'
pow'er·less
pow'wow'

prac'ti·ca·bil'i·ty
prac'ti·ca·ble
prac'ti·cal
prac'ti·cal'i·ty
prac'ti·cal·ly
prac'tice
prac'ticed
prac·ti'tion·er
prae·no'men
prae'tor
prag·mat'ic
prag'ma·tism
prai'rie
praise'wor'thy
pra'line
pranc'ing
pran'di·al
prat'ing
pra·tique'
prat'tle
prax'is
preach'er
preach'ing
preach'y
pre·am'ble
preb'end
pre·car'i·ous
pre·cau'tion
pre·cau'tion·ar'y
pre·cede'
pre·ced'ence
pre·ce'dent,
  pre'ce·dent
pre·ced'ing
pre'cept

pre·cep'tor
pre·ces'sion
pre'cinct
pre·ci'os'i·ty
pre'cious
prec'i·pice
pre·cip'i·tant
pre·cip'i·tate'
pre·cip'i·ta'tion
pre·cip'i·tous
pré'cis
pre·cise'
pre·ci'sion
pre·clude'
pre·clu'sion
pre·clu'sive
pre·co'cious
pre·coc'i·ty
pre'con·ceive'
pre'con·cep'tion
pre·cur'sor
pre·cur'so·ry
pre·da'cious
pred'a·to'ry
pred'e·ces'sor
pre·des'ti·na'tion
pre·des'tine
pre·de'ter·mi·na'tion
pre·de'ter·mine
pred'i·ca·ble
pre·dic'a·ment
pred'i·cate'
pred'i·cat'ed
pred'i·ca'tion
pred'i·ca'tive

pre·dict'
pre·dict'a·ble
pre·dic'tion
pre·dic'tive
pre·dic'tor
pre·di·lec'tion
pre·dis·pose'
pre·dis·po·si'tion
pre·dom'i·nance
pre·dom'i·nant
pre·dom'i·nate'
pre·fab'ri·cate'
pre·fab'ri·ca'tion
pref'ace
pref'a·to'ry
pre'fect
pre·fec'tu·ral
pre·fec·ture
pre·fer'
pref'er·a·bil'i·ty
pref'er·a·ble
pref'er·ence
pref'er·en'tial
pre·fer'ment
pre·fer'ring
pre·fig·u·ra'tion
pre·fig'ure
pre'fix
preg'na·bil'i·ty
preg'na·ble
preg'nan·cy
preg'nant
pre·hen'sile
pre'his·tor'ic
pre'his·tor'i·cal·ly

pre·judge'
prej'u·dice
prej'u·di'cial
prel'ate
pre·lim'i·nar'y
prel'ude
pre'ma·ture'
pre'ma·tur'i·ty
pre·med'i·cal
pre·med'i·tate'
pre·med·i·ta'tion
pre'mier
pre·miere'
prem'ise
pre'mi·um
pre'mo·ni'tion
pre·mon'i·to'ry
pre·na'tal
pre·oc'cu·pa'tion
pre·oc'cu·pied'
pre'or·dain'
pre'or·di·na'tion
pre·paid'
prep'a·ra'tion
pre·par'a·to'ry
pre·pare'
pre·par'ed·ness
pre·pay'
pre·pon'der·ant
pre·pon'der·ate'
prep'o·si'tion
pre·pos·sess'
pre·pos·sess'ing
pre·pos'ter·ous
pre'puce

pre·req'ui·site
pre·rog'a·tive
pres'age
Pres'by·te'ri·an
pre'school'
pre'sci·ence
pre'sci·ent
pre·scribe'
pre·scrip'tion
pre·scrip'tive
pres'ence
pres'ent
pre·sent'a·ble
pres'en·ta'tion
pre·sen'ti·ment
pres'ent·ly
pre·sent'ment
pres'er·va'tion
pre·serv'a·tive
pre·serve'
pres'i·den·cy
pres'i·dent
pres'i·den'tial
pre·sid'i·o'
pre·sid'i·um
press'ing
pres'sor
press'room'
pres'sure
pres'sur·ize'
pres·tige'
pres·ti'gious
pres'to
pre·sum'a·bly
pre·sume'

pre·sump'tion
pre·sump'tive
pre·sump'tu·ous
pre'sup·pose'
pre·tence'
pre·tend'
pre·tend'er
pre·tense'
pre·ten'sion
pret'er·ite
pre'ter·nat'u·ral
pre'text
pre·to'ri·an
pret'ti·ness
pret'ty
pret'zel
pre·vail'
prev'a·lence
prev'a·lent
pre·var'i·cate'
pre·var'i·ca'tor
pre·vent'
pre·vent'a·ble
pre·ven'tion
pre·ven'tive
pre'view'
pre'vi·ous
pre'vi·ous'ly
pre'war'
pri'a·pism
price'less
prick'le
prick'ly
pride'ful
priest'ess

priest'hood
priest'ly
prig'gish
pri'ma·cy
pri'ma don'na
pri'ma fa'ci·e'
pri'mage
pri'mal
pri·ma'ri·ly
pri'ma·ry
pri'mate
prim'er
prim'ing
pri·mip'a·ra
prim'i·tive
pri'mo·gen'i·ture
pri·mor'di·al
prim'rose'
prince'ly
prin'cess
prin'ci·pal
prin'ci·pal'i·ty
prin'ci·pal·ly
prin·cip'i·um
prin'ci·ple
print'a·ble
print'er
print'ing
pri'or
pri'or·ate
pri'or·ess
pri·or'i·ty
pri'or·y
pris·mat'ic
pris'on

pris'on·er
pris'sy
pris·tine'
pri'va·cy
pri'vate
pri'va·teer'
pri·va'tion
priv'a·tive
priv'i·lege
priv'y
prob'a·bil'i·ty
prob'a·ble
pro'bate
pro·ba'tion
pro·ba'tion·ar'y
pro'ba·tive
prob'ing
prob'i·ty
prob'lem
prob'lem·at'ic
pro·bos'cis
pro·caine'
pro·ce'dur·al
pro·ce'dure
pro·ceed'
pro·ceed'ing
proc'ess
pro·ces'sion
pro·ces'sion·al
pro·claim'
proc'la·ma'tion
pro·cliv'i·ty
pro·con'sul
pro·cras'ti·nate'
pro·cras'ti·na'tion

pro'cre·ant
pro·cre·ate'
pro·cre·a'tion
proc·tol'o·gy
proc'tor
pro·cur'a·ble
pro·cur'ance
proc'u·ra'tion
proc'u·ra'tor
pro·cure'
pro·cure'ment
pro·cur'er
prod'i·gal
prod'i·gal'i·ty
pro·di'gious
prod'i·gy
pro·duce'
pro·duc'er
prod'uct
pro·duc'tion
pro·duc'tive
pro'duc·tiv'i·ty
prof'a·na'tion
pro·fane'
pro·fan'i·ty
pro·fess'
pro·fessed'
pro·fes'sion
pro·fes'sion·al·ism
pro·fes'sor
pro·fes·so'ri·al
prof'fer
pro·fi'cien·cy
pro·fi'cient
pro'file

prof'it
prof'it·a·ble
prof'it·eer'
prof'li·gate
pro for'ma
pro·found'
pro·fun'di·ty
pro·fuse'
pro·fu'sion
pro·gen'i·tor
prog'e·ny
pro·ges'ter·one'
prog·no'sis
prog·nos'tic
prog·nos'ti·cate'
prog·nos'ti·ca'tion
pro'gram
pro'gramme
pro'gram·mer
prog'ress
pro·gres'sion
pro·gres'sive
pro·hib'it
pro'hi·bi'tion
pro·hib'i·tive
proj'ect
pro·jec'tile
pro·jec'tion
pro·jec'tion·ist
pro·jec'tor
pro'lan
pro·lapse'
pro'late
pro'le·gom'e·non
pro·lep'sis

pro'le·tar'i·an
pro'le·tar'i·at
pro·lif'er·ate'
pro·lif'er·a'tion
pro·lif'er·ous
pro·lif'ic
pro·lif'i·cal·ly
pro'line
pro·lix'
pro·lix'i·ty
pro'logue
pro·long'
pro'lon·ga'tion
pro·long'ing
prom'e·nade'
pro·me'the·an
pro·me'thi·um
prom'i·nence
prom'i·nent
prom'i·nent·ly
prom'is·cu'i·ty
pro·mis'cu·ous
prom'ise
prom'is·ing
prom'is·so'ry
prom'on·to'ry
pro·mote'
pro·mot'er
pro·mo'tion
pro·mo'tion·al
prompt'er
prompt'ing
promp'ti·tude'
pro·mul'gate
pro'mul·ga'tion

pro·na'tion
pro·na'tor
pro·nom'i·nal
pro'noun
pro·nounce'
pro·nounced'
pro·nounce'ment
pron'to
pro·nun'ci·a'tion
proof'read'
pro'pae·deu'tic
prop'a·gan'da
prop'a·gan'dist
prop'a·gan'dize
prop'a·gate'
prop'a·gat'ing
prop'a·ga'tion
prop'a·ga'tor
pro'pane
pro·pel'
pro·pel'lant
pro·pel'ler
pro·pen'si·ty
prop'er
prop'er·ly
prop'er·tied
prop'er·ty
pro'phase'
proph'e·cy
proph'e·sy'
proph'et
pro·phet'ic
pro'phy·lac'tic
pro'phy·lax'is
pro·pin'qui·ty

pro·pi'ti·ate'
pro·pi'ti·a'tion
pro·pi'tious
pro·po'nent
pro·por'tion
pro·por'tion·al
pro·por'tion·al·ly
pro·por'tion·ate
pro·por'tion·ment
pro·pos'al
pro·pose'
prop'o·si'tion
pro·pound'
pro·pri'e·tar'y
pro·pri'e·tor
pro·pri'e·tress
pro·pri'e·ty
pro·pul'sion
pro·pul'sive
pro ra'ta
pro·rat'a·ble
pro'rate'
pro'ro·ga'tion
pro·rogue'
pro·sa'ic
pro·sa'i·cal·ly
pro·sce'ni·um
pro·scribe'
pro·scrip'tion
pro·scrip'tive
pros'e·cute'
pros'e·cut'ing
pros'e·cu'tion
pros'e·cu'tor
pros'e·lyte'

pros'e·lyt·ize'
pros'i·ness
pro'sit
pro·sod'ic
pros'o·dy
pros'pect
pro·spec'tive
pros'pec·tor
pro·spec'tus
pros'per
pros·per'i·ty
pros·per·ous
pros'tate
pros'the·sis
pros·thet'ic
pros'tho·don'ti·a
pros'ti·tute'
pros'ti·tu'tion
pros'trate
pros'trat·ed
pros·tra'tion
pros'y
pro·tag'o·nist
pro'ta·mine'
pro'te·an
pro·tect'
pro·tec'tion
pro·tec'tion·ism
pro·tec'tive
pro·tec'tor
pro·tec'tor·ate
pro'té·gé'
pro'tein
pro tem'po·re'
pro'te·ol'y·sis

pro·test', pro'test
Prot'es·tant
Prot'es·tant·ism
prot'es·ta'tion
pro'tha·la'mi·on
proth'e·sis
pro'to·col'
pro'ton
pro'to·plasm
pro'to·plas'mic
pro'to·typ'al
pro'to·type'
pro'to·typ'ic
pro'to·zo'an
pro'to·zo'ic
pro·tract'
pro·trac'tile
pro·trac'tion
pro·trac'tor
pro·trude'
pro·trud'ing
pro·tru'sion
pro·tu'ber·ant
prov'a·ble
prov'en
prov'e·nance
prov'en·der
prov'erb
pro·ver'bi·al
pro·vide'
pro·vid'ed
prov'i·dence
prov'i·dent
prov'i·den'tial
prov'ince

pro·vin'cial
pro·vin'cial·ism
pro·vin'ci·al'i·ty
pro·vi'sion
pro·vi'sion·al
pro·vi'so
pro·voc'a·tive
pro·voke'
pro·vok'ing
prov'ost
prow'ess
prowl'er
prox'i·mal
prox'i·mate
prox·im'i·ty
prox'y
pru'dence
pru'dent
pru·den'tial
prud'er·y
prud'ish
pru'ri·ence
pru'ri·ent
prus'sic
pry'ing
psalm'book'
psal'mo·dy
psal'ter
pseu'do
pseu'do·nym'
pseu·don'y·mous
pseu'do·po'di·um
pso·ri'a·sis
pso·ri·at'ic
psy'che

psy'che·del'ic
psy·chi·at'ric
psy·chi'a·trist
psy·chi'a·try
psy'chic
psy'chi·cal
psy'cho·a·nal'y·sis
psy'cho·an'a·lyst
psy'cho·an'a·lyt'ic
psy'cho·an'a·lyze
psy'cho·bi·ol'o·gy
psy'cho·dra'ma
psy'cho·gen'e·sis
psy'cho·log'i·cal
psy·chol'o·gist
psy·chol'o·gize'
psy·chol'o·gy
psy'cho·mo'tor
psy'cho·path'
psy'cho·path'ic
psy'cho·pa·thol'o·gy
psy·cho'sis
psy'cho·so·mat'ic
psy'cho·ther'a·py
psy·chot'ic
pter·i·dol'o·gy
pter'o·dac'tyl
Ptol'e·ma'ic
pto'maine
pu'ber·ty
pu'bes
pu·bes'cence
pu·bes'cent
pub'ic
pu'bis

pub'lic
pub'li·can
pub'li·ca'tion
pub'li·cist
pub·lic'i·ty
pub'li·cize'
pub'lic·ly
pub'lish
pub'lish·er
puck'er
puck'ish
pud'ding
pud'dle
pu·den'dum
pudg'y
pueb'lo
pu'er·ile
pu'er·il'i·ty
pu·er'per·al
puff'er·y
puf'fin
pu'gil·ism
pu'gil·ist
pu'gil·is'tic
pug·na'cious
pug·nac'i·ty
pu'is·sance
pu'is·sant
pul'ing
pull'back'
pul'let
pul'ley
pul'mo·nar'y
pulp'i·ness
pul'pit

pulp'wood'
pulp'y
pul'que
pul'sate
pul·sa'tion
pul·sim'e·ter
pul'ver·i·za'tion
pul'ver·ize'
pu'ma
pum'ice
pum'mel
pump'er·nick'el
pump'kin
pun'cheon
punch'ing
punc·ta'tion
punc·til'i·o'
punc·til'i·ous
punc'tu·al
punc·tu·al'i·ty
punc'tu·ate'
punc·tu·a'tion
punc'ture
pun'dit
pun'gen·cy
pun'gent
pu'ni·ness
pun'ish
pun'ish·a·ble
pun'ish·ment
pu'ni·tive
pun'kah
pun'ster
pu'ny
pu'pa

pu'pal
pu·pa'tion
pu'pil
pup'pet
pup'pet·eer'
pup'pet·ry
pup'py
pur'blind'
pur'chase
pur'chas·ing
pur'dah
pure'bred'
pu·rée'
pure'ly
pur'fle
pur·ga'tion
pur'ga·tive
pur'ga·to'ry
purg'ing
pu'ri·fi·ca'tion
pu'ri·fi'er
pu'ri·fy'
Pu·rim'
pu'rine
pu'rism
pur'ist
Pu'ri·tan
pu'ri·tan'i·cal
Pu'ri·tan·ism
pu'ri·ty
pur'lieu
pur·loin'
pur'ple
pur'plish
pur·port'

pur·port'ed
pur'pose
pur'pose·ful
pur'pos·ive
purs'er
purs'lane
pur·su'ance
pur·su'ant
pur·sue'
pur·suit'
pur'sui·vant
pu'ru·lent
pur·vey'
pur·vey'ance
pur·vey'or
pur'view
push'cart'
push'er
push'ing

pu'sil·la·nim'i·ty
pu'sil·lan'i·mous
puss'y·foot'
pus'tu·lant
pus'tule
pu'ta·tive
pu'tre·fac'tion
pu'tre·fy'
pu'trid
put·tee'
put'ter
put'ty
puz'zle
puz'zle·ment
puz'zler
py·e'mi·a
pyg'my
py'lon

py·lo'rus
py'or·rhe'a
py'or·rhe'al
pyr'a·mid
py·ret'ic
pyr'e·tol'o·gy
py'rex
py·rim'i·dine'
py'rite
py'ro·chem'i·cal
py'ro·gen'ic
py·rog'ra·phy
py'ro·ma'ni·a
py'ro·ma'ni·ac
py·ro'sis
py'ro·tech'nics
pyr'rhic
py'thon

Q

quack′er•y
quack′ing
quad′ra•ge•nar′i•an
quad′ran•gle
quad•ran′gu•lar
quad′rant
quad′rate
quad•rat′ic
quad′ra•ture
quad′ren′ni•al
quad′ri•lat′er•al
qua•drille′
quad•ril′lion
quad•riv′i•um
quad′ru•ped′
quad•ru′pe•dal
quad′ru•ple
quad′ru•plet
quad•ru′pli•cate′
quag′mire′
qua′hog
Quak′er
quak′ing
quak′i•ness
quak′y
qual′i•fi•ca′tion
qual′i•fied′
qual′i•fi′er
qual′i•fy′
qual′i•ta′tive
qual′i•ty

quan′da•ry
quan′tic
quan′ti•fi•ca′tion
quan′ti•fy′
quan′ti•ta′tive
quan′ti•ty
quan′tum
qua′qua•ver′sal
quar′an•tine′
quar′rel
quar′rel•ing
quar′rel•ling
quar′rel•some
quar′ri•er
quar′ry
quar′ter
quar′ter•age
quar′ter•back′
quar′tered
quar′ter•ing
quar′ter•ly
quar′ter•mas′ter
quar•tet′
quar′tile
quar′to
quartz′ite
qua′si
qua•ter′na•ry
qua′train
qua′tre
qua′ver

quea′si•ness
quea′sy
queen′hood′
queen′li•ness
queen′ly
queer′ness
quell′ing
quench′ing
quer′u•lous
que′ry
ques′tion
ques′tion•a•ble
ques′tion•naire′
quet•zal′
quib′ble
quick′en
quick′ie
quick′lime′
quick′ly
quick′sand′
quick′sil′ver
quick′step′
quid′di•ty
quid′nunc′
qui•es′cence
qui•es′cent
qui′et
qui′et•ist
qui′e•tude
qui•e′tus
quilt′ing

qui′na·ry
quin′cunx
quin·dec′a·gon′
qui′nine
quin′qua·ge·nar′i·an
quin′sy
quin·tes′sence
quin′tes·sen′tial
quin·tet′
quin·til′lion

quin′tu·ple
quin′tu·plet
quip′ster
quirk′y
quis′ling
quit′claim′
quit′tance
quit′ter
quiv′er
quix·ot′ic

quix·ot′i·cal·ly
quiz′zer
quiz′zi·cal
Quon′set
quo′rum
quo′ta
quot′a·ble
quo·ta′tion
quo·tid′i·an
quo′tient
quo war·ran′to

R

rab′bet
rab′bi
rab·bin′i·cal
rab′bin·ist
rab′bit
rab′bit·ry
rab′ble
rab′ble·ment
Rab′e·lai′si·an
rab′id
ra·bid′i·ty
ra′bies
rac·coon′
race′course′
ra·ceme′
ra·ce′mic
rac′er
race′way′
ra′cial
ra′cial·ism
ra′cial·ly
rac′i·ly
rac′ing
rac′ism
rac′ist
rack′et
rack′et·eer′
rac′on·teur′
rac′quet
rac′y
ra′dar

ra′dar·scope′
ra′di·al
ra′di·al·ly
ra′di·an
ra′di·ance
ra′di·ant
ra′di·ate′
ra′di·a′tion
ra′di·a′tor
rad′i·cal
ra′di·cal·ism
rad′i·cel′
rad′i·ces′
rad′i·cle
ra′di·i′
ra′di·o′
ra′di·o·ac′tive
ra′di·o·ac·tiv′i·ty
ra′di·o·graph′
ra′di·og′ra·pher
ra′di·o·i′so·tope′
ra′di·ol′o·gy
ra′di·om′e·ter
ra′di·o·ther′a·py
rad′ish
ra′di·um
ra′di·us
ra′dix
ra′don
raf′fi·a
raff′ish

raf′fle
raft′er
raft′ing
rag′a·muf′fin
rag′ged
rag′lan
ra·gout′
rag′pick′er
rag′tag′
rag′time′
rag′weed′
raid′er
rail′ing
rail′ler·y
rail′road′
rail′way′
rain′bow′
rain′coat′
rain′fall′
rain′proof′
rain′y
rai′sin
ra′jah
rake′hell′
rak′ish
ral′ly
Ram′a·dan′
ram′ble
ram′bler
ram′bling
ram·bunc′tious

ram'e·kin
ram'e·quin
ram'i·fi·ca'tion
ram'ify'
ram'jet'
ram'page
ramp'ant
ram'part
ram'rod'
ram'shack'le
ra'mus
ranch'er
ran'cho
ran'cid
ran·cid'i·ty
ran'cor
ran'cor·ous
ran'dom
rand'y
rang'er
rang'y
ra'ni
ran'kle
ran'kled
ran'sack
ran'som
ra·pa'cious
ra·pac'i·ty
rap'id
ra·pid'i·ty
ra'pi·er
rap'ine
rap'ist
rap'per
rap·port'

rap'proche'ment'
rap·scal'lion
rap·to'ri·al
rap'ture
rap'tur·ous
rare'bit
rar'e·fac'tion
rar'e·fy'
rare'ly
rar'i·ty
ras'cal
ras·cal'i·ty
ras·cal·ly
rash'er
rasp'ber'ry
rasp'y
ras'ter
rat'a·fi'a
rat'al
rat'bite'
ratch'et
rath'er
raths'kel'ler
rat'i·fi·ca'tion
rat'i·fi'er
rat'i·fy'
rat'ing
ra'tio
ra'ti·oc·i·na'tion
ra'tion
ra'tion·al
ra'tion·ale'
ra'tion·al·ism
ra'tion·al·ist
ra'tion·al'i·ty

ra'tion·al·i·za'tion
ra'tion·al·ize'
ra·toon'
rats'bane'
rat·tan'
rat'ter
rat'tle
rat'tled
rat'tler
rat'tle·snake'
rat'tle·trap'
rat'trap'
rat'ty
rau'cous
rav'age
rav'el
rav'el·ing
rav'el·ling
rav'en
rav'en·ing
rav'e·nous
rav'in
ra·vine'
rav'ing
ra·vi·o'li
rav'ish
rav'ish·ment
raw'boned'
raw'hide'
ray'less
ray'on
ra'zor
ra'zor·back'
razz'ing
re·act'

re·act'ant
re·ac'tion
re·ac'tion·ar'y
re·ac'tive
re·ac'tor
read'a·bil'i·ty
read'a·ble
re'ad·dress'
read'er
read'i·ly
read'i·ness
read'ing
re'ad·just'
re'ad·just'ment
re'ad·mis'sion
re'ad·mit'
read'y
re'af·fir·ma'tion
re·a'gent
re'al
re'al·ism
re'al·ist
re'al·is'ti·cal·ly
re·al'i·ty
re'al·i·za'tion
re'al·ize'
re'al·ly
re'al·tor
re'al·ty
ream'er
re·an'i·mate'
reap'er
re·ar'ma·ment
re'ar·range'
re'ar·range'ment

rear'ward'
rea'son
rea'son·a·bil'i·ty
rea'son·a·ble
rea'son·ing
re'as·sur'ance
re'as·sure'
re'bate
reb'el, re·bel'
re·bel'lion
re·bel'lious
re·birth'
re·born'
re·bound',
  re'bound
re·buff'
re·buke'
re·buk'ing
re'bus
re·but'
re·but'tal
re·cal'ci·trance
re·cal'ci·trant
re'ca·les'cence
re·call', re'call
re·cant'
re'can·ta'tion
re·cap', re'cap'
re'ca·pit'u·late'
re'ca·pit'u·la'tion
re·cap'ture
re'cast', re'cast'
re·cede'
re·ceipt'
re·ceiv'a·ble

re·ceive'
re·ceiv'er
re·ceiv'er·ship'
re'cent
re·cep'ta·cle
re·cep'ti·ble
re·cep'tion
re·cep'tion·ist
re·cep'tive
re·cep'tiv'i·ty
re·cep'tor
re·cess', re'cess
re·ces'sion
re·ces'sion·al
re·ces'sive
re·cher'ché
re·cid'i·vism
re·cid'i·vist
rec'i·pe
re·cip'i·ent
re·cip'ro·cal
re·cip'ro·cate'
re·cip'ro·ca'tive
re'ci·proc'i·ty
re·cit'al
rec'i·ta'tion
rec'i·ta·tive'
re·cite'
reck'less
reck'on
reck'on·ing
re·claim'
re·claim'ant
rec'la·ma'tion
re·cline'

re·cluse', re'cluse
re·clu'sive
rec'og·ni'tion
rec'og·niz'a·ble
re·cog'ni·zance
rec'og·nize'
re·coil'
rec'ol·lect'
rec'ol·lec'tion
re'com·mence'
rec'om·mend'
rec'om·men·da'tion
rec'om·pense'
rec'on·cil'a·ble
rec'on·cile'
rec'on·cil'i·a'tion
rec'on·dite'
re'con·di'tion
re·con'nais·sance
rec'on·noi'ter
re'con·sid'er
re'con·sign'ment
re'con·struct'
re'con·struc'tion
re'con·ver'sion
re·cord', re'cord
re·cord'er
re·cord'ing
re·count', re'count
re·coup'
re·coup'ment
re'course
re·cov'er
re·cov'er·y
rec're·ate'

rec're·a'tion
re'cre·a'tive
re·crim'i·nate'
re·crim'i·na'tion
re'cru·desce'
re'cru·des'cence
re·cruit'
rec'tal
rec'tan·gle
rec·tan'gu·lar
rec'ti·fi'a·ble
rec'ti·fi·ca'tion
rec'ti·fy'
rec'ti·lin'e·ar
rec'ti·tude'
rec'tor
rec'to·ry
rec'tum
rec'tus
re·cum'ben·cy
re·cum'bent
re·cu'per·ate'
re·cu'per·a'tion
re·cu'per·a'tive
re·cur'
re·cur'rence
re·cur'rent
rec'u·sant
re·dact'
re·dac'tion
re·dac'tor
red'bait'ing
red'bud'
red'cap'
red'den

re·deem'
re·deem'a·ble
re·deem'er
re·demp'tion
re·demp'tive
re'de·pos'it
re'de·vel'op
re'de·vel'op·ment
red'head'
red'in·gote'
re'di·rect'
re'di·rec'tion
red'o·lent
re·dou'ble
re·doubt'a·ble
re·dound'
re·dress', re'dress
re·duce'
re·duc'er
re·duc'i·ble
re·duc'ing
re·duc'tion
re·duc'tive
re·duc'tor
re·dun'dant
re·du'pli·cate'
red'wood'
reed'i·ness
reed'ing
reed'y
reef'er
reek'ing
reel'ing
re·en'try
re'ex·am'ine

re·fec'to·ry
re·fer'
ref'er·ee'
ref'er·ence
ref'er·en'dum
ref'er·ent
ref'er·en'tial
re·fer'ral
re·fill', re'fill'
re·fine'
re·fined'
re·fine'ment
re·fin'er·y
re·flect'
re·flect'ing
re·flec'tion
re·flec'tive
re·flec'tor
re'flex
re·flex'ive
re'flux'
re'for·est·a'tion
re·form'
ref'or·ma'tion
re·form'a·to·ry
re·formed'
re·form'er
re·fract'
re·frac'tion
re·frac'tive
re·frac'tor
re·frac'to·ry
re·frain'
re·fran'gi·ble
re·fresh'

re·fresh'ing
re·fresh'ment
re·frig'er·ate'
re·frig'er·a'tion
re·frig'er·a'tor
ref'uge
ref'u·gee'
re·ful'gent
re'fund, re·fund'
re·fur'bish
re·fus'al
re·fuse' (say no)
ref'use (trash)
ref'u·ta·ble
ref'u·ta'tion
re·fute'
re·gain'
re'gal
re·gale'
re·gale'ment
re·ga'li·a
re·gard'
re·gard'ing
re·gard'less
re·gat'ta
re'gen·cy
re·gen'er·ate'
re'gent
reg'i·cid'al
reg'i·cide'
re·gime'
reg'i·men'
reg'i·ment
reg'i·men'tal
reg'i·men·ta'tion

re'gion
re'gion·al
re'gion·al·ism
reg'is·ter
reg'is·tered
reg'is·trant
reg'is·trar'
reg'is·tra'tion
reg'is·try
re'gi·us
reg'nant
re·grate'
re·gress, re·gress'
re·gres'sion
re·gres'sive
re·gret'
re·gret'ful
re·gret'ta·bly
reg'u·lar
reg'u·lar'i·ty
reg'u·lar·ly
reg'u·late'
reg'u·la'tion
reg'u·la'tor
reg'u·la·to'ry
reg'u·lus
re·gur'gi·tate'
re·gur'gi·ta'tion
re'ha·bil'i·tate'
re'ha·bil'i·ta'tion
re·hears'al
re·hearse'
reichs'mark'
re'i·fy'
reign'ing

re·im·burse'
re·im·burse'ment
re·in·car·na'tion
re·in·force'
re·in·force'ment
re·in·state'
re·in·sure'
re·it'er·ate'
re·it'er·a'tion
re·it'er·a'tive
re·ject', re'ject
re·jec'tion
re·joice'
re·joic'ing
re·join'
re·join'der
re·ju've·nate'
re·ju've·na'tion
re·lapse'
re·late'
re·lat'ed
re·la'tion
re·la'tion·ship'
rel'a·tive
rel'a·tive·ly
rel'a·tiv·ism
rel'a·tiv·ist
rel'a·tiv'i·ty
re·la'tor
re·lax'
re·lax·a'tion
re'lay, re·lay'
re·lease'
rel'e·gate'
rel'e·ga'tion

re·lent'
re·lent'less
rel'e·vance
rel'e·van·cy
rel'e·vant
re·li'a·bil'i·ty
re·li'a·ble
re·li'a·bly
re·li'ance
re·li'ant
rel'ic
rel'ict, rel·ict'
re·lief'
re·lieve'
re·li'gion
re·li'gion·ist
re·lig'i·os'i·ty
re·li'gious
re·lin'quish
rel'i·quar'y
rel'ish
re·luc'tance
re·luc'tant
re·ly'
re·main'
re·main'der
re·mains'
re·mand'
re·mark'
re·mark'a·ble
re·me'di·a·ble
re·me'di·al
rem'e·di·less
rem'e·dy
re·mem'ber

re·mem'brance
re·mind'
re·mind'er
rem'i·nisce'
rem'i·nis'cence
rem'i·nis'cent
re·miss'
re·mis'sion
re·mit'
re·mit'tance
re·mit'ter
rem'nant
re·mod'el
re·mon'e·tize'
re·mon'strance
re·mon'strant
re·mon'strate
rem'o·ra
re·morse'
re·morse'ful
re·morse'less
re·mote'
re·mov'al
re·move'
re·mu'ner·ate'
re·mu'ner·a'tion
re·mu'ner·a'tive
re'nais·sance'
re'nal
re·nas'cence
re·nas'cent
rend'er
ren'dez·vous'
ren·di'tion
ren'e·gade'

re·nege'
re·new'
re·new'al
ren'net
ren'nin
re·nounce'
ren'o·vate'
ren'o·va'tion
ren'o·va'tor
re·nown'
rent'al
rent'er
re·nun'ci·a'tion
re·nun'ci·a·to'ry
re·or'der
re'or·gan·i·za'tion
re'or'gan·ize'
re·pair'
re·pair'man'
rep'a·ra·ble
rep'a·ra·bly
rep'a·ra'tion
rep'ar·tee'
re·past'
re·pa'tri·ate'
re·pa'tri·a'tion
re·pay'
re·pay'ment
re·peal'
re·peat'
re·peat'ed
re·peat'er
re·pel'
re·pel'lence
re·pel'lent

re·pent'
re·pent'ance
re·pent'ant
re'per·cus'sion
re'per·cus'sive
rep'er·toire'
rep'er·to'ry
rep'e·tend'
rep'e·ti'tion
rep'e·ti'tious
re·pet'i·tive
re·pine'
re·place'
re·place'ment
re·plen'ish
re·plen'ish·ment
re·plete'
rep'li·ca
rep'li·cate
rep'li·ca'tion
re·ply'
re·port'
re·port'er
rep'or·to'ri·al
re·pose'
re·pos'i·to'ry
re'pos·sess'
re'pos·ses'sion
rep're·hend'
rep're·hen'si·ble
rep're·hen'si·bly
rep're·sent'
rep're·sen·ta'tion
rep're·sen·ta'tion·al
rep're·sen'ta·tive

re·press'
re·pressed'
re·pres'sion
re·pres'sive
re·prieve'
rep'ri·mand'
re'print, re·print'
re·pris'al
re·prise'
re·proach'
rep'ro·bate'
rep'ro·ba'tion
re'pro·duce'
re'pro·duc'tion
re'pro·duc'tive
re·proof'
re·prove'
rep'tile
rep·til'i·an
re·pub'lic
re·pub'li·can
re·pub'li·can·ism
re·pu'di·ate'
re·pu'di·a'tion
re·pug'nance
re·pug'nant
re·pulse'
re·pul'sion
re·pul'sive
rep'u·ta·ble
rep'u·ta'tion
re·pute'
re·put'ed
re·quest'
re'qui·em

re'qui·es'cat
re·quire'
re·quire'ment
req'ui·site
req'ui·si'tion
re·quit'al
re·quite'
re·run', re'run
re·sale'
re·scind'
re'script
res'cue
re·search',
    re'search
re·sect'
re·sem'blance
re·sem'ble
re·sem'bling
re·sent'
re·sent'ful
re·sent'ment
res'er·va'tion
re·serve'
re·served'
res'er·voir'
re·ship'ment
re·side'
res'i·dence
res'i·den·cy
res'i·dent
res'i·den'tial
re·sid'u·al
re·sid'u·ar'y
res'i·due'
re·sid'u·um

re·sign'
res'ig·na'tion
re·signed'
re·sil'i·ence
re·sil'i·en·cy
re·sil'i·ent
res'in
res'i·nous
re·sist'
re·sist'ance
re·sist'ant
re·sist'i·ble
re·sis'tor
res ju'di·ca'ta
res'o·lute'
res'o·lu'tion
re·solve'
res'o·nance
res'o·nant
res'o·nate'
re·sorp'tion
re·sort'
re·sound'
re'source,
    re·source'
re·source'ful
re·source'ful·ly
re·spect'
re·spect'a·bil'i·ty
re·spect'a·ble
re·spect'ful
re·spect'ing
re·spec'tive
res'pi·ra'tion
res'pi·ra·to'ry

re·spire'
re·spir'ing
res'pite
re·splend'ence
re·splend'ent
re·spond'
re·spond'ent
re·sponse'
re·spon'si·bil'i·ty
re·spon'si·ble
re·spon'sive
re·spon'sive·ly
res'tau·rant
res'tau·ra·teur'
rest'ful
rest'ing
res'ti·tu'tion
res'tive
rest'less
res'to·ra'tion
re·stor'a·tive
re·store'
re·stor'ing
re·strain'
re·strained'
re·straint'
re·strict'
re·strict'ed
re·stric'tion
re·stric'tive
re·sult'
re·sult'ant
re·sume'
ré'su·mé'
re·sump'tion

re·sur'gence
re·sur'gent
res·ur·rect'
res·ur·rec'tion
re·sus'ci·tate'
re·sus'ci·ta'tion
re·sus'ci·ta'tor
re'tail, re·tail'
re'tail·er
re·tain'
re·tain'er
re·tal'i·ate'
re·tal'i·a'tion
re·tal'i·a·to'ry
re·tard'
re·tar·da'tion
re·tard'ed
re·ten'tion
re·ten'tive
ret'i·cence
ret'i·cent
re·tic'u·la'tion
ret'i·na
ret'i·nal
ret'i·nue'
re·tired'
re·tire'ment
re·tir'ing
re·tort'
re·touch'
re·trace'
re·tract'
re·tract'a·ble
re·trac'tive

re·trac'tion
re·treat'
re·trench'ment
ret·ri·bu'tion
re·trib'u·tive
re·trieve'
re·triev'er
re·triev'ing
ret'ro·ac'tive
ret'ro·grade'
ret'ro·gress'
ret'ro·gres'sion
ret'ro·gres'sive
ret'ro·spect'
ret'ro·spec'tive
re·turn'a·ble
re·turned'
re·turn·ee'
re·un'ion
re'u·nite'
re'u·nit'ed
re·veal'
rev·eil·le
rev'el
rev'e·la'tion
rev'el·ry
re·venge'
rev'e·nue
re·ver'ber·ate'
re·ver'ber·a'tion
re·vere'
rev'er·ence
rev'er·end
rev'er·ent

rev'er·en'tial
rev'er·ie
re·ver'sal
re·verse'
re·vers'i·ble
re·ver'sion
re·vert'
re·vert'ed
re·view'
re·view'er
re·vile'
re·vile'ment
re·vise'
re·vis'er
re·vi'sion
re·vi'sion·ist
re·viv'al
re·viv'al·ism
re·viv'al·ist
re·vive'
re·viv'i·fy'
rev'o·ca·ble
rev'o·ca'tion
re·voke'
re·volt'
re·volt'ing
re·volt'ed
rev'o·lu'tion
rev'o·lu'tion·ar·y
rev'o·lu'tion·ize
re·volve'
re·volv'er
re·volv'ing
re·vue'

re·vul'sion
re·ward'
re·word'
re·write'
rhap·sod'ic
rhap'so·dist
rhap'so·dize'
rhap'so·dy
rhe'ni·um
rhe'o·stat'
rhe'sus
rhet'o·ric
rhe·tor'i·cal
rhe·tor'i·cal·ly
rhet'o·ri'cian
rheu·mat'ic
rheu'ma·tism
rheu'ma·toid
rheum'y
rhi'nal
rhine'stone'
rhi·ni'tis
rhi·noc'er·os
rhi·nol'o·gy
rhi'zome
rho'da·mine'
Rho·de'sian
rho'di·um
rho'do·den'dron
rhom'bic
rhom'boid
rhom·boi'dal
rhom'bus
rhon'chus

rhu'barb
rhym'er
rhyth'mic
rhyth'mi·cal
ri'al
ri·al'to
rib'ald
rib'ald·ry
rib'bing
rib'bon
ri'bo·fla'vin
ric'er
rich'es
rich'ly
rick'ets
rick·ett'si·a
rick'et·y
rick'ey
rick'rack'
ric'o·chet'
ric'tus
rid'dance
rid'den
rid'dle
rid'dling
rid'er
ridge'pole'
rid'i·cule
ri·dic'u·lous
rid'ing
rif'fle
riff'raff'
ri'fle
rig'a·doon'

rig'ger
rig'ging
right'eous
right'eous·ness
right'ful
right'ist
right'ly
rig'id
ri·gid'i·ty
rig'id·ly
rig'ma·role'
rig'or
ri'gor mor'tis
rig'or·ous
rim'y
rin'der·pest'
ring'dove'
ring'er
ring'lead'er
ring'let
ring'mas'ter
ring'toss'
ring'worm'
rins'ing
ri'ot
ri'ot·ous
ri·par'i·an
rip'en
ri·poste'
rip'per
rip'ple
rip'rap'
rip'tide'
ris'er

ris'i·bil'i·ty
ris'i·ble
ris'ing
risk'y
ris·qué'
ris'sole
ri'tar·dan'do
rit'u·al
rit'u·al·ism
rit'u·al·is'tic
rit'u·al·ly
ritz'y
ri'val
ri'val·ry
riv'er
riv'er·side'
riv'et
riv'u·let
road'bed'
road'block'
road'side'
road'way'
roar'ing
roast'er
roast'ing
rob'ber·y
rob'in
ro'bot
ro·bot'ics
ro·bust'
rock'er
rock'et
rock'et·ry
rock'ing

rock'y
ro·co'co
ro'dent
ro·de·o, ro·de'o
rod'o·mon·tade'
roe'buck'
roent'gen
ro·ga'tion
ro'ga·to'ry
ro'guer·y
ro'guish
roist'er
roll'back'
roll'er
rol'lick·ing
roll'ing
ro·maine'
Ro'man
ro·mance',
  ro'mance
Ro'man·esque'
Ro'man·ize'
ro·man'tic
ro·man'ti·cal·ly
ro·man'ti·cism
Ro'me·o
romp'er
ron'deau
ron'do
roof'er
roof'ing
roof'tree'
rook'er·y
rook'ie

room'er
room'i·ness
room'mate'
room'y
roor'back
roost'er
root'stock'
rope'walk'er
rop'i·ness
rop'y
roque'fort
Ror'schach
ro·sa'ceous
ro'sa·ry
ro'se·ate
rose'bush'
rose'mar'y
ro·sette'
rose'wood'
Rosh Ha·sha'na
Ro'si·cru'cian
ros'in
ros'i·ness
ros'in·y
ro·so'lio
ros'ter
ros'trum
ros'y
ro'ta·ry
ro'tate
ro·ta'tion
ro'ta·tor
rot'gut'
ro·tis'ser·ie

ro'to·gra·vure'
ro'tor
rot'ten
rot'ter
ro·tund'
ro·tun'da
ro·tun'di·ty
rou·é'
rough'age
rough'cast'
rough'en
rough'house'
rough'ly
rough'neck'
rough'shod'
rou·lade'
rou·leau'
rou·lette'
round'a·bout'
round'ed
roun'del
roun'de·lay'
round'er
round'house'
round'ly
round'up'
round'worm'
rous'ing
roust'a·bout'
rou·tine'
rov'er
row'an
row'di·ness
row'dy

row'el
row'en
roy'al
roy'al·ist
roy'al·ty
ru·basse'
ru·ba'to
rub'ber
rub'ber·ize'
rub'ber·y
rub'bish
rub'ble
rub'down'
ru·be·fa'cient
ru·bel'la
ru·be'o·la
ru·bes'cent
ru'bi·cund'
ru'bric
ru'by
ruck'sack'
ruck'us
rud'der
rud'dy
ru'di·ment
ru'di·men'ta·ry
rue'ful
ruf'fi·an
ruf'fle
ruf'fled
ruf'fly
ru'gate
rug'by
rug'ged

ru'in
ru'in·ate
ru'in·a'tion
ru'in·ous
rul'er
rul'ing
rum'ba
rum'ble
rum'bling
ru'mi·nant
ru'mi·nate'
ru'mi·na'tor
rum'mage
rum'mer
rum'my
ru'mor
ru'mour
rum'ple
rum'pus
run'a·gate'
run'a·way'
run'back'
ru'nic
run'nel
run'ner
run'ning
runt'y
run'way
ru·pee'
rup'ture
ru'ral
rush'er
rush'ing
rus'set

Rus'sian
rus'tic
rus'ti·cal
rus'ti·cate'
rus·tic'i·ty

rust'i·ness
rus'tle
rus'tler
rust'proof'
rust'y
ru'ta·ba'ga

ru·the'ni·um
ruth'less
ru'tile
rut'tish
rut'ty

S

Sab'ba·tar'i·an
Sab'bath
sab·bat'i·cal
sa'ber
Sa'bine
sa'ble
sa'bot
sab'o·tage'
sab'o·teur'
sab'u·lous
sac·char'ic
sac'cha·ride'
sac'cha·rin
sac'cha·rine
sac'cule
sac'er·do'tal
sa·chet'
sack'cloth'
sack'ing
sa'cral
sac'ra·ment
sac'ra·men'tal
sa'cred
sac'ri·fice'
sac'ri·fi'cial
sac'ri·lege
sac'ri·le'gious
sac'ris·tan
sac'ris·ty
sac'ro·il'i·ac'
sac'ro·sanct'

sa'crum
sad'den
sad'dle
sad'dle·bag'
sad'dler·y
sad'ism
sa·dis'tic
sa·fa'ri
safe'break'er
safe'guard'
safe'keep'ing
safe'ty
saf'flow'er
saf'fron
sa'ga
sa·ga'cious
sa·gac'i·ty
sage'brush'
sag'it·tal
Sag'it·ta'ri·us
sa'hib
sail'boat'
sail'cloth'
sail'ing
sail'or
saint'ed
saint'li·ness
saint'ly
sa'ke
sa·laam'
sal'a·ble

sa·la'cious
sal'ad
sal'a·man'der
sa·la'mi
sal'a·ried
sal'a·ry
sale'a·ble
sales'clerk'
sales'man·ship
sales'per'son
sales'room'
sa'li·ence
sa'li·ent
sa·li'na
sa'line
sa·lin'i·ty
sa·li'va
sal'i·var'y
sal'i·vate'
sal'i·va'tion
sal'low
sal'ly
sal'ma·gun'di
sal'mi
salm'on
sal'mo·nel'la
sa·lon'
sa·loon'
sal'si·fy'
salt'cel'lar
salt'i·er

salt′pe′ter
salt′y
sa·lu′bri·ous
sal′u·tar′i·ly
sal′u·tar′y
sal′u·ta′tion
sa·lu′ta·to′ry
sa·lute′
sa·lut′ing
sal′vage
sal·va′tion
salv′ing
sal′vo
Sa·mar′i·tan
sam′ba
sam′o·var
sam′pan
sam′ple
sam′pler
sam′pling
sam′u·rai
san′a·tive
san·a·to′ri·um
sanc′ti·fi·ca′tion
sanc′ti·fied
sanc′ti·fy·ing
sanc′ti·mo′ni·ous
sanc′ti·mo′ny
sanc′tion
sanc′ti·ty
sanc′tu·ar′y
sanc′tum
san′dal
san′dal·wood′
sand′bag′

sand′i·er
sand′pa′per
sand′stone′
sand′wich
sand′y
san′er
sane′ly
sang·froid′
san′gui·nar′y
san′guine
san′i·tar′i·um
san′i·tar′i·ly
san′i·tar′y
san′i·ta′tion
san′i·ty
sa′pi·ence
sa′pi·ent
sap′ling
sa·pon′i·fi·ca′tion
sa·pon′i·fy
sap′per
sap′ping
sap′phire
sap′py
sap′suck′er
sap′wood′
sar′casm
sar·cas′tic
sar·cas′ti·cal·ly
sar·co′ma
sar·coph′a·gus
sar·dine′
sar·don′ic
sar·don′i·cal·ly
sa′ri

sa·rong′
sar′sa·pa·ril′la
sar·to′ri·al
sa·shay′
sa·shay′ing
sas′sa·fras
Sa′tan
sa·tan′ic
sa′tan·ism
satch′el
sat′ed
sa·teen′
sat′el·lite
sa′ti·a·bil′i·ty
sa′ti·a·ble
sa′ti·ate
sa′ti·a′tion
sa·ti′e·ty
sat′in
sat′in·wood′
sat′in·y
sat′ire
sa·tir′i·cal
sat′i·rist
sat′i·rize′
sat′i·riz′ing
sat′is·fac′tion
sat′is·fac′to·ri·ly
sat′is·fac′to·ry
sat′is·fy′
sat′is·fy′ing
sa′trap
sat′u·ra·ble
sat′u·rate′
sat′u·rat′ed

sat'u·rat'ing
sat'u·ra'tion
Sat'ur·day
Sat'ur·na'li·an
sat'ur·ine'
sat'yr
sauce'pan'
sau'cer
sau'ci·ly
sau'cy
sauer'kraut'
saun'ter
saun'ter·ing
sau'ri·an
sau'sage
sau·té'
sau·téed'
sau·terne'
sav'age
sav'age·ly
sav'age·ry
sa·vant'
sav'ior
sa'vor
sa'vored
sa'vor·y
sav'vy
saw'dust'
saw'horse'
saw'yer
sax'i·frage
sax'o·phone'
sax'o·phon'ist
say'ing
scab'bard

scab'bing
scab'by
sca'bies
sca'brous
scaf'fold
scaf'fold·ing
scal'age
scal'a·wag
scald'ing
sca·lene'
scal'ing
scal'lion
scal'lop
scal'pel
scalp'er
scal'y
scan'dal
scan'dal·ize'
scan'dal·iz'ing
scan'dal·ous
scan'di·um
scan'sion
scant'i·ly
scant'i·ness
scant'ling
scant'y
scape'goat'
scap'u·la
scap'u·lar
scar'ab
scarce'ly
scar'ci·ty
scare'crow'
scare'mon'ger
scar'i·fi·ca'tion

scar'i·fy'
scar'let
scar'y
scath'ing
scat'o·log'i·cal
sca·tol'o·gy
scat'ter
scat'ter·brained'
scat'ter·ing
scav'enge
scav'eng·er
sce·na'ri·o
scen'er·y
sce'nic
scep'ter
sched'ule
sche'ma
sche·mat'ic
sche·mat'i·cal·ly
sche'ma·tize'
scher·zan'do
scher'zo
schil'ler
schil'ling
schis·mat'ic
schiz'oid
schiz'o·phre'ni·a
schiz'o·phren'ic
schnau'zer
schol'ar
schol'ar·ly
schol'ar·ship'
scho·las'tic
scho·las'ti·cism
scho'li·ast'

school'book'
school'ing
school'room'
school'yard'
schoon'er
sci·at'ic
sci·at'i·ca
sci'ence
sci'en·tif'ic
sci'en·tif'i·cal·ly
sci'en·tism
sci'en·tist
sci'en·tol'o·gy
scil'i·cet'
scim'i·tar
scin·til·late'
scin·til·lat'ing
scin·til·la'tion
sci'on
sci're fa'ci·as'
scir'rhus
scis'sile
scis'sion
scis'sors
scle'ra
scle·ro'sis
scle·rot'ic
scoff'er
scold'ing
scoop'ful'
scoot'er
sco·pol'a·mine'
scorch'er
scorch'ing
scorn'ful

Scor'pi·o'
scor'pi·on
Scot'tish
scoun'drel
scour'ing
scout'ing
scout'mas'ter
scowl'ing
scrab'ble
scrag'gly
scram'ble
scrap'book'
scrap'er
scrap'per
scrap'ple
scrap'py
scratch'es
scratch'ing
scrath'y
scrawn'i·ness
scrawn'y
scream'er
scream'ing
screech'ing
screech'y
screen'ing
screen'play'
screen'writ'ing
screw'ball'
screw'driv'er
screw'y
scrib'al
scrib'ble
scrib'bler
scrim'mage

scrimp'ing
scrimp'y
scrim'shaw'
scrip'tur·al
scrip'ture
scrive'ner
scrof'u·la
scrof'u·lous
scroll'work'
scro'tal
scro'tum
scroung'ing
scrub'bing
scrub'by
scrump'tious
scru'ple
scru'pu·los'i·ty
scru'pu·lous
scru'ti·nize'
scru'tin·y
scu'ba
scuf'fle
scul'ler·y
scul'lion
sculp'tor
sculp'tur·al
sculp'ture
scum'ble
scum'my
scup'per
scur·ril'i·ty
scur'ri·lous
scur'ry
scur'vy
scut'tle

scut'tle·butt'
sea'board'
sea'far'er
sea'far'ing
sea'go'ing
seal'er
seal'ing
seal'skin'
sea'man
sea'man·ship'
seam'stress
seam'y
sé'ance
sea'plane'
search'ing
search'light'
sea'scape'
sea'shore'
sea'side'
sea'son
sea'son·a·ble
sea'son·a·bly
sea'son·al
sea'son·ing
seat'ing
sea'ward
sea'weed'
sea'wor'thi·ness
sea'wor'thy
se·ba'ceous
se'cant
se·cede'
se·ces'sion
se·ces'sion·ist
se·clude'

se·clud'ed
se·clu'sion
sec'ond
sec'ond·ar'y
sec'ond·hand'
sec'ond·ly
se'cre·cy
se'cret
sec're·tar'i·al
sec're·tar'i·at
sec're·tar'y
sec·rete'
se·cre'tion
se·cre'tive
sec·tar'i·an
sec·tar'i·an·ism
sec'ta·ry
sec'tion
sec'tion·al
sec'tion·al·ism
sec'tor
sec'u·lar
sec'u·lar·ist
sec'u·lar'i·ty
sec'u·lar·i·za'tion
sec'u·lar·ize'
se·cure'
se·cu'ri·ty
se·dan'
se·date'
se·da'tion
sed'a·tive
sed'en·tar'y
Se'der
sed'i·ment

sed'i·men'ta·ry
sed'i·men·ta'tion
se·di'tion
se·di'tious
se·duce'
se·duc'er
se·duc'tion
se·duc'tive
sed'u·lous
se'dum
seed'bed'
seed'er
seed'i·ness
seed'ling
seed'time'
seed'y
see'ing
seem'ing
seem'ing·ly
seem'li·ness
seem'ly
seep'age
seer'suck'er
see'saw'
seg'ment
seg·men'tal
seg·men·ta'tion
seg'ment·ed
se'go
seg're·gate'
seg're·gat'ed
seg're·ga'tion
se'gue
seign'ior·y
seis'mal

seis'mic
seis'mism
seis'mo·graph'
seis·mog'ra·phy
seis'mo·log'i·cal
seis·mol'o·gy
seiz'a·ble
seiz'ing
sei'zure
sel'dom
se·lect'
se·lec'tion
se·lec'tive
se·lec'tiv'i·ty
se·lect'man
se·le'nic
sel'e·nite'
se·le'ni·um
sel'e·nol'o·gy
self'hood
self'ish
self'less
sell'er
sell'ing
sell'out'
selt'zer
sel'vage
se·man'tic
se·man'tics
sem'a·phore'
sem'blance
se'men
se·mes'ter
sem'i·an'nu·al
sem'i·au'to·mat'ic

sem'i·cir'cle
sem'i·cir'cu·lar
sem'i·co'lon
sem'i·con·duc'tor
sem'i·fi·nal
sem'i·nal
sem'i·nar'
sem'i·nar'y
sem'i·na'tion
se'mi·ol'o·gy
se'mi·ot'ic
sem'i·pre'cious
sem'i·qua'ver
sem'i·skilled'
Se·mit'ic
sem'i·tone'
sem'i·trop'i·cal
sem'o·li'na
sem'per fi·de'lis
sem'per par·a'tus
sem'pi·ter'nal
sen'ate
sen'a·tor
sen'a·to'ri·al
send'er
se·nes'cence
se·nes'cent
sen'es·chal
se'nile
se·nil'i·ty
sen'ior
sen·ior'i·ty
sen'sate
sen·sa'tion
sen·sa'tion·al·ism

sen·sa'tion·al·is'tic
sense'less
sen'si·bil'i·ty
sen'si·ble
sen'si·tive
sen'si·tiv'i·ty
sen'si·tize
sen·so'ri·um
sen'so·ry
sen'su·al
sen'su·al·ist
sen'su·al'i·ty
sen'su·ous
sen'tence
sen·ten'tial
sen·ten'tious
sen'tience
sen'tient
sen'ti·ment
sen'ti·men'tal
sen'ti·men·tal'i·ty
sen'ti·men'tal·ize'
sen'ti·nel
sen'try
sep'a·ra·ble
sep'a·rate'
sep'a·ra'tion
sep'a·ra'tist
sep'a·ra'tor
se'pi·a
sep'sis
Sep·tem'ber
sep'te·nar'y
sep·tet'
sep'tic

sep·til'lion
sep'ti·mal
sep'tu·a·ge·nar'i·an
sep'tum
sep'tu·ple
sep'ul·cher
se·pul'chral
sep'ul·ture
se'quence
se'quent
se·quen'tial
se·ques'ter
se·ques'tered
se·ques·tra'tion
se'quin
se·quoi'a
se·rag'lio
se·ra'pe
ser'aph
ser'a·phim'
ser'e·nade'
ser'en·dip'i·ty
se·rene'
se·ren'i·ty
serf'dom
ser'geant
se'ri·al
se'ri·al·ly
se'ries
ser'if
se'ri·o·com'ic
se'ri·ous
ser'mon
ser'mon·ize'
se·rol'o·gy

se'rous
ser'pent
ser'pen·tine'
ser'rate
ser'rat·ed
ser'ru·late'
se'rum
ser'vant
serv'er
serv'ice
serv'ice·a·ble
ser'vice·man'
ser'vi·ette'
ser'vile
ser·vil'i·ty
ser'vi·tor
ser'vi·tude'
ses'a·me'
ses'qui·cen·ten'ni·al
ses'sile
ses'sion
ses·tet'
ses·ti'na
set'screw'
set·tee'
set'ter
set'ting
set'tle
set'tle·ment
set'tler
set'up'
sev'en
sev'en·teen'
sev'en·teenth'
sev'enth

sev'en·ti·eth
sev'en·ty
sev'er
sev'er·a·ble
sev'er·al
sev'er·ance
se·vere'
se·ver'i·ty
sew'age
sew'er
sew'er·age
sew'ing
sex'a·ge·nar'i·an
sex·en'ni·al
sex'i·ly
sex'i·ness
sex·ol'o·gy
sex'tant
sex·tet'
sex·til'lion
sex'ton
sex'tu·ple
sex'u·al
sex'u·al'i·ty
sex'u·al·ly
sex'y
sfor·zan'do
shab'bi·ness
shab'by
shack'le
shad'ing
shad'ow
shad'ow·less
shad'ow·y
shad'y

shaft'ing
shag'gi·ness
shag'gy
sha·green'
shake'down'
shak'en
shak'er
Shake·spear'e·an
shak'i·ly
shak'ing
shak'y
shal'lop
shal·lot'
shal'low
shal'y
sha'man
sha'man·ism
sham'bles
shame'faced'
shame'fac'ed·ly
shame'ful
shame'less
sham·poo'
sham'rock
shang'hai
shan'ty
shan'ty·town'
shape'less
shape'ly
shap'er
share'crop'ping
share'hold'er
shark'skin'
sharp'en
sharp'ened

sharp'en·er
sharp'shoot'er
shat'ter
shat'tered
shat'ter·proof'
shav'en
shav'ing
shear'ing
shear'ling
shear'wa'ter
sheath'ing
she·bang'
shed'der
shed'ding
sheep'cote'
sheep'fold'
sheep'herd'er
sheep'ish
sheep'skin'
sheet'ing
shek'el
shel·lac'
shel·lack'ing
shell'fish'
shell'shocked'
shel'ter
shelv'ing
she·nan'i·gans
shep'herd
sher'bet
sher'iff
sher'ry
shib'bo·leth
shield'ing
shift'i·er

shift'y
shil·le'lagh
shil'ling
shim'mer
shim'mer·ing
shim'my
shin'gle
shin'i·ness
shin'ing
shin'y
ship'board'
ship'ment
ship'per
ship'ping
ship'shape'
ship'wreck'
shirk'er
shirk'ing
shirt'ing
shirt'waist'
shiv'er
shiv'er·ing
shock'er
shock'ing
shod'di·ness
shod'dy
shoe'horn'
shoe'lace'
shoe'mak'er
shoe'string'
shoot'ing
shop'lift'er
shop'ping
shop'talk'
shop'worn'

shor'ing
short'age
short'cake'
short'com'ings
short'en·ing
short'hand'
short'ly
short'stop'
shot'gun'
shoul'der
shout'ed
shout'ing
shov'el
shov'eled
shov'elled
shov'ing
show'down'
show'er
show'er·ing
show'ing
show'man
show'man·ship'
show'y
shrap'nel
shred'ded
shred'der
shrewd'ly
shrewd'ness
shrew'ish
shriek'ing
shrill'ness
shril'ly
shrink'age
shriv'el
shriv'en

shroud'ed
shrub'ber·y
shud'der
shuf'fle
shuf'fle·board'
shuf'fling
shut'down'
shut'out'
shut'ter
shut'tle
shut'tle·cock'
shy'lock
shy'ly
shy'ster
Si'a·mese'
sib'i·lance
sib'i·lant
sib'ling
sib'yl
sick'en·ing
sick'le
sick'ly
side'board'
side'burns'
sid'ed
si·de're·al
side'swipe'
side'walk'
side'ways'
sid'ing
si'dle
si'dled
sieg'es
si·en'na
si·er'ra

si·es'ta
sift'er
sift'ing
sigh'ing
sight'less
sight'see'ing
sig'nal
sig'naled
sig'nal·ing
sig'nalled
sig'nal·ling
sig'nal·ly
sig'na·to'ry
sig'na·ture
sig'net
sig·nif'i·cance
sig·nif'i·cant
sig'ni·fi·ca'tion
sig'ni·fied'
sig'ni·fy'
sig'ni·fy'ing
sign'post'
si'lage
si'lence
si'lenc·er
si'lent
si'lent·ly
si·lex
sil'hou·ette'
sil'hou·et'ted
sil'i·ca
sil'i·cate
sil'i·con
sil'i·co'sis
silk'en

silk'worm'
silk'y
sil'li·ness
sil'ly
si'lo
sil'ver
sil'ver·smith'
sil'ver·ware'
sil'ver·y
sim'i·an
sim'i·lar
sim'i·lar'i·ty
sim'i·le'
si·mil'i·tude'
sim'mer
sim'mered
sim'o·ny
sim'per
sim'ple
sim'ple·ton
sim'plex
sim·plic'i·ty
sim'pli·fi·ca'tion
sim'pli·fi'er
sim'pli·fy'
sim·plis'tic
sim'ply
sim'u·la'crum
sim'u·late'
sim'u·la'tion
sim'u·la'tor
si'mul·cast'
si'mul·ta·ne'i·ty
si'mul·ta'ne·ous
sin·cere'

sin·cere'ly
sin·cer'i·ty
sin'ci·put'
si'ne·cure'
si'ne di'e
si'ne qua non
sin'ew
sin'ew·y
sin'ful
sing'er
sing'ing
sin'gle
sin'glet
sin'gle·ton
sin'gly
sing'song'
sin'gu·lar
sin'gu·lar'i·ty
sin'is·ter
sin'is·tral
sink'er
sink'hole'
sink'ing
sin'ner
sin'u·ate'
sin'u·ous
si'nus
si'nus·i'tis
si'phon
sip'pet
sip'ping
si'ren
si·re'ni·an
sir'loin
si·roc'co

sir'up
sir'up·y
si'sal
sis'sy
sis'ter
sis'ter·hood'
sis'ter·ly
sis'trum
si·tol'o·gy
sit'ter
sit'ting
sit'u·ate'
sit'u·at'ed
sit'u·a'tion
sit'u·a'tion·al
si'tus
six'fold'
six'teen'
six'teenth'
six'ti·eth
six'ty
siz'a·ble
siz'ing
siz'zle
siz'zling
skald'ic
skat'ing
ske·dad'dle
skel'e·tal
skel'e·ton
skep'tic
skep'ti·cal
skep'ti·cism
sker'ry
sketch'book'

sketch'i·ness
sketch'y
skew'er
skid'ding
ski'er
ski'ing
skil'let
skill'ful
skim'mer
skim'ming
skimp'i·ness
skimp'y
skin'flint'
skin'ner
skin'ny
skin'tight'
skip'per
skir'mish
skir'mish·es
skit'ter
skit'tish
skit'tle
skiv'er
skiv'vy
skul·dug'ger·y
skull'cap'
sky'div'ing
sky'lark'
sky'light'
sky'line'
sky'rock'et
sky'scrap'er
slack'en
slack'er
sla'lom

slan'der
slan'der·ous
slang'y
slant'wise'
slap'dash'
slap'jack'
slap'stick'
slash'er
slash'ing
slat'ing
slat'tern
slat'tern·ly
slaugh'ter
slaugh'ter·house'
slaugh'ter·ous
slave'hold'ing
slav'er
slav'er·y
slav'ey
slav'ish
slea'zi·ness
slea'zy
sled'der
sled'ding
sleep'er
sleep'i·ness
sleep'ing
sleep'walk'er
sleep'y
sleet'y
sleeve'less
sleigh'ing
slen'der
slic'er
slick'er

slide'way'
slid'ing
slight'ing
slight'ly
slim'mer
slim'i·ness
slim'y
sling'shot'
slink'y
slip'knot'
slip'page
slip'per
slip'per·y
slip'sheet'
slip'shod'
slith'er
slith'er·y
sliv'er
slob'ber
slob'ber·ing
slo'gan
slop'ing
slop'pi·ly
slop'pi·ness
slop'py
sloth'ful
slouch'ing
slov'en·li·ness
slov'en·ly
slow'down'
sludg'y
slug'gard
slug'ger
slug'gish
sluice'way'

slum'ber
slum'ber·ous
slum'ming
slur'ry
slush'y
slut'tish
sly'ly
smack'ing
small'er
small'ish
small'pox'
smart'en
smart'ing
smash'up'
smat'ter
smat'ter·ing
smear'case'
smear'y
smell'er
smell'ing
smell'y
smelt'er
smil'ing
smirk'ing
smith'y
smit'ten
smock'ing
smog'gy
smoke'house'
smoke'less
smok'er
smok'i·ness
smok'ing
smok'y
smol'der

smooth'bore'
smor'gas·bord'
smoth'er
smudg'i·ness
smudg'y
smug'gle
smug'gler
smug'gling
smut'ty
snaf'fle
sna·fu'
snag'gle·tooth'
snag'gy
snake'skin'
snak'y
snap'drag'on
snap'per
snap'ping
snap'pish
snap'py
snarl'ing
snatch'ing
sneak'er
sneak'ing
sneak'y
sneer'ing
sneez'ing
snick'er
snif'fle
snif'fling
snif'ter
snip'er
snip'ing
snip'py
sniv'el

sniv'el·ing
sniv'el·ling
snob'ber·y
snob'bish
snor'kel
snow'ball'
snow'bank'
snow'fall'
snow'flake'
snow'plow'
snow'shoe'
snow'y
snub'bing
snuff'box'
snuf'fle
snug'gle
soak'ing
soap'box'
soap'i·ness
soap'stone'
soap'suds'
soap'y
so'ber
so·bri'e·ty
so'bri·quet'
soc'cer
so'cia·bil'i·ty
so'cia·ble
so'cia·bly
so'cial
so'cial·ism
so'cial·ist
so'cial·i·za'tion
so'cial·lize
so·ci'e·tal

so·ci'e·ty
so'ci·o·log'i·cal
so'ci·ol'o·gy
sock'et
So·crat'ic
so'da
so·dal'i·ty
sod'den
so'di·um
sod'om·y
so'fa
so'far
soft'ball'
sof'ten
soft'heart'ed
soft'ware'
soft'y
sog'gi·ness
sog'gy
soil'age
soi·ree'
so'journ
sol'ace
so'lar
so·lar'i·um
so'lar·ize'
so·la'ti·um
sol'der
sol'der·ing
sol'dier
sol'dier·ly
sol'dier·y
sol'e·cism
sole'ly
sol'emn

so·lem'ni·ty
sol'em·nize'
so'le·noid'
sol·feg'gio
so·lic'it
so·lic'i·ta'tion
so·lic'i·tor
so·lic'i·tous
so·lic'i·tude'
sol'id
sol'i·dar'i·ty
so·lid'i·fy'
so·lid'i·ty
sol'i·dus
so·lil'o·quy
sol'ip·sism
sol'ip·sist
sol'i·taire'
sol'i·tar'i·ness
sol'i·tar'y
sol'i·tude'
so'lo
so'lo·ist
sol'stice
sol·sti'tial
sol'u·bil'i·ty
sol'u·ble
so·lu'tion
solv'a·ble
sol'ven·cy
sol'vent
so'ma
so·mat'ic
so'ma·to·log'i·cal
so'ma·tol'o·gy

som'ber
som·bre'ro
some'bod'y
some'how'
some'one'
som'er·sault'
some'thing'
some'time'
some'what'
some'where'
som·nam'bu·lant
som·nam'bu·lism
som·nil'o·quy
som'no·lence
som'no·lent
so'nance
so'nar
so·na'ta
so·na·ti'na
song'ster
song'stress
son'ic
son'net
son'ny
so·nor'i·ty
son'o·rous
soon'er
sooth'say'er
soot'i·ness
soot'y
soph'ism
soph'ist
so·phis'ti·cal
so·phis'ti·cate'
so·phis'ti·cat'ed

so·phis'ti·ca'tion
soph'is·try
soph'o·more'
soph'o·mor'ic
so'po·rif'ic
sop'ping
so·pra'no
sor'cer·er
sor'cer·y
sor'did
sor'did·ly
sore'ly
sor'ghum
so·ri'tes
so·ror'i·ty
so·ro'sis
sor'rel
sor'row
sor'row·ful
sor'ry
sor'ti·lege
sou'bise'
sou·brette'
souf'flé'
soul'ful
soul'less
sound'er
sound'ing
sound'less
sound'ly
soup'con'
soup'y
sour·dine'
sour'dough'
sou'sa·phone'

sou·tane'
south'bound'
south'east'
south'east'er·ly
south'east'ern
south'er·ly
south'ern
south'ern·er
south'ing
south'ward
south'west'
south'west'ern
sou've·nir'
sov'er·eign
sov'er·eign·ty
so'vi·et
soy'bean'
space'craft'
space'man
spac'er
space'ship'
spa'cial
spac'ing
spa'cious
spade'work'
spa·ghet'ti
span'drel
span'gle
span'iel
Span'ish
spank'ing
span'ner
spare'ly
spare'ribs'
spar'ing

spar'ing·ly
spark'ing
spar'kle
spar'kler
spar'kling
spar'row
spar'tan
spas·mod'ic
spas·mod'i·cal·ly
spas'tic
spas'ti·cal·ly
spa'tial
spa'tial·ly
spat'ter
spat'u·la
spat'u·late
spav'in
speak'er
speak'ing
spear'head'
spear'mint'
spe'cial
spe'cial·ist
spe·ci·al'i·ty
spe'cial·i·za'tion
spec'ial·ize'
spe'cial·ly
spe'cial·ty
spe'cie
spe'cies
spe·cif'ic
spec'i·fi·ca'tion
spec'i·fic'i·ty
spec'i·fy'
spec'i·men

spe'cious
speck'le
spec'ta·cle
spec'ta·cled
spec·tac'u·lar
spec'ta·tor
spec'ter
spec'tral
spec'tro·graph'
spec'trum
spec'u·late
spec'u·la'tion
spec'u·la'tive
spec'u·la'tor
spec'u·lum
speech'i·fy'
speech'less
speech'less·ly
speech'mak'er
speed'boat'
speed'er
speed'i·ly
speed'ing
speed·om'e·ter
speed'way'
speed'y
spe'le·ol'o·gy
spell'bind'
spell'bind'er
spell'bound'
spell'er
spell'ing
spel'ter
spe·lunk'er
Spen·ce'ri·an

spend'er
spend'thrift'
Spen·se'ri·an
sper'ma·ce'ti
sper'ma·to·zo'a
sper'ma·to·zo'on
sphag'num
spher'i·cal
spher'ics
sphe'roid
sphinc'ter
sphyg'mic
sphyg'mus
spic·ca'to
spic'er·y
spic'i·ness
spic'u·late'
spic'ule
spic'y
spi'der
spi'der·y
spig'ot
spike'nard
spik'y
spill'way'
spin'ach
spi'nal
spin'dle
spin'dling
spin'dly
spin'drift'
spine'less
spin'na·ker
spin'ner
spin'ning

spin'off'
spin'ster
spin'y
spi'ral
spi'rant
spir'it
spir'it·ed
spir'it·ism
spir'it·less
spir'it·u·al
spir'it·u·al·ism
spir'it·u·al·ly
spi'ro·chete'
spi·rom'e·ter
spite'ful
spit'fire'
spit'ter
spit'ting
spit'tle
spit·toon'
splash'board'
splash'ing
splash'y
splat'ter
splay'foot'
splen'did
splen'dor
sple·net'ic
splen'ic
splic'ing
splin'ter
splin'ter·y
split'ting
splotch'y
splut'ter

spoil′age
spoil′sport′
spo′ken
spokes′man
spokes′per′son
spo′li·ate′
spo′li·a′tion
spon·da′ic
spon′dee
sponge′cake′
spon′gy
spon′sion
spon′son
spon′sor
spon′sor·ship′
spon′ta·ne′i·ty
spon′ta′ne·ous
spoof′ing
spook′y
spoon′bill′
spoon′er·ism
spoon′fed′
spo·rad′ic
spo·rad′i·cal·ly
spo′ro·zo′an
sport′i·ness
sport′ing
spor′tive
sports′man·like′
sports′wear′
sport′y
spot′less
spot′light′
spot′ted
spot′ter

spot′ty
spous′al
sprawl′ing
spray′ing
spread′er
spright′li·ness
spright′ly
spring′board′
spring′er
spring′i·ness
spring′time′
spring′y
sprin′kle
sprin′kler
sprin′kling
sprock′et
spu·mes′cent
spu·mo′ni
spu′mous
spum′y
spunk′y
spu′ri·ous
spurn′ing
sput′nik
sput′ter
spu′tum
squab′ble
squab′bling
squad′ron
squal′id
squall′ing
squall′y
squal′or
squa′mate
squa′mous

squan′der
squar′ing
squar′ish
squash′y
squat′ter
squat′ty
squawk′ing
squeak′i·ness
squeak′y
squeal′ing
squeam′ish
squee′gee
squeez′a·ble
squeez′ing
squir′rel
squirt′ing
stab′bing
sta′bile
sta·bil′i·ty
sta′bi·li·za′tion
sta′bi·lize′
sta′bi·liz′er
sta′ble
stac·ca′to
sta′di·a
sta′di·um
stage′coach′
stage′craft′
stage′hand′
stag′ger
stag′ing
stag′nant
stag′nate
stag·na′tion
stag′y

stain'less
stair'case'
stair'way'
sta·lac'tite
sta'lag
sta·lag'mite
stale'mate'
stalk'ing
stall'ing
stal'lion
stal'wart
sta'men
stam'i·na
stam'mer
stam'mer·ing
stam·pede'
stamp'er
stamp'ing
stan'chion
stand'ard
stand'ard·i·za'tion
stand'ar·dize'
stand·ee'
stand'ing
stand'off'
stand'point'
stand'still'
stan'nous
stan'num
stan'za
stan·za'ic
sta'pes
staph'y·lo·coc'cus
sta'ple
sta'pler

sta'pling
star'board'
starch'i·ness
starch'y
star'dom
star'fish'
star'gaz'er
star'gaz'ing
star'let
star'light'
star'ling
star'ri·ness
star'ry
start'er
star'tle
star'tling
star·va'tion
starve'ling
starv'ing
sta'sis
state'craft'
stat'ed
state'hood
state'li·ness
state'ly
state'ment
state'side'
states'man
states'man·ship'
stat'ic
sta'tion
sta'tion·ar'y
sta'tion·er
sta'tion·er'y
sta'tion·mas'ter

stat'ism
stat'ist
sta·tis'tic
sta·tis'ti·cal
sta·tis'ti·cal·ly
stat'is·ti'cian
stat'u·ar'y
stat'ue
stat'u·esque'
stat'u·ette'
stat'ure
sta'tus
sta'tus quo
stat'ute
stat'u·to'ry
stay'ing
stead'fast'
stead'i·ly
stead'i·ness
stead'y
stead'y·ing
steal'ing
stealth'i·ly
stealth'i·ness
stealth'y
steam'boat'
steam'er
steam'ship'
steam'tight'
steam'y
ste·ap'sin
ste'a·rin
ste'a·tite'
steel'work'
steel'work'er

steel'y
steel'yard'
stee'ple
stee'ple·chase'
stee'ple·chas'er
steer'age
steer'ing
steers'man
ste'le
stel'lar
stel'late
stel'lu·lar
stem'mer
stem'ming
stem'ware'
sten'cil
sten'cil·er
sten'cil·ler
sten'o·graph'
ste·nog'ra·pher
sten'o·graph'ic
ste·nog'ra·phy
ste·no'sis
sten'o·type'
sten·to'ri·an
step'child'
step'fa'ther
step'lad'der
step'moth'er
step'par'ent
step'per
step'ping·stone'
step'wise'
ster'e·o
ster'e·o·phon'ic

ster'e·op'ti·con
ster'e·o·scope'
ster'e·o·scop'ic
ster'e·o·type'
ster'e·o·typ'ic
ster'ile
ste·ril'i·ty
ster'i·li·za'tion
ster'i·lize'
ster'i·liz'er
ster'ling
ster'nal
stern'most
ster'num
ster'oid
ster'to·rous
steth'o·scope'
steth'o·scop'ic
ste·thos'co·py
ste've·dore'
stew'ard
stew'ard·ess
stew'ard·ship'
stick'er
stick'i·ness
stick'ing
stick'le
stick'ler
stick'pin'
stick'y
stiff'en
sti'fle
sti'fling
stig'ma
stig'ma·ta

stig'ma·tism
stig'ma·tize'
stil·bes'trol
sti·let'to
still'birth'
still'born'
stilt'ed
Stil'ton
stim'u·lant
stim'u·late'
stim'u·la'tion
stim'u·la'tor
stim'u·lus
sting'er
stin'gi·ness
sting'ing
stin'gy
stink'ing
sti'pend
sti·pen'di·ar'y
stip'pled
stip'pling
stip'u·late'
stip'u·la'tion
stip'u·la·to'ry
stip'ule
stir'ring
stir'rup
stitch'ing
sto'a
stock·ade'
stock'hold'er
stock'i·ness
stock'ing
stock'man

stock'y
stock'yard'
stodg'i·ness
stodg'y
sto'gie
sto'gy
sto'i·cal
sto'i·cal·ly
stok'er
stok'ing
stol'en
stol'id
sto'ma
stom'ach
sto·mat'ic
stone'cut'ter
stone'ma'son
stone'wall'
stone'ware'
ston'i·ness
ston'y
stop'gap'
stop'o'ver
stop'per
stor'age
store'house'
store'keep'er
store'room'
sto'ried
storm'i·ly
storm'i·ness
storm'y
stor'y
stove'pipe'
stow'age

stow'a·way'
stow'ing
stra·bis'mus
strad'dle
strad'dling
straf'ing
strag'gle
strag'gler
straight'a·way'
straight'en
straight'for'ward
strain'er
strain'ing
strait'ened
strange'ly
strang'er
stran'gle
stran'gler
stran'gling
stran'gu·late'
stran'gu·la'tion
strap'ping
strat'a·gem
stra·te'gic
strat'e·gy
strat'i·fi·ca'tion
strat'i·fied'
strat'i·fy'
strat'i·fy'ing
strat'o·sphere'
stra'tum
straw'ber'ry
stray'ing
streak'y
stream'er

stream'let
stream'lined'
stream'lin'ing
strength'en
stren'u·ous
stren'u·ous·ly
strep'to·coc'cic
strep'to·coc'cus
strep'to·my'cin
stress'ful
stretch'er
stretch'ing
stri'ate
stri'at·ed
strick'en
strict'ly
strict'ness
stric'ture
stri'den·cy
stri'dent
strid'ing
strid'u·late'
strid'u·la'tion
strife'torn'
strik'er
strik'ing
strin'gen·cy
strin'gent
string'ing
string'y
strip'ing
strip'ling
strip'ping
striv'en
striv'ing

strok'ing
stroll'er
strong'hold'
strong'ly
stron'ti·um
stro'phe
stroph'ic
strop'ping
struc'tur·al
struc'tur·al·ly
struc'ture
struc'tured
stru'del
strug'gle
strug'gling
strum'ming
strum'pet
strut'ted
strych'nine
stub'bi·ness
stub'ble
stub'bly
stub'born
stub'born·ness
stub'by
stuc'co
stud'ded
stu'dent
stud'ied
stu'di·o'
stu'di·ous
stud'y
stuff'i·ness
stuff'ing
stuff'y

stul'ti·fied'
stul'ti·fy'
stum'ble
stum'bling·block'
stump'y
stun'ning
stunt'ed
stunt'ing
stu·pe·fac'tion
stu·pe·fied'
stu·pe·fi'er
stu·pe·fy'
stu·pen'dous
stu·pid'i·ty
stu'pid·ly
stu'por
stur'di·ness
stur'dy
stur'geon
stut'ter
styl'ing
styl'ish
styl·ist
sty·lis'tic
styl'i·za'tion
styl'ized
styl'lus
sty'mied
sty'ro·foam'
sua'sion
suave'ly
sua'vi·ty
sub·al'tern
sub'a·tom'ic
sub'com·mit'tee

sub·con'scious
sub·con'tract,
  sub'con·tract'
sub'di·vide
sub'di·vi'sion
sub·due'
sub·du'ing
sub'head'ing
sub'ject
sub·jec'tion
sub·jec'tive
sub'jec·tiv'i·ty
sub'ju·gate'
sub'ju·ga'tion
sub·junc'tive
sub'lease'
sub·let'
sub'li·mate'
sub·li·ma'tion
sub·lime'
sub·lim'i·nal
sub·ma·chine'
sub'ma·rine'
sub·merge'
sub·merse'
sub·mer'sion
sub·mis'sion
sub·mis'sive
sub·mit'
sub·mit'ting
sub·or'di·nate'
sub·or'di·na'tion
sub·orn'
sub'plot'
sub·poe'na

sub'ro·ga'tion
sub·scribe'
sub·scrip'tion
sub'se·quent
sub'se·quent·ly
sub·ser'vi·ent
sub·side'
sub·sid'i·ar'y
sub·sid'ing
sub'si·dize'
sub'si·dy
sub·sist'
sub·sis'tence
sub'stance
sub·stand'ard
sub·stan'tial
sub·stan'ti·al'i·ty
sub·stan'tial·ly
sub·stan'ti·ate'
sub'stan·tive
sub'sti·tute'
sub'sti·tu'tion
sub·sume'
sub'ter·fuge'
sub'ter·ra'ne·an
sub'ter·ra'ne·ous
sub'tle
sub'tle·ty
sub·tract'
sub·trac'tion
sub'trop'i·cal
sub'urb
sub·ur'ban
sub·ur'ban·ite'
sub·ur'bi·a

sub·vene'
sub·ven'tion
sub·ver'sion
sub·ver'sive
sub·vert'
suc·ceed'
suc·cess'
suc·cess'ful
suc·ces'sion
suc·ces'sive
suc·ces'sor
suc·cinct'
suc'cor
suc'co·tash'
suc'cu·bus
suc'cu·lence
suc'cu·lent
suc·cumb'
suck'er
suck'le
suck'ling
su'crose
suc'tion
su·dar'i·um
su'da·to'ry
sud'den
sud'den·ly
su'dor·if'ic
suds'y
su'et
suf'fer
suf'fer·a·ble
suf'fer·ance
suf'fer·ing
suf·fice'

suf·fi'cien·cy
suf·fi'cient
suf'fix
suf'fo·cate'
suf'fo·ca'tion
suf'frage
suf'fra·gist
suf·fuse'
suf·fu'sion
Su'fism
sug'ar
sug'ared
sug'ar·y
sug·gest'
sug·gest'i·bil'i·ty
sug·gest'i·ble
sug·ges'tion
sug·ges'tive
su'i·cid'al
su'i·cide'
suit'a·ble
suit'a·bly
suit'case'
suit'or
Suk'koth'
sul'cate
sul'cus
sul'fa
sul'fate
sul'fide
sul·fon'ic
sul'fur
sul'fu·rate
sul'fu·rous
sulk'y

sul'len
sul'ly
sul'ly·ing
sul'phu·rous
sul'tan
sul'tan·ate
sul'tri·ness
sul'try
sum'ma cum
   lau'de
sum'ma·ri·ly
sum'ma·ri·za'tion
sum'ma·rize'
sum'ma·ry
sum'ma'tion
sum'mer
sum'mer·y
sum'mit
sum'mon
sum'mon·ing
sum'mons
sump'tu·ar'y
sump'tu·ous
sun'burn'
sun'dae
Sun'day
sun'der
sun'di'al
sun'down'
sun'fish'
sun'flow'er
sunk'en
sun'ni·ness
sun'ny
sun'rise'

sun'set'
sun'shine'
sun'stroke'
su'per
su'per·a·ble
su'per·a·bun'dance
su'per·an'nu·at'ed
su·perb'
su·perb'ly
su'per·cil'i·ous
su'per·e'go
su'per·er'o·gate'
su'per·e·rog'a·to'ry
su'per·fi'cial
su'per·fi'ci·al'i·ty
su'per·fi'cial·ly
su·per'flu·ous
su'per·heat'
su'per·im·pose'
su'per·im'po·si'tion
su'per·in·tend'
su'per·in·tend'ent
su·pe'ri·or
su·pe'ri·or'i·ty
su·per'la·tive
su'per·mar'ket
su'per·nat'u·ral
su'per·nu'mer·ar'y
su'per·pow'er
su'per·sede'
su'per·son'ic
su'per·sti'tion
su'per·sti'tious
su'per·struc'ture
su'per·vene'

su'per·vise'
su'per·vi'sion
su'per·vi'sor
su'per·vi'so·ry
su·pine'
sup'per
sup·plant'
sup·plant'ing
sup'ple
sup'ple·ment
sup'ple·men'ta·ry
sup'pli·ant
sup'pli·cant
sup'pli·cate'
sup·ply'
sup·port'
sup·port'a·ble
sup·port'er
sup·port'ing
sup·por'tive
sup·pose'
sup·pos'ed·ly
sup'po·si'tion
sup·pos'i·to'ry
sup·press'
sup·pressed'
sup·pres'sion
sup·pres'sive
sup'pu·rate'
sup'pu·ra'tive
su·prem'a·cy
su·preme'
sur·cease'
sur'charge'
sur'cin'gle

sure'ly
sure'ty
sur'face
sur'fac·ing
surf'board'
sur'feit
surf'ing
sur'geon
sur'ger·y
sur'gi·cal
sur'gi·cal·ly
surg'ing
sur'ly
sur·mise'
sur·mount'
sur'name
sur·pass'
sur'plice
sur'plus
sur·prise'
sur·pris'ing
sur·re'al·ism
sur·re'al·ist
sur·re'al·is'tic
sur·ren'der
sur'rep·ti'tious
sur'rey
sur'ro·gate'
sur·round'
sur·round'ing
sur'tax'
sur·veil'lance
sur·vey', sur'vey
sur·vey'or
sur·viv'al

sur·vive'
sur·vi'vor·ship'
sus·cep'ti·bil'i·ty
sus·cep'ti·ble
sus·pect', sus'pect
sus·pect'ing
sus·pend'
sus·pend'ed
sus·pend'ers
sus·pense'
sus·pense'ful
sus·pen'sion
sus·pi'cion
sus·pi'cious
sus·pi·ra'tion
sus·pire'
sus·tain'
sus'te·nance
su'sur·a'tion
sut'ler
su'tra
sut·tee'
su'ture
su'ze·rain
swab'bing
swad'dle
swad'dling
swag'ger
swal'low
swa'mi
swamp'y
swap'ping
swarm'ing
swarth'i·ness
swarth'y

swash'buck'ler
swash'buck'ling
swas'ti·ka
swat'ting
swear'ing
sweat'er
sweat'i·ness
sweat'y
sweep'er
sweep'ing
sweep'stakes'
sweet'bread'
sweet'en·er
sweet'meat'
swell'ing
swel'ter
swift'er
swift'ly
swill'ing
swim'ming
swin'dle
swin'dler
swin'dling
swine'herd'
swing'ing
swin'ish
switch'back'
switch'yard'
swiv'el
swiz'zle
swol'len
sword'fish'
swords'man
syb'a·rite'
syb'a·rit'ic

syc'a·more'
syc'o·phan·cy
syc'o·phant
sy·co'sis
syl·lab'ic
syl·lab'i·fi·ca'tion
syl'la·ble
syl'la·bus
syl'lo·gism
syl'lo·gize'
syl'van
sym'bi·o'sis
sym'bi·ot'ic
sym'bol
sym·bol'ic
sym'bol·ism
sym'bol·ist
sym'bol·ize'
sym·met'ri·cal
sym'me·try
sym'pa·thet'ic
sym'pa·thize'
sym'pa·thy
sym·phon'ic

sym'pho·ny
sym·po'si·um
symp'tom
symp'to·mat'ic
syn'a·gogue'
syn·apse'
syn·ap'sis
syn·chron'ic
syn'chro·nism
syn'chro·nize'
syn'chro·nous
syn'co·pate'
syn'co·pa'tion
syn'cre·tism
syn'cre·tize'
syn'dic
syn'di·cal·ism
syn'di·cate'
syn'di·ca'tion
syn·ec'do·che
syn'er·gism
syn'er·gy
syn'es·the'si·a
syn'od

syn'o·nym
syn·on'y·mous
syn·op'sis
syn·op'tic
syn·tac'tic
syn'tax
syn'the·sis
syn'the·size'
syn'the·siz'ing
syn·thet'ic
syn·thet'i·cal·ly
syph'i·lis
syph'i·lit'ic
syr·inge'
sy'rup
sy'rup·y
sys·tal'tic
sys'tem
sys'tem·at'ic
sys'tem·a·tize'
sys·tem'ic
sys'to·le'
sys·tol'ic

T

ta·bas'co
tab'by
tab'er·nac'le
ta'bes
tab'la·ture
ta'ble
tab'leau tab·leau'
ta'ble·cloth'
ta'ble·spoon'
tab'let
tab'loid
ta·boo'
tab'u·lar
tab'u·late'
tab'u·lat'ing
tab'u·la'tor
ta·chom'e·ter
tach'y·car'di·a
tac'it
tac'i·turn
tack'i·ness
tack'le
tack'ling
tack'y
tact'ful
tac'tic
tac'ti·cal
tac·ti'cian
tac'tile
tact'less
tad'pole'

taf'fe·ta
taff'rail'
taf'fy
tag'ging
tail'board'
tail'gate'
tail'ing
tai'lor
tai'lor·made'
tail'spin'
taint'ed
tak'en
tak'er
tak'ing
tal'cum
tale'bear'ing
tal'ent
tal'ent·ed
tal'is·man
talk'a·tive
talk'ie
talk'ing
talk'y
tall'er
tall'est
tal'low
tal'ly
tal'on
ta'lus
ta·ma'le
tam'a·rind'

tam'a·risk'
tam'bour
tam'bou·rine'
tam'er
tam'ing
tamp'er
tam'pon
tan'a·ger
tan'dem
tan'ge·lo'
tan'gent
tan·gen'tial
tan'ge·rine'
tan'gi·bil'i·ty
tan'gi·ble
tan'gle
tan'gled
tan'go
tang'y
tank'age
tank'ard
tank'er
tan'ner
tan'ner·y
tan'nic
tan'ning
tan'ta·lize'
tan'ta·liz'ing
tan'ta·mount'
tan'trum
Tao'ism

tap'er
tap'es·try
tape'worm'
tap'i·o'ca
tap'ing
ta'pir
tap'per
tap'ping
tap'room'
tap'root'
tar'an·tel'la
ta·ran'tu·la
tar'di·ness
tar'dy
tar'get
tar'iff
tar'nish
tar'pau·lin
tar'pon
tar'ra·gon'
tar'ry
tar'ry·ing
tar'sal
tar'sus
tar'tan
tar'tar
tar'tare
tart'ness
task'mas'ter
tas'sel
tas'seled
tas'selled
taste'ful
taste'less
tast'er

tast'y
tat'ter
tat'tered
tat'ting
tat'tle
tat'tler
tat·too'
taunt'ing
tau'rine
taut'en
tau'to·log'i·cal
tau·tol'o·gy
tav'ern
tav'ern·er
taw'dri·ness
taw'dry
taw'ni·ness
taw'ny
tax'a·ble
tax·a'tion
tax'eme
tax'i
tax'i·der'mist
tax'i·der'my
tax'is
tax'o·nom'ic
tax·on'o·my
tax'pay'er
teach'a·ble
teach'er
teach'ing
tea'cup'
tea'ket'tle
team'mate'
team'ster

team'work'
tea'pot'
tear'drop'
tear'ful
tear'ing
tea'room'
tear'y
teas'er
teas'ing
tea'spoon'
tech'nic
tech'ni·cal
tech'ni·cal'i·ty
tech'ni·cal·ly
tech·ni'cian
tech'ni·col'or
tech'nics
tech·nique'
tech·noc'ra·cy
tech'no·crat'
tech'no·log'i·cal
tech·nol'o·gy
tec·ton'ic
ted'dy
te'di·ous
te'di·um
teen'ag'er
tee'ter
teeth'ing
tee·to'tal
tee·to'tal·er
teg'men
teg'u·ment
tel'a·mon'
tel'e·cast'

tel'e·com·mu'ni·ca'
   tion
tel'e·gram'
tel'e·graph'
tel'e·graph'ic
te·leg'ra·phy
tel'e·lec'tric
tel'e·o·log'i·cal
tel'e·ol'o·gy
tel'e·path'i·cal·ly
te·lep'a·thy
tel'e·phone'
tel'e·phon'ic
tel'e·pho'to
tel'e·pho'to·graph'
tel'e·print'er
tel'e·ran'
tel'e·scope'
tel'e·scop'ic
tel'e·type'
tel'e·vise'
tel'e·vi'sion
tel'ic
tell'er
tell'ing
tell'tale'
tel·lu'ri·an
tel·lu'ri·um
te·mer'i·ty
tem'per
tem'per·a
tem'per·a·ment
tem'per·a·men'tal
tem'per·ance
tem'per·ate

tem'per·a·ture
tem'pered
tem'pest
tem·pes'tu·ous
tem'plate
tem'ple
tem'po
tem'po·ral
tem'po·ral'i·ty
tem'po·rar'y
tem'po·rize'
tem'po·riz'ing
temp·ta'tion
tempt'er
tempt'ing
tempt'ress
ten'a·bil'i·ty
ten'a·ble
te·na'cious
te·nac'i·ty
ten'an·cy
ten'ant
ten'ant·ry
tend'ance
tend'en·cy
ten·den'tious
ten'der (soft, offer
   to pay)
tend'er (one who
   tends)
ten'der·foot'
ten'der·ize'
ten'der·loin'
ten'di·nous
ten'don

ten'dril
ten'e·ment
ten'e·men'ta·ry
ten'et
ten'fold'
Ten'nes·se'an
ten'nis
ten'on
ten'or
tense'ly
ten'sile
ten'sion
ten'sor
ten'ta·cle
ten'ta·tive
tent'ed
ten'ter·hooks'
ten'u·ous
ten'ure
te'pee
tep'id
ter'a·tism
ter'a·tol'o·gy
ter'bi·um
ter'cel
ter·cen'te·nar'y
ter'cet, ter·cet'
ter'gi·ver·sate'
ter'gum
ter'ma·gant
ter'mi·na·ble
ter'mi·nal
ter'mi·nal·ly
ter'mi·nate'
ter'mi·na'tion

ter'mi·na'tor
ter'mi·nol'o·gy
ter'mi·nus
ter'mite
term'less
term'or
ter'na·ry
ter'nate
terp'si·cho·re'an
ter'race
ter'ra cot'ta
ter·rain'
ter'ra in·cog'ni·ta
ter'ra·my'cin
ter·rar'i·um
ter·res'tri·al
ter'ret
ter'ri·ble
ter'ri·bly
ter'ri·er
ter·rif'ic
ter·rif'i·cal·ly
ter'ri·fy'
ter'ri·fy'ing
ter'ri·to'ri·al
ter'ri·to'ri·al'i·ty
ter'ri·to'ri·al·ly
ter'ri·to'ry
ter'ror
ter'ror·ism
ter'ror'ist
ter'ror·ize'
ter'ry
ter'ti·ar'y
ter·va'lent

tes'se·late'
tes'se·lat'ed
tes'ta·ment
tes'ta·men'ta·ry
tes'tate
tes'ta·tor
test'er (one who
    tests)
tes'ter (bed can-
    opy)
tes'ti·cle
tes'ti·fied'
tes'ti·fi'er
tes'ti·fy'
tes'ti·ly
tes'ti·mo'ni·al
tes'ti·mo'ny
tes·tos'ter·one'
tes·tu'do
tes'ty
te·tan'ic
tet'a·nus
teth'er
teth'ered
tet'ra·chlo'ride
tet'rad
tet'ra·gon'
te·trag'o·nal
Tet'ra·gram'ma·ton'
tet'ra·he'dron
te·tral'o·gy
te·tram'e·ter
tet'ra·va'lent
Teu·ton'ic
Tex'an

text'book'
tex'tile
tex'tu·al
tex'tu·al·ism
tex'ture
tex'tured
tha·lam'ic
thal'a·mus
thal'li·um
than'a·to·pho'bi·a
thank'ful
thank'ing
thank'less
thanks'giv'ing
thau'ma·tol'o·gy
thau'ma·turge'
thau'ma·tur'gy
thaw'ing
the'a·ter
the'a·tre
the·at'ri·cal
the·at'ri·cal'i·ty
the·at'rics
the'ism
the·is'tic
the·mat'ic
the·mat'i·cal·ly
them·selves'
the'nar
thence'forth'
thence'for'ward
the'o·cen'tric
the·oc'ra·cy
the'o·crat'
the'o·crat'ic

the·od'i·cy
the·og'o·ny
the·o·lo'gi·an
the·o·log'i·cal
the·ol'o·gy
the·oph'a·ny
the'o·rem
the·o·ret'i·cal·ly
the·o·re·ti'cian
the'o·rist
the'o·rize'
the'o·ry
the·os'o·phy
ther'a·peu'tic
ther'a·pist
ther'a·py
there'a·bouts'
there·af'ter
there·by'
there'fore'
there·in'
there·of'
there·to'
there·with'
ther'mal
ther'mal·ly
ther'mic
therm'i'on
ther'mo·chem'is·try
ther'mo·dy·nam'ic
ther·mom'e·ter
ther'mo·nu'cle·ar
ther'mos
ther'mo·stat'
ther'mo·trop'ic

ther·mot'ro·pism
the·sau'rus
the'sis
thes'pi·an
the'ta
thi'a·mine'
thick'en
thick'en·ing
thick'et
thick'ness
thiev'er·y
thiev'ing
thim'ble
thim'ble·rig'
think'a·ble
think'ing
think'tank'
thin'ner
thi'ol
thi·on'ic
thirst'y
thir'teen'
thir'teenth'
thir'ti·eth
thir'ty
this'tle
this'tle·down'
thith'er
tho·rac'ic
tho'rax
tho'ri·um
thorn'i·ness
thorn'y
tho'ron
thor'ough

thor'ough·bred'
thor'ough·fare'
thor'ough·ly
thor'ough·ness
thought'ful
thought'less
thou'sand
thou'sandth
thrall'dom
thrash'er
thrash'ing
thra·son'i·cal
thread'bare'
threat·en
threat'en·ing
three'fold'
three'some
thren'o·dy
threash'er
thresh'ing
thresh'old
thrift'y
thrill'er
thrill'ing
thriv'ing
throat'i·ness
throat'y
throb'bing
throm·bo'sis
throm'bus
throt'tle
throt'tling
through·out'
throw'a·way'
throw'back'

thrust'ing
thu'li·um
thumb'nail'
thumb'tack'
thump'ing
thun'der
thun'der·bolt'
thun'der·ous
thun'der·show'er
thun'der·struck'
Thurs'day
thy'mus
thy'roid
thy·rox'ine
thyr'sus
thy·self'
tib'i·a
tick'er
tick'et
tick'ing
tick'le
tick'ling
tick'lish
tid'al
tid'bit'
tid'dly·winks'
tide'wa'ter
ti'dings
ti'dy
ti'ger
ti'ger·ish
tight'en
tight'rope'
ti'gress
til'de

tile'fish'
til'ing
till'age
till'er
till'ing
tilt'ed
tim'ber
tim'ber·land'
tim'bre
time'less
time'li·ness
time'ly
time'piece'
tim'id
ti·mid'i·ty
tim'ing
tim'or·ous
tim'o·thy
tim'pa·ni
tinc'ture
tin'der
tinge'ing
tin'gling
ti'ni·er
tink'er
tin'kle
tin'ner
tin'ny
tin'sel
tin'smith'
ti'ny
tip'per
tip'pet
tip'ping
tip'ple

tip'sy
tip'toe'
ti'rade
tire'some
tir'ing
tis'sue
ti'tan
ti·tan'ic
ti·ta'ni·um
tith'ing
tit'il·late'
ti'tle
ti'tled
tit'mouse'
ti'trate
tit'ter
tit'ter·ing
tit'u·lar
toad'stool'
toast'er
toast'mas'ter
to·bac'co
to·bac'co·nist
to·bog'gan
to·bog'gan·ing
toc·ca'ta
toc'sin
tod'dle
tod'dler
tod'dy
tof'fee
to'ga
to·geth'er
to·geth'er·ness
toil'ing

to'ken
tol'er·a·ble
tol'er·ance
tol'er·ant
tol'er·ate'
toll'gate'
toll'ing
tol'u·ene'
tom'a·hawk'
to·ma'to
tom'boy'
tomb'stone'
tom'cat'
to·mor'row
ton'al
to·nal'i·ty
tone'less
ton'ic
to·night'
ton'nage
ton·neau'
ton'sils
ton'sil·lec'to·my
ton·sil·li·tis
ton·so'ri·al
ton'sure
tool'ing
tooth'ache'
tooth'some
tooth'y
to'paz
top'coat'
top'ic
top'i·cal
to·pog'ra·phy

top'per
top'ping
top'ple
top'pling
top'side'
top'soil'
to'rah
torch'bear'er
tor'e·a·dor'
tor'ment,
    tor·ment'
tor·men'tor
tor·na'do
tor·pe'do
tor'pid
tor'por
tor'rent
tor·ren'tial
tor'rid
tor'sion
tor'so
tor·til'la
tor'toise
tor'tu·ous
tor'ture
tor'tured
toss'ing
to·tal'i·tar'i·an
to·tal'i·ty
to'tem
tot'ing
tot'ter
tot'ter·ing
tou'can
touch'down'

touch'ing
touch'y
tough'en
tou·pee'
tour'ism
tour'ist
tour'na·ment
tour'ney
tour'ni·quet
tou'sle
tou'sled
tout'ed
tow'el
tow'er
tow'head'
tow'line'
town'ship
towns'peo'ple
tox·e'mi·a
tox·e'mic
tox'ic
tox·ic'i·ty
tox'i·col'o·gist
tox'i·col'o·gy
tox'in
trac'er·y
tra'che·a
trac'ing
track'er
track'ing
trac'ta·ble
trac'tile
trac'tion
trac'tor
trade'mark'

trad'er
trades'man
tra·di'tion
tra·di'tion·al
tra·duce'
tra·duced'
traf'fic
traf'fick·ing
tra·ge'di·an
trag'e·dy
trag'ic
trag'i·cal·ly
trag'i·com'e·dy
trail'er
trail'ing
train·ee'
train'er
train'ing
traips'ing
trai'tor
trai'tor·ous
tra·jec'to·ry
tram'mel
tram'ple
tram'po·line
tram'way'
tran'quil
tran'quil·ize'
tran'quil·iz'er
tran·quil'li·ty
trans·act'
trans·ac'tion
trans·ac'tion·al
trans'at·lan'tic
tran·scend'

tran·scend'ent
tran'scen·den'tal
tran·scribe'
tran'script'
tran·scrip'tion
tran'sept
trans·fer, trans·fer'
trans·fer·a·ble
trans'fer·ence
trans·ferred,
  trans·ferred'
trans·fig'u·ra'tion
trans·fig'ure
trans·fix'
trans·form'
trans'for·ma'tion
trans'for·ma'tion·al
trans·form'a·tive
trans·form'er
trans·fuse'
trans·fu'sion
trans·gress'
trans·gres'sion
trans·gres'sor
tran'sien·cy
tran'sient
tran·sis'tor
trans'it
tran·si'tion
tran'si·tive
tran'si·to'ry
trans·late,
  trans·late'
trans·lat·ed,
  trans·lat'ed

trans·la'tion
trans·lu'cent
trans·mi'grate
trans·mis'si·ble
trans·mis'sion
trans·mit'
trans·mit'ter
trans·mut'a·ble
trans'mu·ta'tion
trans·mute'
tran'som
trans·par'en·cy
trans·par'ent
tran·spire'
trans'plant,
  trans·plant'
trans'port,
  trans·port'
trans'por·ta'tion
trans·pose'
trans'po·si'tion
trans·verse'
trans·ves'tite
tra·peze'
trap'e·zoid'
trap'per
trap'pings
trau'ma
trau·mat'ic
trau'ma·tize'
trav'el
trav'eled
trav'el·er
trav'el·ing
trav'e·logue'

tra·verse′, tra′verse
trav′es·ty
trawl′er
treach′er·ous
treach′er·y
trea′cle
trea′dle
tread′mill′
trea′son
treas′ure
treas′ur·er
treas′ur·y
trea′tise
treat′ment
trea′ty
tre′ble
tre′foil
trek′ker
trel′lis
trem′ble
trem′bling
tre·men′dous
trem′or
trem′u·lous
trench′ant
trench′er
tre·pan′
tres′pass
tres′pass·er
tres′tle
tri′ad
tri′al
tri′an′gle
tri·an′gu·lar
tri·an′gu·late′

tri·an′gu·la′tion
trib′al
tribes′man
trib′u·la′tion
tri·bu′nal
trib′une
trib′u·tar′y
trib′ute
tri′ceps
trich′i·no′sis
trick′i·ness
trick′le
trick′ster
trick′y
tri·col′or
tri′cot
tri′cy·cle
tri′dent
tri·en′ni·al
tri′fle
tri′fling
tri·fo′cal, tri′fo′cal
trig′ger
trig′o·no·met′ric
trig′o·nom′e·try
tri·lat′er·al
tri·lin′gual
tril′lion
tril′lionth
tril′o·gy
tri·mes′ter
trim′e·ter
trim′mer
trim′mings
trin′i·ty

trink′et
tri′o
tri·par′tite
trip′ham′mer
tri′ple
tri′plet
trip′li·cate
tri′pod
trip′per
trip′pet
trip′ping
trip′tych
tri′reme
tri·sect′
trit′u·rate′
tri′umph
tri·um′phant
tri·um′vi·rate
tri·va′lence
tri·va′lent
triv′et
triv′i·a
triv′i·al
triv′i·al′i·ty
triv′i·um
tro·cha′ic
tro′chee
trog′lo·dyte′
troi′ka
trol′ley
trol′lop
trom′bone
trom′bon·ist
troop′er
troph′ic

tro'phy
trop'ic
trop'i·cal
tro'pism
tro·pol'o·gy
trop'o·sphere'
trot'line'
trot'ter
trou'ba·dour'
trou'ble
trou'ble·mak'er
trou'ble·some
trou'bling
troup'er
trou'sers
trous·seau'
tro'ver
trow'el
tru'an·cy
tru'ant
truck'er
truck'ing
truck'le
truc'u·lent
trudg'ing
truf'fle
tru'ism
trum'pet
trum'pet·er
trun'cate
trun'cat·ed
trun'cheon
trun'dle
truss'ing
trus·tee'

trus·tee'ship
trust'ing
trust'wor'thy
trust'y
truth'ful
try'ing
try'out'
tryp'sin
tset'se
tub'al
tu'ber
tu'ber·cle
tu·ber'cu·lar
tu·ber'cu·lin
tu·ber'cu·lo'sis
tube'rose'
tu'ber·ous
tub'ing
tu'bu·lar
Tues'day
tug'boat'
tu·i'tion
tu la·re'mi·a
tu'lip
tu'lip·wood'
tum'ble
tum'bler
tum'brel
tu'me·fac'tion
tu'me·fy'
tu·mes'cence
tu'mid
tu'mor
tu'mor·ous
tu'mult

tu·mul'tu·ous
tu'mu·lus
tu'na
tune'ful
tun'er
tung'sten
tu'nic
tun'nel
tun'neled
tun'nelled
tu'pe·lo'
tur'ban
tur'bid
tur'bine
tur'bo·jet'
tur'bu·lence
tur'bu·lent
tur'gid
tur·gid'i·ty
tur'key
tur'mer·ic
tur'moil
turn'a·bout'
turn'buck'le
turn'coat'
turn'ing
tur'nip
turn'o'ver
turn'stile'
turn'ta'ble
tur'pen·tine'
tur'quoise
tur'ret
tur'ret·ed
tur'tle

tus'sle
tu'te·lage
tu'te·lar'y
tu'tor
tu·to'ri·al
tut'ti
tux·e'do
twad'dle
twee'dle
tweet'er
tweez'ers
twen'ti·eth
twen'ty
twid'dle
twi'light'

twin'ing
twin'kle
twin'kling
twist'ing
twit'ter
two'fold'
tym'pa·ni
tym·pan'ic
type'script'
type'writ'er
type'writ'ten
ty'phoid
ty·phoon'
ty'phus

typ'i·cal
typ'i·fi·ca'tion
typ'i·fy'
typ'ist
ty·pog'ra·phy
ty·pol'o·gy
ty·ran'ni·cal
tyr'an·nize'
ty·ran'no·saur'
tyr'an·nous
tyr'an·ny
ty'rant
tza·ri'na
tzar'ist

U

ud'der
u·dom'e·ter
u'do·met'ric
u·dom'e·try
ug'li·fy'
ug'li·ness
ug'ly
u'ku·le'le
ul'cer·ate'
ul'cer·a'tion
ul'cer·ous
ull'age
ul'nar
ul·te'ri·or
ul'ti·mate
ul'ti·ma'tum
ul'ti·mo'
ul'tra·ma·rine'
ul'tra·mi'cro·scope'
ul'tra·mod'ern
ul'tra·vi'o·let
ul'u·lant
ul'u·la'tion
um'bel
um'bel·late
um'ber
um·bil'i·cal
um'bra
um'brage
um·brel'la
um'laut

um'pire
un'ac·com'pa·nied
un'ac·count'a·ble
un'af·fect'ed
u·nan'i·mous
un·armed'
un'as·sum'ing
un'a·wares'
un'be·known'
un·bri'dled
un·can'ny
un·cer'tain
un'ci·al
un'ci·form'
un'cle
un·com·mit'ted
un'con·di'tion·al
un·con'scious
unc'tion
unc'tu·ous
un·dec'a·gon'
un'der
un'der·cur'rent
un'der·es'ti·mate'
un'der·grad'u·ate
un'der·hand'ed
un'der·lie'
un'der·mine'
un'der·score'
un'der·stand'
un'der·stand'a·ble

un'der·stand'ing
un'der·stood'
un'der·stud'y
un'du·late'
un'du·la'tion
un·du'ly
un·earth'ly
un·eas'y
un'em·ploy'ment
un·gain'ly
un'guent
un'gu·la
un'gu·late
un·hinged'
u'ni·cam'er·al
u'ni·corn'
u'ni·cy'cle
u'ni·fi·ca'tion
u'ni·form'
u'ni·formed'
u'ni·form'i·ty
u'ni·fy
u'ni·lat'er·al
un'im·peach'a·ble
un'ion
un'ion·ism
un'ion·i·za'tion
un'ion·ize'
u·nip'a·rous
u·nique'
u'ni·son

u'nit
U'ni·tar'i·an
u'ni·tar'y
u·nite'
u·nit'ed
u'ni·ty
u'ni·va'lent
u'ni·ver'sal
u'ni·ver·sal'i·ty
u'ni·ver·sal·ly
u'ni·ver'si·ty
un·kempt'
un·like'li·hood'
un·like'ly
un·mit'i·gat'ed
un·nat'u·ral
un·nec'es·sar'y
un·rav'el
un·rea'son·a·ble
un're·mit'ting
un·rest'
un·rul'i·ness
un·rul'y
un·til'
un·told'
un·u'su·al
un·wield'y
up·braid'
up'bring'ing
up·date', up'date'
up·heav'al
up·hold'
up·hol'ster
up·hol'ster·er

up·hol'ster·y
up·lift', up'lift'
up·on'
up'per
up'per·class'man
up'per·most'
up'right'
up'ris'ing
up'roar'
up·roar'i·ous
up·set', up'set'
up'side'
up'si·lon'
up'stage'
up'state'
up'swing'
up'town'
u·ran'ic
u·ra'ni·um
u'ra·nog'ra·phy
ur'ban
ur·bane'
ür·ban'i·ty
ur'ban·i·za'tion
ur'chin
u·re'mi·a
u·re'mic
u·re'ter
u're·thane'
u're'thra
ur'gen·cy
ur'gent
u'ri·nal
u'ri·nar'y

u'ri·na'tion
u'rine
u·rol'o·gy
ur'sine
us'a·bil'i·ty
us'a·ble
us'age
use'ful
ush'er
ush'er·ette'
u'su·al
u'su·al·ly
u'su·fruct'
u'su·rer
u·su'ri·ous
u'sur·pa'tion
u·surp'er
u'su·ry
U'tah·an
u·ten'sil
u'ter·ine
u'ter·us
u'tile
u·til'i·tar'i·an
u·til'i·ty
u'til·ize'
ut'most'
u·to'pi·an
ut'ter
ut'ter·ance
ut'ter·most'
u've·a
ux·o'ri·al
ux·o'ri·ous

V

va'can·cy
va'cant
va'cate'
va·ca'tion
vac'ci·nate'
vac'ci·na'tion
vac·cine'
vac'il·late'
vac'il·lat'ing
vac'il·la'tion
va·cu'i·ty
vac'u·ole'
vac'u·ous
vac'u·um
va'de me'cum
vag'a·bond'
va·gar'y
va·gi'na
vag'i·nal
va'gran·cy
va'grant
va'gus
vain'glo'ri·ous
vain'ly
val'ance
val'e·dic'tion
val'e·dic'to·ri·an
val'e·dic'to·ry
va'lence
val'en·tine'
val'et

val'e·tu'di·nar'i·an
val'iant
val'id
val'i·date'
val'i·da'tion
va·lid'i·ty
va·lise'
val'ley
val'or·i·za'tion
val'or·ize'
val'or·ous
val'u·a·ble
val'u·a'tion
val'ue
val'ued
val'vate
val'vu·lar
vam'pire
vam'pir·ism
va·na'di·um
van'dal·ism
van'dal·ize'
van'guard
va·nil'la
van·il'lin, van·il'lin
van'ish
van'ish·ing
van'i·ty
van'quish
van'tage
vap'id

va'por
va'por·im'e·ter
va'por·i·za'tion
va'por·ize'
va'por·iz'er
va'por·ous
var'i·a·ble
var'i·ance
var'i·ant
var'i·a'tion
var'i·cose'
var'i·cos'i·ty
var'ied
var'i·e·gate'
va·ri'e·ty
va·ri'o·la
var'i·o'rum
var'i·ous
var'nish
var'si·ty
var'y
vas'cu·lar
vas'cu·lum
vas·ec'to·my
vas'e·line'
vas'o·mo'tor
vas'sal
vas'sal·age
Vat'i·can
vaude'ville
vault'ed

270

vault′ing
vec′tion
vec′tor
veg′e·ta·ble
veg′e·tal
veg′e·tar′i·an
veg′e·tate′
veg′e·ta′tion
veg′e·ta′tive
ve′he·mence
ve′he·ment
ve′hi·cle
ve·hic′u·lar
ve·la′men
ve′lar
vel′lum
ve·loc′i·ty
vel′vet
vel′vet·een′
ve′nal
ve·nal′i·ty
ve·na′tion
vend·ee′
ven·det′ta
vend′ing
ven′dor
ve·neer′
ven′er·a·ble
ven′er·ate′
ven′er·a′tion
ve·ne′re·al
ven′er·y
Ve·ne′tian
venge′ance
venge′ful

ve′ni·al
ve′ni·al′i·ty
ven′i·son
ven′om
ven′om·ous
ve′nous
ven′ter
ven′ti·late′
ven′ti·la′tion
ven′tral
ven′tri·cle
ven·tric′u·lar
ven·tril′o·quism
ven′ture
ven′ture·some
ven′tur·ous
ven′ue
ve·ra′cious
ve·rac′i·ty
ve·ran′da
ve·ran′dah
ver′bal
ver′bal·ize′
ver′bal·ly
ver·ba′tim
ver·be′na
ver·bi·age
ver·bose′
ver·bos′i·ty
ver′dan·cy
ver′dant
ver′dict
ver′di·gris′
ver′dure
ver′i·fi′a·ble

ver′i·fi·ca′tion
ver′i·fy′
ver′i·sim′i·lar
ver′i·si·mil′i·tude′
ver′i·ta·ble
ver′i·ty
ver′mi·cel′li
ver·mic′u·lar
ver·mil′ion
ver′min
Ver·mont′er
ver·mouth′
ver·nac′u·lar
ver′nal
Ver′ner
ver′ni·er
ve·ron′i·ca
ver′sant
ver′sa·tile
ver′sa·til′i·ty
ver′si·fi′er
ver′si·fy′
ver′sion
ver′sus
ver′te·bra
ver′te·brate′
ver′tex
ver′ti·cal
ver′ti·cal·ly
ver′ti·ces
ver·tig′i·nous
ver·ti·go′
ves′i·cant
ves′i·cle
ves′per

ves'per·tine
ves'pi·ar'y
ves'sel
ves'tal
vest'ed
ves'tige
ves·tig'i·al
vest'ment
ves'try
ves'ture
vet'er·an
vet'er·i·nar'i·an
vet'er·i·nar'y
ve'toed
vex·a'tion
vex·a'tious
vi'a·bil'i·ty
vi'a·ble
vi'a·duct'
vi'al
vi·at'i·cum
vi'bran·cy
vi'brant
vi'brate'
vi·bra'tion
vi·bra'to
vic'ar
vic'ar·age
vi·car'i·ous
vice'ge'rent
vice'roy
vice ver'sa
vi·cin'i·ty
vi'cious
vi·cis'si·tude'

vic'tim
vic'tim·ize'
Vic·to'ri·an
vic·to'ri·ous
vic'to·ry
vict'ual
vi·cu'ña
vid'e·o'
view'point'
vig'i·lance
vig'i·lant
vig'i·lan'te
vi·gnette'
vig'or
vig'or·ous
vil'i·fi·ca'tion
vil'i·fy'
vil'lage
vil'lag·er
vil'lain
vil'lain·ous
vil'lain·y
vin'ai·grette'
vin'ci·bil'i·ty
vin'ci·ble
vin'di·cate'
vin'di·ca'tion
vin·dic'tive
vin'e·gar
vin'e·gar·y
vine'yard
vin'i·cul'ture
vi'nous
vin'tage
vint'ner

vi'nyl
vi·o'la
vi'o·la·ble
vi'o·late'
vi'o·la'tion
vi'o·lence
vi'o·lent
vi'o·let
vi'o·lin'
vi'o·lin'ist
vi'ol·ist, vi·ol'ist
vi'per
vi·ra'go
vir'gin
vir'gin·al
vir·gin'i·ty
vir'gule
vir'i·des'cent
vir'ile
vi·ril'i·ty
vi·ro'sis
vir'tu·al
vir'tu·al·ly
vir'tue
vir'tu·os'i·ty
vir'tu·o'so
vir'tu·ous
vir'u·lence
vir'u·lent
vi'rus
vi'sa
vis'age
vis'cer·a
vis'cer·al
vis'cid

vis'cose
vis·cos'i·ty
vis'cous
vis'i·bil'i·ty
vis'i·ble
vi'sion
vi'sion·ar'y
vis'it
vis'i·tant
vis'i·ta'tion
vis'i·tor
vis'or
vis'ta
vis'u·al
vis'u·al·i·za'tion
vis'u·al·ize'
vi'tal
vi'tal'i·ty
vi'tal·ize'
vi'ta·min
vi'ti·ate'
vit're·ous
vit'ri·fy'
vit'ri·ol
vit'ri·ol'ic
vi·tu'per·a'tive
vi·va'cious
viv'id
vi·vip'a·rous
viv'i·sec'tion
viv'i·sec'tion·ist

vix'en
vo·cab'u·lar'y
vo'cal
vo·cal'ic
vo'cal·ize'
vo·ca'tion
voc'a·tive
vo·cif'er·ate'
vo·cif'er·ous
vod'ka
void'ance
void'ed
vol'a·tile
vol'a·til'i·ty
vol·can'ic
vol'can·ize'
vol·ca'no
vo·li'tion
vo·li'tion·al·ly
vol'ley
vol'ley·ball'
volt'age
vol·ta'ic
volt·tam'e·ter
volt'me·ter
vol'u·ble
vol'ume
vol'u·met'ric
vo·lu'mi·nous
vol'un·tar'i·ly
vol'un·tar'y

vol'un·teer'
vo·lup'tu·ar'y
vo·lup'tu·ous
vo·lute'
vom'it
vom'i·tor'y
vo·ra'cious
vo·rac'i·ty
vor'tex
vor'ti·ces
vo'ta·ry
vo'tive
vouch'er
vouch·safe'
vow'el
voy'age
vo·yeur'
vo·yeur'ism
vul'can·i·za'tion
vul'can·ized'
vul'gar
vul·gar'i·ty
vul'gar·ize'
vul'ner·a·bil'i·ty
vul'ner·a·ble
vul'pine
vul'ture
vul'tur·ous
vul'va
vy'ing

W

wack'y
wad'ding
wad'dle
wad'ing
wa'fer
waf'fle
wag'er
wag'gish
wag'gle
wag'on
wag'on·er
wain'scot·ing
wain'scot·ting
waist'coat'
wait'er
wait'ress
waiv'er
wake'ful
wake'ful·ness
wak'en
wall'board'
wal'let
wall'eyed'
wall'flow'er
wal'lop
wal'low
wal'nut
wal'rus
wan'der
wan'der·ing
wan'der·lust'

wan'ton
war'ble
war'bler
ward'en
ward'er
ward'robe'
ware'house'
war'fare'
war'like'
war'lock'
war'mon'ger
warn'ing
war'rant
war'ran·tee'
war'ran·tor'
war'ran·ty
war'ren
war'ri·or
wash'a·ble
wasp'ish
was'sail
wast'age
waste'ful
waste'land'
wast'rel
watch'ful
watch'word'
wa'ter
wa'tered
wa'ter·shed'
wa'ter·works'

wa'ter·y
watt'age
wat'tle
watt'me'ter
wa'ver
wav'i·ness
wav'y
wax'en
wax'y
way'far'er
way'far'ing
way'lay'
way'side'
way'ward
weak'en·ing
weak'ling
weak'ness
wealth'y
weap'on
weap'on·ry
wear'a·ble
wea'ri·ness
wear'ing
wea'ri·some
wea'ry
wea'sel
weath'er
weath'ered
weav'er
web'bing
we'ber

274

wed'ded
wed'ding
wedg'ie
wed'lock
weed'y
week'day'
week'end'
week'ly
weep'er
weep'ing
wee'vil
weigh'bridge'
weight'i·ness
weight'lift'ing
wel'come
wel'fare
wel'kin
well'spring'
wel'ter
wel'ter·weight'
were'wolf'
west'bound'
west'er·ly
west'ern
west'ward
weth'er
wet'land'
whale'bone'
whal'ing
wharf'age
wharf'in·ger
what·ev'er
wheat'ear'
wheat'en
whee'dle

whee'dling
wheel'bar'row
wheel'er
wheez'ing
when·ev'er
where·as'
where·at'
where·of'
where·ev'er
where'with·al'
wher'ry
wheth'er
whet'stone'
which·ev'er
whif'fle
whim'per
whim'si·cal
whim'si·cal'i·ty
whim'sy
whin'ny
whip'cord'
whip'per·snap'per
whip'pet
whirl'i·gig'
whirl'pool'
whirl'wind'
whisk'er
whis'ky
whis'per
whis'per·ing
whis'tle
whis'tler
whis'tling
white'cap'
white'ness

whit'en·ing
white'wash'
whith'er
whit'tle
who·dun'it
who·ev'er
whole'ness
whole'sale'
whole'some
whom·ev'er
whoop'ing
whop'ping
wick'ed
wick'er
wick'et
wide'spread'
wid'ow
wid'ow·er
wid'ow·hood'
wield'y
wife'ly
wig'gle
wig'gly
wig'wam
wild'cat'
wild'cat'ter
wil'der·ness
wild'fire'
wil'i·ness
will'ful
will'ing
wil'low
wil'low·y
wilt'ed
wim'ble

wim'ple
wind'age
wind'break'er
wind'er
wind'fall'
wind'ing
wind'jam'mer
wind'lass
wind'mill'
win'dow
wind'row'
wind'up'
wind'ward
wind'y
wine'glass'
win'er·y
wine'skin'
wink'er
win'ning
win'now
win'now·er
win'some
win'ter
win'ter·green'
win'ter·ize'
win'try
wip'er
wire'less
wire'pho'to
wir'y
wis'dom
wise'a'cre
wise'crack'
wish'bone'
wish'ful

wis·te'ri·a
wist'ful
witch'craft'
witch'er·y
with·draw'
with·draw'al
with·drawn'
with'er
with'ers
with·hold'
with·hold'ing
with·in'
with·out'
with·stand'
wit'less
wit'ness
wit'nessed
wit'ti·cism
wit'ti·ly
wit'ting·ly
wit'ty
wiz'ard
wiz'ard·ry
wiz'en
wiz'ened
wob'ble
wob'bly
woe'ful
wolf'ram·ite'
wolfs'bane'
wol'ver·ine'
wom'an
wom'an·hood'
wom'an·ize'
wom'an·ly

wom'bat
wom'en
won'der
won'der·ful
won'der·land'
won'drous
wont'ed
wood'chuck'
wood'craft'
wood'en
wood'land
wood'peck'er
wood'work'
woof'er
wool'en
wool'gath'er·ing
wool'ly
Worces'ter·shire'
word'age
word'i·ness
word'less
word'play'
word'y
work'a·ble
work'bench'
work'book'
work'er
work'ing
work'man·like'
work'man·ship'
work'shop'
world'li·ness
world'ly
worm'wood'
wor'ri·some

wor'ry
wors'en
wor'ship
wor'ship·ful
wor'sted
worth'less
wo'ven
wran'gle
wran'gler
wrap'per
wrap'ping

wrath'ful
wreath'ing
wreck'age
wreck'er
wreck'ing
wres'tle
wres'tler
wres'tling
wretch'ed
wrig'gle

wrig'gly
wring'er
wrin'kle
wrin'kled
wrist'band'
writ'er
writ'ing
wrong'do'ing
wrong'head'ed
Wy·o'ming·ite'

X

xan′thic
xan′tho·phyll
xan′thous
xe′ni·a
xe·nog′a·my
xen′o·gen′e·sis
xen′o·lith

xe′non
xen′o·pho′bi·a
xe′ro·der′ma
xe·roph′i·lous
xe′ro·phyte′
xiph′oid
xy′lem

xy′lene
xy′lic
xy′lo·graph′
xy·log′ra·phy
xy′lo·phone′
xy·loph′o·nist
xy′lose

Y

yacht'ing
yachts'man
Ya'hoo
yam'mer
Yan'kee
Yan'kee·ism
yard'age
yard'arm'
yard'mas'ter
yard'stick'
yar'row
yash·mak'
yean'ling
year'book
year'ling
year'long
year'ly
yearn'ing
yeast'y
yel'low

yel'low·ish
yel'low·y
Yem'en·i
Yem'en·ite
yeo'man
yeo'man·ry
ye·shi'va
yes'ter·day'
yes'ter·eve'
yes'ter·morn'
yes'ter·year'
Yid'dish
yield'ing
yo'del
yo'del·er
yo'del·ler
yo'ga
yo'gi
yo'gurt
yo'kel

yok'ing
yolk'y
Yom Kip'pur
yon'der
york'er
young'er
young'ish
young'ling
young'ster
your·self'
youth'ful
yowl'ing
yt·ter'bi·um
yt'tri·um
yu·an'
yuc'ca
Yu'go·sla'vi·an
yule'tide'
yum'my

279

Z

za′ba·glio′ne
zaf′fer
zai′ba·tsu′
za′ny
zeal′ot
zeal′ot·ry
zeal′ous
ze′bra
ze′brine
ze′bu
zed′o·a′ry
Zeit′geist′
ze·na′na
ze′nith
ze′o·lite′
zeph′yr
zep′pe·lin
ze′ro
zest′ful
zest′y
ze′ta
zeug′ma
zib′el·ine′
zig′gu·rat
zig′zag′

zil′lion
zinc′ite
zin·cog′ra·phy
zin′cous
zin′ni·a
Zi′on·ism
Zi′on·ist
zip′per
zip′py
zir′con
zir·co′ni·um
zith′er
zlo′ty
zo·an′thro·py
zo′di·ac
zo·di′a·cal
zom′bie
zon′al
zo·na′tion
zon′ing
zo′o·chem′is·try
zo′o·ge·og′ra·phy
zo·og′ra·phy
zo′oid
zo·ol′a·try

zo′o·log′i·cal
zo·ol′o·gist
zo·ol′o·gy
zo′o·mor′phism
zo′o·pho′bi·a
zo′o·phyte′
zo′o·spore′
zo·ot′o·my
Zo′ro·as′tri·an·ism
zos′ter
zuc·chi′ni
zwie′back′
zwit′ter
zwit′ter·i·on′ic
zy·go′ma
zy′go·mat′ic
zy·go′sis
zy′gote
zy′mase
zy′mo·gen
zy·mol′o·gy
zy·mol′y·sis
zy·mo′sis
zy·mot′ic
zy′mur·gy